Nina Pindham is a barrister with a wide-ranging practice specialising in environmental law matters in the context of planning applications, including infrastructure, energy, minerals development, hazardous substances consent, waste, EIA, SEA, agriculture, water, air quality, and nature conservation issues. She has represented clients before the High Court, Court of Appeal, Supreme Court, and Inter-American Court of Human Rights. She has also represented the UK Government in international environmental law proceedings before the United Nations. She is ranked as one of the country's top-rated barristers by the Legal 500, Chambers and Partners, the ENDS Report, and Planning Magazine.

A Practical Guide to Biodiversity Net Gain

A Practical Guide to Biodiversity Net Gain

Nina Pindham

Barrister

Law Brief Publishing

Published 2024 by Law Brief Publishing, an imprint of Law Brief Publishing Ltd
30 The Parks
Minehead
Somerset
TA24 8BT

www.lawbriefpublishing.com

Paperback: 978-1-916698-08-6

PREFACE

This book is intended to serve as a helpful guide for those making and determining applications for planning permission under the Town and Country Planning Act 1990 (with a brief look ahead to applications for development consent under the Planning Act 2008).

When the regime is so complex that not even legal databases are able to adequately display the current law, there is a large volume of guidance spread across many websites, and when there are inconsistencies with existing policy, a guide through the entire biodiversity net gain regime which looks to identify and explain inconsistencies, complete gaps, and most importantly, display everything in one integrated source of information is an essential tool to ensure the consistent, correct, and efficient operation of this extremely important world-leading biodiversity net gain regime.

The law stated in this book is believed to be up-to-date and correct as of 1 October 2024.

Nina Pindham
October 2024

CONTENTS

CHAPTER ONE

INTRODUCTION

Ecologists tolerate margins of error that would give aeronautical engineers heart palpitations. Nature is complex, unpredictable and quite often wholly uncontrollable. While policy-based biodiversity net gain ("BNG") regimes are decades-old, why, until now, was there no equivalent in law?[1] Is it possible to achieve the laudable aim of improving biodiversity by means as rigid, specific, and severe as the law? One answer is clear enough: previous efforts have not worked to stem the crisis of biodiversity loss even in nations where BNG policies have existed for decades. David Attenborough noted in his forward to the Dasgupta Review:[2]

> "We are facing a global crisis. We are totally dependent upon the natural world. It supplies us with every oxygen-laden breath we take and every mouthful of food we eat. But we are currently damaging it so profoundly that many of its natural systems are now on the verge of breakdown…Today, we ourselves, together with the livestock we rear for food, constitute 96% of the mass of all mammals on the planet. Only 4% is everything else – from elephants to badgers, from moose to monkeys."

The European Union's Explanatory Memorandum proposing a regulation on nature restoration (2022/0195) concluded "[d]espite EU

---

1 Research carried out by my brilliant pupil, Hannah Taylor investigating the basis for the regime (law or policy) and the stated aim (no net loss or biodiversity gain).

2 Available at https://www.gov.uk/government/publications/final-report-the-economics-of-biodiversity-the-dasgupta-review. Last accessed 1 October 2024.

and international efforts, biodiversity loss and the degradation of ecosystems continue at an alarming rate[3]…The outlook for biodiversity and ecosystems is bleak and shows that the current approach is not working."[4]

Closer to home for legal practitioners, Holgate J. (as he then was) noted in *Vistry Homes Limited v Secretary of State for Levelling Up, Housing and Communities, St Albans City and District Council, Colney Heath Parish Council* [2024] EWHC 2088 (Admin):

> "139. Global decline in biodiversity is described in the literature as a matter of great concern. It was discussed at the UN COP 26 meeting in November 2021. The nations involved adopted the Glasgow Climate Pact. Paragraph 38 emphasises the importance of protecting, conserving and restoring nature and ecosystems including the protection of biodiversity.
>
> 140. A report by the House of Commons Environment Audit Committee in June 2021 ('Biodiversity in the UK: Bloom or bust?' HC 136) referred to the UK as being one of the most nature-depleted countries in the world."

And so, all eyes are on England's world-leading approach.[5] With thanks to my publishers for prohibiting any citation of academic articles, to avoid disappointment it must be said this book has no intellectual pretensions, contains no original research, and suggests no improvements. Rather, it aims to set out for those making and

---

[3] Page 1, first sentence.

[4] Page 2, final paragraph.

[5] Within my direct knowledge, in 2024 alone it has been subject to presentations and discussion at the UN Convention on Biological Diversity's COP16 in Cali, Colombia; biodiversity sessions during New York Climate Week; and the UN Framework Convention on Climate Change's COP29 in Baku, Azerbaijan.

determining planning applications what England's BNG regime is and how it works, in the simplest possible terms. As I and my patient publisher have learned, that was a daunting enough task.

General Overview

The genesis of the BNG regime is the Environment Act 2021. It comprises the framework for a series of enabling and amending provisions, concerning both primary and secondary legislation, supplemented through policy and guidance issued from two separate government departments, critical contributions from statutory advisers to government and professional organisations, all spread across numerous websites. All of this will be referred to here as the BNG regime. The BNG regime is, in short, incredibly complex. The aim, however, is simple: to achieve a measurable post-development improvement in biodiversity.

Given the complexity of the regime, it is worth clarifying the status within the framework for decision makers. When the provision in question arises in law (whether as a section in an Act, a regulation in Regulations, or an article in an Order), that must be obeyed. When the provision in question arises as a matter of policy or guidance (whether national, as a paragraph in the national planning policy framework, ("NPPF"), or planning practice guidance, ("PPG"), or local in the form of development plan policy, supplementary planning documents, or the like), then that should be obeyed unless material considerations indicate otherwise. The BNG regime involves an awful lot of all of the above. To (hopefully) keep the legal distinction between what must be done and what should be done clear, this book aims to always cite the source of the provision in question and, although it comes at a cost to flow and readability, where the source is legal that is not generally footnoted.

It is also worth clarifying, at the outset, the terms used. Throughout this book references to the PPG are, unless otherwise specified, to the PPG on Biodiversity Gain, published jointly by MHCLG and DEFRA[6] although readers must also be aware of, and check, the DEFRA-only "collection" of guidance on BNG.[7] For convenience, applicants for planning permission and those submitting a biodiversity gain plan for approval are referred to as "developers" even though their identity will vary in reality. Landowners, habitat bank operators, local planning authorities selling biodiversity units, and all other providers of offsite BNG are collectively referred to as "landowners". Those making decisions under the Town and Country Planning Act 1990, whether local planning authorities, combined authorities, a mayor, the Secretary of State, or an inspector, are collectively referred to as "planning authorities".

How does the BNG regime work to achieve this goal? First, s.98 and Schedule 14 to the Environment Act 2021 inserted s.90A and Schedule 7A into the Town and Country Planning Act 1990. Together these impose (from 12 February 2024) a mandatory condition on every non-exempt planning permission granted under Part 3 of the Town and Country Planning Act 1990 requiring the provision of at least 10% BNG for at least 30 years (for the condition see paragraph 13(2) of Schedule 7A, "the biodiversity gain condition").

The BNG regime does not apply to any planning permission granted after 12 February 2024 when the application was made before 12 February 2023 (reg.s 2 and 3 of the Environment Act 2021 (Commencement No.8 and Transitional Provisions) Regulations 2024). This does not mean the BNG regime must be treated as irrelevant in such decisions: the Court of Appeal has accepted that future legislative provisions may be relevant to a decision maker (*R (Cala Homes (South)*

6 https://www.gov.uk/guidance/biodiversity-net-gain. Last accessed 1 September 2024.

7 https://www.gov.uk/government/collections/biodiversity-net-gain See also overview https://www.gov.uk/guidance/understanding-biodiversity-net-gain. Last accessed 1 September 2024.

Limited) v Secretary of State for Communities and Local Government [2011] EWCA Civ 639 where the point was not ultimately disputed ([20] and [33]).

However, decision makers should be very cautious if taking the BNG regime into account for development which is not caught by the BNG regime, as no fewer than three cases have already alleged an unlawful retrospective application of the BNG regime, two successfully. In *NRS Saredon Aggregates Limited v Secretary of State for Levelling Up, Housing and Communities* [2023] EWHC 2795 (Admin) Eyre J. held the decision-maker was not entitled to reduce the weight that would otherwise be given to the first 10% of the BNG to be provided by applying the not-yet-in-force legislative requirement ([55] to [56]). In *R (Weston Homes plc) v Secretary of State for Levelling Up, Housing and Communities* [2024] EWHC 2089 Admin the reasoning for the weight given to BNG improvements, in the context of the new legislation, was deemed unlawfully inadequate. An argument on retrospective application was also made in *Vistry Homes* but did not succeed.

From 2025 the BNG regime is intended to be applied to nationally significant infrastructure projects, ("NSIPs"). This will be achieved through amendments to the Planning Act 2008 (Schedule 15 of the Environment Act 2021, when it enters into force, will insert what will be Schedule 2A to that Act, and make consequential amendments). The government has previously stated a commitment to making BNG mandatory for NSIPs from late November 2025.[8]

It is important to point out the BNG regime with which this book is concerned should be distinguished from the provision of other

---

8 See DEFRA blog post https://defraenvironment.blog.gov.uk/2023/11/29/the-biodiversity-net-gain-statutory-instruments-explained/#:~:text=We%20have%20committed%20to%20BNG,NSIP%20guidance%2C%20in%20September%202024. Last accessed 1 October 2024.

biodiversity gains and the general biodiversity objective under s.40(A1) of the Natural Environment and Rural Communities Act 2006. The statutory metric, for example, is not intended to represent a comprehensive model of all aspects of biodiversity. By using habitat as a proxy, animal species presence and/or abundance are not accounted for in the metric. Protected sites and species are dealt with separately from the BNG regime. These other regimes and measures of biodiversity value are nonetheless crucial in ecological terms, and therefore remain important for developers and decision makers to consider alongside the BNG regime.

The Biodiversity Gain Objective

Schedule 7A, paragraph 1(1) of the Town and Country Planning Act 1990 confirms the legislation provides for "grants of planning permission in England to be subject to a condition to secure that the biodiversity gain objective is met." So, what is the biodiversity gain objective and how does one meet it?

Schedule 7A, paragraph 2(1) provides the biodiversity gain objective is met if "the biodiversity value attributable to the development exceeds the pre-development biodiversity value of the onsite habitat by at least the relevant percentage". The relevant percentage is 10% (Schedule 7A, paragraph 2(3)). Thus, in a nutshell, the biodiversity gain objective means development granted planning permission must provide for at least a 10% increase above the pre-development biodiversity value of the onsite habitat.

The relevant percentage for the purposes of the BNG regime can be changed, but only by way of law (as secondary legislation in the form of regulations: paragraph 2(4) of Schedule 7A), and only after a draft of the instrument containing the regulations has been laid before, and approved by a resolution of, each House of Parliament (s.333(3AA) of the Town and Country Planning Act 1990). It is crucial to understand the 10% is measured against the cumulative total pre-development onsite habitat biodiversity value (this is all land within the red line plan[9]), irrespective of whether or not that specific habitat will or might be impacted by the development.[10]

In addition to exemptions, there are transitional arrangements which disapply the biodiversity condition from certain planning permissions, as well as special modifications for other planning permissions or where irreplaceable habitat is present on the development site (see Exemptions, Special Cases, and Irreplaceable Habitats chapters below).

The development subject to the BNG regime comprises all "development for which planning permission is granted" (Schedule 7A, paragraphs 2(1) and 5(1)). This is limited to planning permission granted on an application made under Part 3 of the Town and Country Planning Act 1990 (reg.2(2) of the Environment Act 2021 (Commencement No. 8 and Transitional Provisions) Regulations 2024). Permission granted by way of development order, and other limited exemptions, are not caught by the BNG regime (see Exemptions chapter below).

There are three ways to achieve BNG in order to satisfy the gain objective. First, generating onsite "units" (a quantified biodiversity value uplift within the red line boundary of the development site, Schedule 7A paragraph 12(1) refers to onsite habitat as that on "land to which the planning permission relates"); second, generating offsite units (biodiversity gains created on land outside the red line plan); and thirdly and finally statutory biodiversity credits (buying credits from Natural England as a measure of last resort if onsite or offsite options are not feasible).

9 The DEFRA guidance confirms "onsite" means within the red line plan: https://www.gov.uk/guidance/understanding-biodiversity-net-gain. Last accessed 1 September 2024.

10 DEFRA guidance https://www.gov.uk/guidance/understanding-biodiversity-net-gain. Last accessed 1 September 2024.

In each case, the statutory metric (an online Excel-based tool published by the Secretary of State for the Environment, Food and Rural Affairs) is used "for measuring, for the purposes of [Schedule 7A], the biodiversity value or relative biodiversity value of habitat or habitat enhancement" (Schedule 7A, paragraph 4(1); see also Schedule 7A, paragraph 3). Because of the importance of the metric it must be laid before Parliament (Schedule 7A, paragraph 4(6)), and is subject to procedural conditions in the event of any update (consultation and transitional arrangements: paragraphs 4(4) and 4(5)).

The statutory metric uses habitat as a proxy measurement for biodiversity value in order to generate numeric biodiversity units in one of three non-interchangeable types of habitat comprising either area habitat, watercourse, or hedgerow units. 10% BNG must be achieved for every one of the three types of habitat; in other words, gains in one type of habitat cannot offset the provision of less than 10% net gain in another form of habitat type.

As to the baseline date from which the gain is to be measured, Schedule 7A provides for six options depending on the circumstances (see Relevant Date section in the Statutory Metric chapter below).

The Biodiversity Gain Hierarchy

The biodiversity gain hierarchy is as central to the BNG regime as the biodiversity gain condition and objective: the condition achieves the objective through application of the hierarchy. Article 37A of the Town and Country Planning (Development Management Procedure) (England) Order 2015 gives the definition:

> *"37A. Meaning of biodiversity gain hierarchy*
>
> In this Part, 'biodiversity gain hierarchy' means the following actions in the following order of priority-

(a) in relation to onsite habitat with a habitat distinctiveness score, applied in the statutory metric, equal to or higher than four-

(i) avoiding adverse effects of the development, or

(ii) insofar as those adverse effects cannot be avoided, mitigating those effects;

(b) in relation to any onsite habitat which is adversely affected by the development, compensating for that adverse effect by-

(i) habitat enhancement of onsite habitat;

(ii) insofar as there cannot be that enhancement, creation of onsite habitat;

(iii) insofar as there cannot be that creation, the availability of registered offsite biodiversity gain for allocation to the development;

(iv) insofar as registered offsite biodiversity gain cannot be allocated to the development, the purchase of biodiversity credits."

The effect of the statutory definition of the biodiversity gain hierarchy is summarised by the PPG, which sets out the prioritised list:[11]

- First, in relation to onsite habitats which have a medium, high and very high distinctiveness (a score of four or more according to the statutory metric), avoiding adverse effects from development and, if adverse effects cannot be avoided, mitigating those effects; and then

- Second, in relation to all onsite habitats which are adversely affected by the development, adverse effects should be compensated by prioritising, in this order of priority where

[11] Summarised from PPG paragraph: 008 Reference ID: 74-008-20240214.

possible: (1) enhancement of existing onsite habitats, (2) creation of new onsite habitats, (3) allocation of registered offsite gains and finally (4) purchase of statutory biodiversity credits.

"Habitat enhancement" means enhancement of the biodiversity of habitat (as defined by paragraph 12(2) of Schedule 7A to the Town and Country Planning Act 1990).

It is important to note the hierarchy, like much of the BNG regime, does not apply to irreplaceable habitats (see the Irreplaceable Habitats chapter below). Where it does apply, developers are obliged to explain how the biodiversity gain hierarchy has been applied in their biodiversity gain plan, including any reasons for not following the order of priority (article 37C(2)(e) of the Town and Country Planning (Development Management Procedure) (England) Order 2015). Planning authorities are then obliged to consider the application of the hierarchy when determining whether to approve the biodiversity gain plan (article 37D(2)(a) of the Town and Country Planning (Development Management Procedure) (England) Order 2015), including any reason why the biodiversity gain hierarchy is not to be applied, and if no reason is given, the absence of an explanation must be taken into account by the planning authority (article 37D(2)(b)). The various means of BNG delivery within the hierarchy are not mutually exclusive, so a developer can meet their BNG requirement through a combination of them, but they must apply the hierarchical order of the options where possible.[12]

Because the application of the biodiversity gain hierarchy is a mandatory material consideration, decision makers should give reasons if they do not approve the biodiversity gain because of a failure in relation to the biodiversity gain hierarchy (or if it is rejected for any other reason). These

12 DEFRA guidance https://www.gov.uk/guidance/understanding-biodiversity-net-gain#ways-to-achieve-bng-on-site-units-off-site-units-and-statutory-biodiversity-credits. Last accessed 1 September 2024.

reasons should meet the legal standard,[13] obviously, and enable the developer to know what they did wrong and why the plan was rejected as a consequence of that failure. Further and in any event, when a biodiversity gain plan is rejected for any reason the planning authority is legally obliged to give reasons stating "clearly and precisely their full reasons for the determination, specifying all elements of the biodiversity gain plan which are relevant to the determination" (article 37D(5) of the Town and Country Planning (Development Management Procedure) (England) Order 2015).

The biodiversity gain hierarchy is separate from, but relevant to, the mitigation hierarchy set out in paragraph 186(a) of the NPPF.[14] Thus, there is a separate requirement for decision makers to refuse a planning application if significant harm to biodiversity resulting from the development cannot be avoided (through locating on an alternative site with less harmful impacts), adequately mitigated, or, as a last resort, compensated for. Clearly, avoiding, mitigating and if necessary compensating for harms to biodiversity through the BNG regime can be

---

13 Reasons for the decision must be intelligible and adequate, enabling one to understand why the matter was decided as it was and what conclusions were reached on the 'principal important controversial issues'. A decision maker's reasoning must not give rise to a substantial doubt as to whether they went wrong in law, for example by misunderstanding a relevant policy or by failing to reach a rational decision on relevant grounds. But the reasons need refer only to the main issues in the dispute, not to every material consideration (per Lord Brown in *South Bucks District Council and another v Porter* (No. 2) [2004] 1 W.L.R. 1953, at page 1964B-G).

14 Which provides: "[w]hen determining planning applications, local planning authorities should apply the following principles: a) if significant harm to biodiversity resulting from a development cannot be avoided (through locating on an alternative site with less harmful impacts), adequately mitigated, or, as a last resort, compensated for, then planning permission should be refused".

relevant to application of the paragraph 186(a) policy but other biodiversity impacts may also be relevant.[15]

Biodiversity Gain as Material Consideration

BNG will often be a material consideration when determining a planning application, and planning authorities may consider whether the biodiversity gain condition is capable of being discharged during determination (developers are likely to want this answer early as well). It would accordingly be helpful for developers and planning authorities to engage in early discussion of the prospective contents of the biodiversity gain plan and other relevant requirements. There is helpful case law on how to take account of BNG as a benefit of development (see Planning Authority Governance chapter below).

Maintenance, Monitoring and Enforcement Responsibilities

Developers must ensure habitats they enhance and/or create in order to achieve the biodiversity gain objective are maintained for at least 30 years, whether that is onsite or offsite. Legal agreements are necessary to outline responsibilities for habitat enhancement and/or creation, monitoring, and reporting for all offsite provision of BNG (Schedule 7A, paragraphs 10(1) and 10(3) of the Town and Country Planning Act 1990). A legal agreement or condition is also expressly required by statute for all "significant" onsite habitat provision (Schedule 7A, paragraphs 9(1)-(3)). The legal agreements can take the form of either an agreement under s.106 of the Town and Country Planning Act 1990 or conservation covenant as defined by s.118 and executed under s.117 of the Environment Act 2021 (see Legal Agreements chapter below). Additional planning conditions and legal agreements may also be used to secure the necessary provision, maintenance and monitoring of non-significant onsite BNG for at least 30 years. As to the monitoring interval, a

[15] This is recognised in the PPG at paragraph: 008 Reference ID: 74-008-20240214.

monitoring interval regime at years 1, 5, 10, 20 and 30 is generally accepted as the minimum industry standard, although every case will require specific attention to the appropriate monitoring interval regime and this may need to be adjusted.

If conditions or a s.106 agreement are used the enforcing body will be the local planning authority. If a conservation covenant is used, the enforcing body will be the designated responsible body (which may also be a local planning authority). Further details on enforcement are set out in the Planning Authority Governance and Legal Agreements chapters below.

CHAPTER TWO

EXEMPTIONS

The first more detailed chapter deals with exemptions because there is no point reading further if the regime does not apply. At the time of writing, it is understood the government is looking very carefully at means to resolve potential issues in relation to exemptions, as local planning authorities are reporting dramatic shifts in the kinds of applications coming forward and the number of applications subject to the BNG regime has fallen short of expectations. Some consider the exemptions regime is the predominant reason why, although it is more likely to be a combination of factors.

This chapter is structured in the form of permissions / categories of development to which the BNG regime does not apply, although, as will be seen, the boundary of those categories is sometimes unclear.

Applications Prior to BNG Regime Entering into Force

All planning permissions where the application was made before 12 February 2024 are exempt from the BNG regime, as the legislation does not act retrospectively. For this purpose an application is "made" at the earliest moment when it is received by the local planning authority, not when it is sent nor when it is validated. The Court of Appeal explained in *Camden London Borough Council v ADC Estates Ltd* (1991) 61 P.&C.R. 48 this is because an application is not made in a vacuum, rather, the purpose is to convey information, and information cannot be conveyed until the recipient has received it: per Nourse L.J. at page 55 "it is very difficult to see how an application can ever be made by A to B without B having notice of it". If the application is made on or after 12 February 2024, it is caught by the BNG regime, subject to the below exemptions.

Section 73 Applications

The commencement date has consequences for planning permissions granted by way of an application under s.73 of the Town and Country Planning Act 1990 (application for planning permission for the development of land without complying with conditions subject to which the original planning permission was granted). Regulation 4(1) of the Environment Act 2021 (Commencement No.8 and Transitional Provisions) Regulations 2024 (labelled as a "transitional provision") exempts s.73 permissions in two cases: where (1) the application for the *original* permission to which the s.73 planning permission relates was made before 12 February 2024; or (2) the *original* permission to which the s.73 planning permission relates was granted before 12 February 2024.

The Environment Act 2021 (Commencement No.8 and Transitional Provisions) Regulations 2024 confirm that the "original planning permission to which the section 73 planning permission relates" is defined as a planning permission which is the first in a sequence of two or more planning permissions, where the second and any subsequent planning permissions are s.73 planning permissions (reg.4(2)(b)). It is important that the phrase "to which... [the s.73 permission] relates" is included in this express statutory definition, because "relates" is duly restricted to one thing: the first planning permission in the sequence. This means any s.73 application made on or after 12 February 2024 which is itself premised on a s.73 permission is not exempt, whatever the dates in the sequence may be, because the exemption in reg.4(1) only applies to s.73 applications premised on the "original planning permission" as defined.

The Explanatory Notes to the Regulations are unhelpful in that they do not contemplate a linked series of s.73 consents, and refer to "any" subsequent s.73 permission:

> "[t]he transitional provision in regulation 4 provides that where the application for planning permission was made, or planning permission was granted, for a development before 12th February 2024 the biodiversity gain planning condition also does not apply to any subsequent planning permission for that development granted on an application made under section 73 of the 1990 Act (determination of applications to develop land without compliance with conditions previously attached)."

For the reasons set out above, it is considered the Explanatory Notes are not comprehensively useful, because the actual wording of the provision distinguishes s.73 applications in relation to an "original" parent permission from s.73 applications premised on a s.73 permission. The former are captured by the transitional provision in reg.4, but not the latter.

Small Development Section 73 Applications

The commencement date was extended for small development to 2 April 2024, so applications made and permissions granted for small development before 2 April 2024 are not subject to the BNG regime.

Small development is defined as "development which is not major development within the meaning of article 2(1) of the Town and Country Planning (Development Management Procedure) (England) Order 2015" (see reg.3(3) of the Biodiversity Gain Requirements (Exemptions) Regulations 2024). Article 2(1) defines "major" development as:

> "development involving any one or more of the following-
> (a) the winning and working of minerals or the use of land for mineral-working deposits;
> (b) waste development;
> (c) the provision of dwellinghouses where-

(i) the number of dwellinghouses to be provided is 10 or more; or

(ii) the development is to be carried out on a site having an area of 0.5 hectares or more and it is not known whether the development falls within sub-paragraph (c)(i);

(d) the provision of a building or buildings where the floor space to be created by the development is 1,000 square metres or more; or

(e) development carried out on a site having an area of 1 hectare or more"

The DEFRA guidance is more helpful in terms of positively defining small sites, as there are many developments outside the above definition that are also not small development. A small development means:[16]

- residential development where the number of dwellings is between 1 and 9 on a site of an area 1 hectare or less, or if the number of dwellings is unknown, the site area is less than 0.5 hectares
- commercial development where floor space created is less than 1,000 square metres or total site area is less than 1 hectare
- development that is not the winning and working of minerals or the use of land for mineral-working deposits
- development that is not waste development.

Permissions granted under s.73 in relation to small development are also exempt in two situations: where (1) the application for the *original* permission was made before 2 April 2024; or (2) the *original* permission

16 DEFRA guidance https://www.gov.uk/guidance/biodiversity-metric-calculate-the-biodiversity-net-gain-of-a-project-or-development#:~:text=Small%20developments%20are%20only%20required%20to%20achieve%20BNG%20from%202%20April%202024.%C2%A0%C2%A0. Last accessed 1 October 2024.

was granted before 2 April 2024 (reg.3(2) of the Biodiversity Gain Requirements (Exemptions) Regulations 2024).

Although it is much less common to see a linked series of s.73 permissions arising from one original "parent" permission in the case of small development, the Biodiversity Gain Requirements (Exemptions) Regulations 2024 set out the same position as above in the case of s.73 permissions related to major development. They too define the "original planning permission to which the section 73 planning permission relates" as a planning permission which is the first in a sequence of two or more planning permissions, where the second and any subsequent planning permissions are s.73 planning permissions (reg.3(3)). Thus, any s.73 application relating to small development made on or after 2 April 2024 which is itself premised on a s.73 permission is not exempt.

Section 73A Planning Permissions

All retrospective planning permissions granted under s.73A of the Town and Country Planning Act 1990 are expressly excluded from the BNG regime (reg.2(2) of the Environment Act 2021 (Commencement No.8 and Transitional Provisions) Regulations 2024).

The De Minimus Impact Exemption

Developments that have a *de minimus* impact on onsite habitat are exempt from BNG requirements, provided two conditions are met. The first condition is that the development does not impact an onsite priority habitat (reg.4(2) of the Biodiversity Gain Requirements (Exemptions) Regulations 2024). "Priority habitat" means a habitat specified in a list published under s.41 of the Natural Environment and Rural Communities Act 2006.[17] The second condition is that the development

[17] By reg.4(4) of the Biodiversity Gain Requirements (Exemptions) Regulations 2024. This list is available at

impacts (a) less than 25 square metres of onsite habitat that has a biodiversity value greater than zero (anything multiplied by zero is zero anyway), and (b) less than 5 metres in length of any onsite linear habitat (whether hedgerow or watercourse) (reg.4(3)).

For the purposes of the *de minimus* exemption regulation a habitat is "impacted" where the habitat is lost or degraded such that there is a decrease in the biodiversity value of that habitat (reg.4(4)(b)). Biodiversity value is determined through application of the statutory metric. A decrease in biodiversity value would result from a negative unit score attributable to a change in habitat type, extent, or condition.

There is a question over how to assess the area of impact for the purposes of this exemption. Here the precautionary principle is helpful in navigating a solution to the question in the (as yet) absence of an explicit answer in government policy. The precautionary principle is now a mandatory consideration for all government environmental policy.[18] The Environmental Principles Policy Statement provides "[t]he precautionary principle is applicable where there is plausible evidence of a risk that a particular policy could cause serious or irreversible damage to the environment, alongside a lack of scientific certainty about the likelihood or severity of this damage". Because works involved in the implementation of a planning permission may lead to permanent onsite biodiversity harm beyond the building footprint, all onsite land (the *de minimus* exemption only applies to onsite land) which may be adversely impacted by construction, occupation, decommissioning, and any other ancillary aspects of carrying out the development should be considered

---

https://www.gov.uk/government/publications/habitats-and-species-of-principal-importance-in-england. Last accessed 1 September 2024.

18 Environmental Principles Policy Statement, a mandatory consideration when making policy by s.19(1) of the Environment Act 2021. Available at: https://www.gov.uk/government/publications/environmental-principles-policy-statement/environmental-principles-policy-statement. Last accessed 1 September 2024.

when assessing possible impact for the purposes of the *de minimus* exemption, having regard to all evidence on the location of development on the site and the means of possible impacts, so far as possible.

It should be noted the statutory metric applies a time frame for impacts, which may be relevant to whether or not there is any "impact" at all for the purposes of the *de minimus* exemption. The User Guide confirms the developer does not need to record a habitat as lost when impacts are temporary and the area can be restored to both:

- baseline habitat type within two years of the initial impact; and
- baseline condition within two years of the initial impact.[19]

Because "impact" is assessed for the purposes of this exemption by reference to a negative unit score leading to a decrease in biodiversity value, and a negative unit score is determined by application of principles in the statutory metric, it appears this means temporary impacts would not count as impacts for the purposes of the *de minimus* exemption.

The PPG provides further guidance on the application of this exemption.[20] This paragraph of the PPG provides that if a developer considers the development benefits from the *de minimis* exemption they "must" state this in their planning application form, and give reasons so that the planning authority can consider whether the proposal is genuinely exempt at the earliest possible stage (the developer has to provide this information with the application for planning permission in relation to all potentially relevant exemptions anyway, unless it is a s.73 application: article 7(1A)(b) of the Town and Country Planning (Development Management Procedure) (England) Order 2015). When

---

19 Statutory Metric User Guide page 34 https://assets.publishing.service.gov.uk/media/669e45fba3c2a28abb50d426/The_Statutory_Biodiversity_Metric_-_User_Guide__23.07.24_.pdf. Last accessed 1 September 2024.

20 PPG paragraph: 004 Reference ID: 74-004-20240214.

providing reasons for the application of the *de minimis* exemption, an applicant should provide "sufficient evidence to support their justification". This said, paragraph 004 in the PPG also confirms where the development would be smaller than 25 square metres, then the description of development, existing and proposed site plans, and the development's area size may comprise sufficient evidence.

Where it cannot be clearly demonstrated through site plans and descriptions whether an onsite habitat would be lost or degraded by the development, i.e. because the location of underground infrastructure or the means of construction are yet to be determined, applicants are "strongly encouraged" to provide a completed metric for the pre-development and post-development value for the onsite habitat and clear plans identifying the nature and size of this pre-development onsite habitat and how much of it will be impacted by the development.[21] The PPG goes on to note this step will be particularly important where the development involves multiple small-scale impacts on onsite habitat in order to avoid the cumulative effect on onsite habitat equating to more than the *de minimis* threshold.

The PPG provides three illustrative scenarios where the *de minimis* exemption would apply:[22]

Scenario 1: A development solely on a sealed surface

> The development is a new commercial building on an existing car park. There are no other habitats (e.g. a green verge or tree) within the red line boundary of the development. The development would be exempted from biodiversity net gain by the *de minimis* exemptions as:
>
> - the development does not impact on any onsite priority habitat;

---

[21] PPG paragraph: 004 Reference ID: 74-004-20240214.

[22] PPG paragraph: 004 Reference ID: 74-004-20240214.

- the car park would be classified as developed land: sealed surface which has a biodiversity value of zero under the statutory metric; and
- there are no other onsite habitats.

Scenario 2: A development which only marginally impacts on a garden habitat

The development is a new residential dwelling largely on the footprint of an existing dwelling which will be demolished but there would be a small loss of a grass lawn (of 20 square metres) in the garden. The red line boundary for the development includes two large trees at the end of the garden which are not affected by the development. The development would be exempted from biodiversity net gain by the *de minimis* exemptions as:

- the development does not impact on any onsite priority habitat;
- the existing dwelling would be classified as a developed land: sealed surface which has a biodiversity value of zero under the statutory metric;
- the grass lawn would be classified as vegetated garden and would have a biodiversity value of greater than zero under the statutory metric but the size of this habitat lost is less than 25 square metres; and
- the trees within the red line boundary would be classified as individual urban trees and would have a biodiversity value of greater than zero under the statutory metric but are not impacted by the development.

Scenario 3: A very small development within an established wood

The development is a new telecommunications mast (taking up 5 square metres of land) within mixed woodland. The development would be exempted from biodiversity net gain by the *de minimis* exemptions as:

- the development does not impact on any onsite priority habitat;
- the woodland would be classified as other woodland: mixed and would have a biodiversity value of greater than zero under the statutory metric, but the size of the habitat impacted is less than 25 square metres.

From the above an order for decision makers can be discerned: (1) is the biodiversity value of the site greater than zero? (2) if so, is there any onsite priority habitat? (3) will any of that priority habitat be impacted by the development, including construction and other ancillary impacts of development, provided those impacts are not temporary? If so, the exemption does not apply. Otherwise, (4) is the total area of all onsite non-priority area habitat that will be impacted less than 25 square metres; and (5) is the total length of impacted onsite linear habitat less than five metres? If the answer to both is yes, the exemption applies.

<u>Householder Applications</u>

These are exempt from the BNG regime (reg.5 of the Biodiversity Gain Requirements (Exemptions) Regulations 2024). The Regulations refer to article 2(1) of the Town and Country Planning (Development Management Procedure) (England) Order 2015, which defines a householder application as follows:

> "(a) an application for planning permission for development for an existing dwellinghouse, or development within the curtilage of such a dwellinghouse for any purpose incidental to the enjoyment of the dwellinghouse, or
>
> (b) an application for any consent, agreement or approval required by or under a planning permission, development order or local development order in relation to such development,

but does not include an application for change of use or an application to change the number of dwellings in a building."

High-Speed Railway Transport Network

Planning permission for development forming part of, or ancillary to, the high speed railway transport network comprising connections between all or any of the places or parts of the transport network specified in section 1(2) of the High Speed Rail (Preparation) Act 2013 is exempt (reg.(6)(1) of the Biodiversity Gain Requirements (Exemptions) Regulations 2024). For this purpose, reg.6(2) provides that "transport network" and "high speed railway transport network" have the same meaning as in the High Speed Rail (Preparation) Act 2013, but that Act does not actually truly define either term. Instead, s.1 provides for expenditure to be incurred for a high speed railway transport network, and s.1(2) says that such a network:

> "(a) involves the construction of railway lines connecting at least-
>
> London,
> Birmingham,
> the East Midlands,
> Sheffield,
> Leeds, and
> Manchester, and
>
> (b) connects with the existing railway transport network as well as with such other parts of the transport network (including roads, footpaths, cycleways, airports and light railways) as the Secretary of State considers appropriate."

This only says what the network may involve (as a minimum), but then goes on to add the network can also include any connection(s) to any other part of the transport network as the Secretary of State considers appropriate. What "transport network" means is not set out at all in the

Act. While Phase 2 of HS2 has been cancelled (for now), the legislation – including the discretionary extension to the network – remains available to be applied. If it is, the boundary of this exemption is likely to be tested.

Biodiversity Gain Site

Planning permission for development which is undertaken solely or mainly for the purpose of fulfilling, in whole or in part, the biodiversity gain condition which applies in relation to another development cannot itself have the biodiversity gain condition imposed on it (reg.7(1) of the Biodiversity Gain Requirements (Exemptions) Regulations 2024). As to what "solely or mainly" means, the Biodiversity Gain Requirements (Exemptions) Regulations 2024 only provide that "no account is to be taken of any facility for the public to access or to use the site for educational or recreational purposes, if that access or use is permitted without the payment of a fee" (reg.7(2)). Otherwise, the application of reg.7(1) will be a matter of judgment for the planning authority.

Self-build and Custom Build Applications

Developments consisting of no more than nine dwellings, on a site no larger than 0.5 hectares, and which comprise exclusively of "self-build or custom housebuilding" dwellings are exempt from BNG requirements (reg.8(1) of the Biodiversity Gain Requirements (Exemptions) Regulations 2024). Self-build or custom housebuilding is the building or completion by:

(a) individuals,
(b) associations of individuals, or
(c) persons working with or for individuals or associations of individuals,

of houses to be occupied as homes by those individuals (by s.1(A1) of the Self-build and Custom Housebuilding Act 2015). The DEFRA-issued guidance cross refers to the PPG on Self-Build and Custom Housebuilding,[23] which says "[o]ff-plan housing, homes purchased at the plan stage prior to construction and without input into the design and layout from the buyer, are not considered to meet the definition of self-build and custom housing."[24] As to the further clarity provided in s.1(A2) of the Self-build and Custom Housebuilding Act 2015, which provides that subsection A1 does not include the building of a house on a plot acquired from a person who builds the house wholly or mainly to plans or specifications decided or offered by that person reg.8(2) of the Biodiversity Gain Requirements (Exemptions) Regulations 2024 only refers to subsection A1 of the Self-build and Custom Housebuilding Act 2015 when defining what exempt "self-build or custom housebuilding" means, which appears to, accordingly, exclude s.1(A2).

Development Order

Development granted planning permission by a development order made under s.59 of the Town and Country Planning Act 1990 is exempt (Schedule 7A, paragraph 17(a)(i) of the Town and Country Planning Act 1990). This includes all permitted development under the Town and Country Planning (General Permitted Development) (England) Order 2015.

Urgent Crown Development

Urgent Crown development granted planning permission under s.293A of the Town and Country Planning Act 1990 is exempt from the BNG regime (Schedule 7A, paragraph 17(a)(ii) of the Town and Country Planning Act 1990).

---

23 https://www.gov.uk/guidance/biodiversity-net-gain-exempt-developments. Last accessed 1 September 2024.

24 https://www.gov.uk/guidance/self-build-and-custom-housebuilding PPG paragraph: 016 Reference ID: 57-016-20210208. Last accessed 1 September 2024.

Permissions Granted Outside of Part 3 of the Town and Country Planning Act 1990

The BNG condition only applies to permissions granted pursuant to applications under Part 3 of the Town and Country Planning Act 1990, and so does not apply to consents and planning permission granted through other routes.

The grant of permission in principle is not within the scope of biodiversity net gain (as it is not a grant of planning permission),[25] but any subsequent technical details consent (which is a grant of planning permission) would be subject to the biodiversity gain condition.

Further, "planning permission" for the purposes of Schedule 7A expressly includes deemed planning permission, (Schedule 7A, paragraph 12(3)), and so development approved this way under the Electricity Act 1989 and the Transport and Works Act 1989, for example, are subject to the BNG regime.

Enforcement appeals seeking planning permission under a ground (a) appeal are also outside the scope of the BNG regime (at present) because control over development by way of enforcement falls under Part 7.

Applications for certificates of the lawfulness of an existing or proposed use or development (which also fall under Part 7 of the Town and Country Planning Act 1990) are not subject to the BNG regime for an additional reason: certificates are not planning permissions.[26]

---

[25] See s.336(1) of the Town and Country Planning Act 1990, which defines planning permission as "permission under Part III or section 293A but does not include permission in principle."

[26] By section 336(1) of the Town and Country Planning Act 1990 (set out in footnote above).

Reserved Matters

The approval of reserved matters in relation to outline planning permission is not subject to the biodiversity gain condition because it is not a grant of planning permission. This is a long standing legal principle, most recently confirmed by Lewison L.J. giving judgment for the Court of Appeal in *R (Fulford Parish Council) v City of York Council v Persimmon Homes (Yorkshire) Limited* [2019] EWCA Civ 1359 at [24]: "[i]n the light of the provisions of the Act and the case law, I accept that the approval of reserved matters is not, itself, a planning permission and that an application for such approval is not, itself, an application for planning permission."

CHAPTER THREE

THE STATUTORY METRIC

The statutory biodiversity metric[27] ("statutory metric") is the official tool for quantifying biodiversity value for the purposes of the BNG regime (Schedule 7A, paragraph 3 of the Town and Country Planning Act 1990). It uses habitat as a proxy for overall biodiversity interest. First, the various onsite habitat types i.e. grassland, culvert, native hedgerow, woodland, open mosaic, etc. are identified and inputted into one of the three separate main habitat modules: area habitat, hedgerow, or watercourse. Then factors like the size, condition, and strategic significance of that habitat are included in the calculation. When habitat enhancement and/or creation is proposed, the metric will also take account of the difficulty of creating or enhancing that specific habitat, the time it takes that habitat to reach its target condition, and the new habitat's distance from where habitat has been lost. Biodiversity value is then quantified in standardized units. The same tool is used to assess existing onsite habitat and proposed BNG, whether onsite or offsite (or that which must be purchased by way of statutory credit).

Applicants for development subject to the biodiversity gain condition must submit a metric assessment with the baseline tab completed alongside their planning application (article 7(1)(c)(iia) and articles 7(1A)(c)(i)-(ii) of the Town and Country Planning (Development Management Procedure) (England) Order 2015). A fully completed statutory metric assessment is also required as part of any biodiversity gain plan, as the biodiversity gain objective of achieving at least a 10%

27 This is an online tool. The two kinds of metric (the standard statutory metric and the small sites metric) and accompanying detailed user guides are available at: https://www.gov.uk/government/publications/statutory-biodiversity-metric-tools-and-guides. Last accessed 1 September 2024.

gain in post-development biodiversity value is measured by comparing the prospective post-development biodiversity value against the pre-development calculation of the onsite habitat's biodiversity value using the metric (see Schedule 7A, paragraph 15 of the Town and Country Planning Act 1990).

It is the planning authority's responsibility to check that the pre-development, post-development and total net change calculations using the statutory metric match, that the developer has satisfied the metric's trading rules, and the habitat evaluations inputted into the metric are accurate.[28]

Pre-Development Biodiversity Value

Pre-development biodiversity value is the total value of all onsite habitat as at the relevant date (which will always be prior to the approval of the biodiversity gain plan), on the development site (i.e. within the red line plan). Once the pre-development biodiversity value has been established it cannot change for that planning permission because it is a historic snapshot. Any change to the pre-development value after permission is granted and the biodiversity gain condition discharged would mean the biodiversity gain plan which was approved and which allowed the permission to be implemented is also wrong, because that will have been based on the pre-development biodiversity value of the development site.

Relevant Date for Calculating Pre-Development Biodiversity Value / Impact of Degradation

The relevant date is to be specified on the planning application form (article 7(1A)(c)(i) of the Town and Country Planning (Development Management Procedure) (England) Order 2015. There are six potential

28 DEFRA guidance. https://www.gov.uk/guidance/biodiversity-net-gain-what-local-planning-authorities-should-do. Last accessed 1 September 2024.

options for the date of the pre-development biodiversity value calculation.

First, if "planning permission is granted on application", then it is the date "of the application" (Schedule 7A, paragraph 5(2)(a) of the Town and Country Planning Act 1990). This includes applications made directly to the Secretary of State under s.62A, 76A and 77 of the Town and Country Planning Act 1990.

Second, "in any other case" the relevant date is the date on which planning permission is granted (Schedule 7A, paragraph 5(2)(b)). An "other case" includes planning permission following an appeal under s.78 of the Town and Country Planning Act 1990 because in this case planning permission is granted on appeal, not on application.

Third, in either of the above situations, the developer and the planning authority may agree an earlier date (Schedule 7A, paragraph 5(3)). That date cannot be any earlier than 12 February 2024 because Schedule 7A does not have retrospective effect. If an earlier date is used, despite being agreed, the reasons for using this date should still be provided on the planning application and the biodiversity gain plan (and overall biodiversity gain plan if the permission relates to phased development) (article 7(1A)(c)(iv) of the Town and Country Planning (Development Management Procedure) (England) Order 2015 for the application; article 37C(4)(a) of the Town and Country Planning (Development Management Procedure) (England) Order 2015 for the biodiversity gain plan).

Fourthly is the situation where unauthorised activity (unauthorised being otherwise than in accordance with planning permission or any other permission specified by the Secretary of State in regulations; none have been published yet) has taken place on or after 30 January 2020.[29] If, as

[29] This is the date when what became the Environment Act 2021 received its first reading in Parliament.

a result of that unauthorised activity, the pre-development biodiversity value of the onsite habitat is lower on the relevant date than it would have otherwise been, then the relevant date is the date immediately before any of the specified activities took place and the pre-development value of the onsite habitat is the biodiversity value immediately before the carrying out of those activities (Schedule 7A, paragraph 5(4) and paragraph 6).

Questions have been raised on whether deliberate destruction of onsite biodiversity through an activity which does not require planning permission, such as tearing up scrubland or in compliance with an environmental permit, would also engage paragraph 6. The language of paragraph 6 does not provide much clarity, because it only refers to activities "otherwise than in accordance with planning permission" (regulations under paragraph 6(a)(ii) are not relevant, yet). The Explanatory Notes say: "[t]hese activities must have been carried out without planning permission, or without an alternative permission…"[30] That appears to support an interpretation that a breach of planning control would be required to engage paragraph 6. However, the PPG is more in line with the text of paragraph 6: "[u]nauthorised degradation of onsite habitat is any degradation which is not in accordance with a previous planning permission."[31] Ultimately the language of the statute is what the courts will have primary regard to.

So, if the tearing up of scrubland was "in accordance" with a previous permission, paragraph 6 is not engaged (but see paragraph 6A). If it is not in accordance with the operative planning permission relating to the site, even if it were in accordance with a permit, then it would engage paragraph 6. In short, paragraph 6 is only concerned with whether the activity was in accordance with <u>planning permission</u>. No doubt this question is one which will be the subject of litigation or further legislation in due course.

---

30 Explanatory Notes to the Environment Act 2021, paragraph 1736.

31 PPG paragraph: 036 Reference ID: 74-036-20240214.

Fifthly, if activities to implement or carry out planning permission are carried out on or after 25 August 2023 on the development site, provided certain criteria are met, then again the date is the date immediately before any of the specified activities took place and the pre-development biodiversity value of the onsite habitat is to be taken to be its biodiversity value immediately before the carrying on of the activities (Schedule 7A, paragraph 6A). The criteria are: (1) on the 'otherwise' relevant date (i.e. either the date of the application or the date of the grant in accordance with Schedule 7A, paragraph 5(2)), either the development for which that other planning permission was granted has not been begun, or that development has begun but has not been completed, and (2) that activity has lowered the biodiversity value of the onsite habitat.

In either the fourth or fifth situation above (so either Schedule 7A, paragraph 6 or 6A applies because onsite habitat has been degraded in a relevant way) if there is insufficient evidence of the biodiversity value of onsite habitat immediately before the carrying on of the activities in question, then the pre-development biodiversity value of the onsite habitat is to be taken to be the highest biodiversity value of the onsite habitat which is reasonably supported by any available evidence immediately before the carrying on of the activities (Schedule 7A, paragraphs 6B(1)-(2)). Examples of this data could be locally available data or nationally available data such as DEFRA's MAGiC map.[32]

Where relevant degradation activities have occurred the planning application must include (by article 7(1A)(v)(aa) of the Town and Country Planning (Development Management Procedure) (England) Order 2015):[33]

- a statement setting out that degradation activities have been carried out;

32 https://magic.defra.gov.uk/magicmap.aspx. Last accessed 1 September 2024.

33 See also PPG paragraph: 036 Reference ID: 74-036-20240214.

- confirmation of the date immediately before these activities were carried out;
- the pre-development biodiversity value of the site on that date; and
- any available supporting evidence of this.

Sixthly and finally, in the event that a site registered as a "biodiversity gain site" is developed the pre-development value of the land is to be assumed as the enhanced value of the registered site, regardless of whether or not the final proposed biodiversity gain has in fact been delivered successfully (Schedule 7A, paragraph 7 of the Town and Country Planning Act 1990). This is a potential incentive not to develop registered BNG sites (as to which sites qualify for registration, see the Offsite chapter below), but even if that does occur, the effect is that overall biodiversity gain is still achieved.

A biodiversity gain site no longer needs to be registered once all obligations are completed, so practically this provision would only apply within the relevant 30-year maintenance period.

Survey Dates

Developers should seek advice from their ecologist on dates to carry out the necessary surveys of the development site well in advance of submitting their planning application. Determining the survey schedule at least a year in advance is advisable. A number of surveys can only take place during a specific time of the year, potentially during a very short window. On the other hand, the survey work should also be completed as close as possible to the submission of the planning application. Surveys carried out earlier can only be used where there has been no material change to the onsite habitat when the planning application is eventually submitted, but this is a matter of expert judgement, and a further survey may need to be conducted to demonstrate there has been no material change. Any material change requires a new survey.[34]

[34] PPG paragraph: 012 Reference ID: 74-012-20240214.

Detailed Overview of Use of Statutory Metric

Using the Metric Tool

Both the person creating the metric assessment (known as the assessor) and the person reviewing the assessment within the planning authority (known as the reviewer) must be a "competent person" with the necessary skills, training and qualifications.[35] This is typically an ecologist (unless the small sites metric is used, see below). The Chartered Institute of Ecology and Environmental Management publishes guidance on hiring suitable consultants, who should at least be trained to British Standard BS 8683:2021 level. Additional good practice guidance is available from CIRIA and IEMA.

In addition, if there is a watercourse on the development site the competent person acting as assessor must be qualified to undertake a river condition assessment,[36] which includes specialised training in using the Modular River Physical survey methodology and restoring watercourse habitats. A river condition assessment is, essentially, a bi-partite assessment: first, there is a desk-based reach-scale assessment which determines the river type, and only then is a site-based survey carried out. This will investigate factors such as physical features including channel dimensions, vegetation, habitats, structural features, and human interventions in order to assess the condition of the river. The User Guide does not specify that the reviewer must also be qualified to undertake a river condition assessment, but this would obviously assist in ensuring

---

35 "Principle 1" of the statutory metric: see User Guide page 19 https://assets.publishing.service.gov.uk/media/669e45fba3c2a28abb50d426/The_Statutory_Biodiversity_Metric_-_User_Guide__23.07.24_.pdf. Last accessed 1 September 2024. For reviewers see page 8.

36 User Guide page 8 https://assets.publishing.service.gov.uk/media/669e45fba3c2a28abb50d426/The_Statutory_Biodiversity_Metric_-_User_Guide__23.07.24_.pdf. Last accessed 1 September 2024.

the information submitted to the planning authority is correct and the biodiversity gain objective will be met.

The metric creates three value outputs (existing, enhanced and created habitat) in relation to three separate kinds of biodiversity units (area habitat, hedgerow, and watercourse). The three kinds of biodiversity unit are calculated in the metric within three completely separate modules, and so cannot be combined for an overall output score. This means developers must achieve at least a 10% for each affected kind of biodiversity unit. It is not possible to combine a 15% hedgerow post-development score with a 5% area habitat score and tell the planning authority the development achieves an "overall" biodiversity gain of 10%.

Also of note is the inclusion of private gardens in the July 2024 metric update. Pre-development habitats within a private garden are now expressly included in the metric baseline, although important features may have to be recorded as individual habitat parcels such as individual trees that have a diameter at breast height[37] greater than 7.5cm and less than or equal to 30cm, hedgerows, other ecologically important habitats such as ponds (a pond qualifies as any waterbody less than two hectares in surface area; two hectares or bigger and it is a lake). These areas can only be recorded as "retained" habitat given the general lack of control over what people do in their private gardens. Post-development private gardens are recorded as "urban – vegetated" or "urban – unvegetated". The creation of private gardens, no matter how expansively verdant, cannot be recorded as anything other than these two types of habitat and can never be recorded as post-development habitat enhancement.

The metric requires that the user includes everything that exists within a development site's red line boundary, as well as all post-development BNG proposal information. This includes all pre-development onsite

37 This is the industry standard language. "Diameter at breast height" technically means 1.3 meters above ground level.

features, whether or not they may be lost, retained or improved, as well as:

- the types of habitat, both present and planned.
- the size of each "habitat parcel" in hectares, or for linear habitats (watercourse and hedgerows, measured as a centre line along the length of the feature) in kilometres.
- the condition of each "habitat parcel" (condition is a measure of the habitat judged against its ecological optimum state – in much the same way that water body status under the Water Framework Directive is assessed). Condition is used to measure variation in the quality of areas of the same habitat type.
- whether the proposed actions for the habitat parcel are mapped in the local nature recovery strategy's local habitat map or identified in other alternative strategies.
- the distinctiveness of the relevant habitat. This is a measure calculated from the type of habitat and its distinguishing features and includes:
    - consideration of species richness and rarity;
    - the extent to which the habitat is protected by designations; and
    - the degree to which a habitat supports species rarely found in other habitats.

A habitat parcel is a smaller area within a site, which contains one type of habitat of the same distinctiveness, condition and strategic significance. If any of these three measures differ, it is a different habitat parcel which must be inputted separately into the metric.

Developers should note the metric is extremely useful as an iterative tool used throughout the planning process – even and perhaps especially at site selection stage – to optimize biodiversity gains onsite, minimize losses, and ensure development is cost-effective. The metric is deliberately designed for repeated use to enable developers to refine their plans based on expert ecological advice. Developers can save various iterations as different versions within the metric so that they can simultaneously assess various potential scenarios based on different layouts for the development and/or different post-development BNG scenarios in order to achieve optimal development with maximum gains at minimal cost.

Rules and Principles

Failure to follow the four metric rules means BNG cannot be claimed, and the biodiversity gain plan cannot be approved.[38]

Rule 1 is that the trading rules must be followed. The trading rules are found at Table 3 of the User Guide to the statutory metric.[39] This sets out what may be proposed for loss based on both distinctiveness of the habitat from very high to very low and its type within either area, hedgerow or watercourse as follows:

[38] User Guide page 13 https://assets.publishing.service.gov.uk/media/669e45fba3c2a28abb50d426/The_Statutory_Biodiversity_Metric_-_User_Guide__23.07.24_.pdf. Last accessed 1 September 2024.

[39] User Guide page 13 https://assets.publishing.service.gov.uk/media/669e45fba3c2a28abb50d426/The_Statutory_Biodiversity_Metric_-_User_Guide__23.07.24_.pdf. Last accessed 1 September 2024.

Table 3 Trading rules (Rule 1) to compensate for losses

Baseline habitat distinctiveness	Area	Hedgerow	Watercourse
Very high	Priority should be given to replacing losses with area habitat units of the same habitat type (see below notes on trading)	Losses must be replaced with hedgerow units of the same habitat type	Priority should be given to replacing losses with watercourse units of the same habitat type (see below notes on trading)
High	Losses must be replaced with area habitat units of the same habitat type	Losses must be replaced with hedgerow units of the same habitat type or of a higher band	Losses must be replaced with watercourse units of the same habitat type
Medium	Losses must be replaced by area habitat units of either medium band habitats within the same broad habitat type or, any habitat from a higher band from any broad habitat type	Losses must be replaced with hedgerow units of the same or of a higher band	Losses must be replaced with watercourse units of the same habitat type
Low	Losses must be replaced with area habitat units of the same or higher band	Losses must be replaced with hedgerow units of the same or of a higher band	Losses must be replaced with watercourse units of a higher band
Very low	Not applicable	Losses must be replaced with hedgerow units of the same or of a higher band	Not applicable

It can be seen that an exchange of larger but lower distinctiveness habitat for smaller but higher distinctiveness habitat is acceptable whereas the reverse is typically not permitted, unless bespoke compensation is agreed between the developer and the LPA.

Once the trading rules have been met, biodiversity net gain requirements can be met by the creation and enhancement of any habitat, provided it is within the relevant module. Helpfully, the metric tool automatically informs users whether the trading rules have been met (in the "headline results" tab).

For very high distinctiveness habitats of any type the trading rules note there is a bespoke compensation option in the statutory metric tool, which provides:[40]

1. priority should be given to replacing losses with units of the same habitat type;
2. if this is not possible, losses should be replaced by appropriate units of the same habitat distinctiveness;
3. if this is not possible, losses should be replaced by appropriate area units of a high habitat distinctiveness.

Where high distinctiveness woodland habitat is present, the trading rules provide that developers should set a realistic target condition for the created woodland, and in most cases given the timeframes and difficulty involved the target condition should be 'poor' or 'moderate'. Enhancement alone where woodland would be lost is not generally acceptable given this will result in an overall reduction in woodland habitat. Instead woodland creation should also be proposed alongside

---

40 User Guide page 15 https://assets.publishing.service.gov.uk/media/669e45fba3c2a28abb50d426/The_Statutory_Biodiversity_Metric_-_User_Guide__23.07.24_.pdf. Last accessed 1 September 2024.

enhancement works to avoid an overall loss of woodland cover.[41] Further, any felled[42] woodland (this is not the same as coppicing or restocking) must be compensated as if the habitat was high distinctiveness woodland, irrespective of its original condition.[43]

Finally, the trading rules provide that for watercourses any compensation for the loss of watercourse units should be on a section of watercourse with similar habitat features (these are to be based on the assumption it were in a natural state). That watercourse should also be of a similar size, function and stream order as the affected watercourse. The User Guide gives examples:[44]

- impacts on headwaters cannot be offset on large lowland rivers
- impacts on canals cannot be offset on rivers
- impacts on ditches cannot be offset on canals or rivers

---

41 User Guide page 16 https://assets.publishing.service.gov.uk/media/669e45fba3c2a28abb50d426/The_Statutory_Biodiversity_Metric_-_User_Guide__23.07.24_.pdf. Last accessed 1 September 2024.

42 See Forestry Commission guidance dated 2 August 2024 "Felling and restocking definitions" at https://www.gov.uk/government/publications/definitions-of-felling-and-restocking-options/felling-and-restocking-definitions. Last accessed 1 September 2024.

43 User Guide page 17 https://assets.publishing.service.gov.uk/media/669e45fba3c2a28abb50d426/The_Statutory_Biodiversity_Metric_-_User_Guide__23.07.24_.pdf. Last accessed 1 September 2024.

44 User Guide page 16 https://assets.publishing.service.gov.uk/media/669e45fba3c2a28abb50d426/The_Statutory_Biodiversity_Metric_-_User_Guide__23.07.24_.pdf. Last accessed 1 September 2024.

Rule 2 is that biodiversity unit outputs for each of the three types of habitat (area, hedgerow, watercourse) must not be summed, traded, or converted between types. The requirement to deliver at least a 10% net gain applies to each type separately.

Rule 3 is that developers must use the statutory metric (or small sites statutory metric for small sites). The output from the metric's calculation is used to assess whether the biodiversity gain objective has been met.

Rule 4 allows deviation from the standard methodology, subject to approval by relevant authorities, when there is a clear ecological justification for the habitat intervention which is not being reflected by the statutory metric. This can only occur when there are exceptional ecological circumstances, defined as when: (1) the site has optimal conditions (such as soil condition, hydrology, nutrient status) for restoration of a wildlife-rich or historic natural habitat, and (2) the project team has the expertise and resource to deliver the habitat with negligible risk of failure (as, ultimately, judged by the planning authority); and one or more of the following is proposed:[45]

1. Highly complex landscape scale habitat changes such as creation of heathland or a heathland grassland mosaic;
2. River re-meandering; and/or
3. Large-scale restoration of natural processes.

There are special techniques within the metric to allow for disapplication of the trading rules in these circumstances. Evidence must be entered directly into the metric (for example, in the user comments) for the reviewer to judge whether Rule 4 ought to be applied and the

[45] User Guide pages 17-18 https://assets.publishing.service.gov.uk/media/669e45fba3c2a28abb50d426/The_Statutory_Biodiversity_Metric_-_User_Guide__23.07.24_.pdf. Last accessed 1 September 2024.

requirements above have been satisfied. The biodiversity gain objective still needs to be met in every Rule 4 case.

In addition to the rules and the trading rules, there are nine principles which must be applied. As noted earlier, and reflected in principle 1, the metric assessment should be completed by a competent person. The remaining principles are:[46]

Principle 2	The use of this statutory metric does not override existing biodiversity protections, statutory obligations, policy requirements, ecological mitigation hierarchy or any other requirements. This includes consenting or licensing processes, for example woodlands.
Principle 3	This statutory metric should be used in accordance with established good practice guidance and professional codes.
Principle 4	This statutory metric is not a complex or comprehensive ecological model and is not a substitute for expert ecological advice.
Principle 5	Biodiversity units are a proxy for biodiversity and should be treated as relative values.
Principle 6	This statutory metric is designed to inform decisions in conjunction with locally relevant evidence, expert input, or guidance.
Principle 7	Habitat interventions need to be realistic and deliverable within a relevant project timeframe.
Principle 8	Created and enhanced habitats should be, where practical and reasonable, local to any impact and deliver strategically important outcomes for nature conservation.

46 Table 4 of the User Guide, page 19 User Guide page 13 https://assets.publishing.service.gov.uk/media/669e45fba3c2a28abb50d426/The_Statutory_Biodiversity_Metric_-_User_Guide__23.07.24_.pdf. Last accessed 1 September 2024.

Principle 9	This statutory metric does not enforce a minimum habitat size ratio for compensation of losses. Proposals should aim to: maintain habitat extent – supporting more, bigger, better and more joined up ecological networks; ensure that proposed or retained habitat parcels are of sufficient size for ecological function.

Habitat Quality Inputs

There are four relevant inputs to habitat quality: size and the three core quality components.

"Size" as a parameter means the area of the habitat to be retained, enhanced, or created, measured in hectares or kilometers. This includes areas of intertidal habitats that are both above water at low tide and under water at high tide as well as individual trees: the statutory metric contains a "tree helper" which generates an area habitat value based on the tree's diameter at breast height (see Table 14 in the User Guide).[47] The measurement of the length of a watercourse and/or hedgerow is to be taken along the centre line, using OS maps where possible. If it is a double hedgerow or a hedgerow bounding green lanes[48] then that is to count as two separate lengths. Further technical guidance on the measurement of hedgerows and the areas adjacent to hedgerows is set out within the User Guide.[49]

47 User Guide page 54 https://assets.publishing.service.gov.uk/media/669e45fba3c2a28abb50d426/The_Statutory_Biodiversity_Metric_-_User_Guide__23.07.24_.pdf. Last accessed 1 September 2024.

48 Green lanes are unsealed, unclassified roads.

49 User Guide page 24 https://assets.publishing.service.gov.uk/media/669e45fba3c2a28abb50d4

The core quality components are distinctiveness, condition, and strategic significance. Taking these in turn:

"Distinctiveness" is a measure based on the type of habitat and its distinguishing features. Each habitat type is sorted into a band depending on the following four factors: total amount of remaining habitat in England (its rarity), proportion of habitat protected through SSSI designation (where less land is protected in SSSIs, it is considered of higher distinctiveness), UK Priority Habitat Status, and finally European Red List Category.[50] The Priority Habitat Inventory (England) is the main source of data to inform Natural England's sorting of habitats into bands for the first of the two criteria listed above (total amount of habitat remaining and % of habitat protected in SSSIs), whereas Priority Habitat Status and the European Red List were used to highlight how rare or endangered a habitat is.

The statutory metric automatically attributes a number to a habitat based on its distinctiveness band, although it should be noted for watercourses the distinctiveness score is attributed based on a specific methodology (see Table 10 of the User Guide for a summary of this methodology).[51] The distinctiveness matrix is:[52]

26/The_Statutory_Biodiversity_Metric_-_User_Guide__23.07.24_.pdf. Last accessed 1 September 2024.

50 Technical Annex 2 to Biodiversity Metric 4.0 page 23 paragraph 3.1.2 https://publications.naturalengland.org.uk/publication/5850908674228224. Last accessed 1 September 2024.

51 User Guide Table 10, page 37 https://assets.publishing.service.gov.uk/media/669e45fba3c2a28abb50d426/The_Statutory_Biodiversity_Metric_-_User_Guide__23.07.24_.pdf. Last accessed 1 September 2024.

52 User Guide Table 5, page 25 https://assets.publishing.service.gov.uk/media/669e45fba3c2a28abb50d426/The_Statutory_Biodiversity_Metric_-_User_Guide__23.07.24_.pdf. Last accessed 1 September 2024.

Very high: 8
High: 6
Medium: 4
Low: 2
Very low (hedgerow module): 1
Very low (area habitat module): 0

Distinctiveness scores are also used elsewhere in the BNG regime to permit or prohibit certain actions.

"Condition" is an assessment of the habitat's ecological quality. Because varying quality habitat require varying responses, it is also used to measure variation between parcels of the same habitat type. Condition assessment sheets are provided in the metric which set out a more simplified version of the methodology used for Common Standards Monitoring, while applying a broader set of attributes.[53] The simplification is designed to allow an assessment to be undertaken with a single visit to a site, using visual indicators of likely wider habitat condition whilst still being objective and measurable.[54]

Just as with distinctiveness, the statutory metric automatically attributes a number to a habitat based on its condition. In relation to watercourse-specific differences, culverts (as defined by the Flood and Water Management Act 2010)[55] do not require a condition assessment. Ditches

---

53 For Common Standards Monitoring see JNCC guidance https://jncc.gov.uk/our-work/common-standards-monitoring-guidance/. Last accessed 1 September 2024.

54 Confirming CSM as the foundation for the condition assessment methodology: Technical Annex 2 to Biodiversity Metric 4.0 page 50 paragraph 4.1.1; reasons for it at paragraph 4.1.2 https://publications.naturalengland.org.uk/publication/5850908674228224. Last accessed 1 September 2024.

55 Schedule 2, paragraph 39 of the Flood and Water Management Act 2010 inserts the definition of culvert into s.72 of the Land Drainage Act 1991

do, using the standard statutory metric condition sheet. For all other watercourses a special assessment called a "river condition assessment" is required to assess condition. All those who carry out a river condition assessment must be accredited as a professional trained to carry them out.

Further, if the site boundary includes the riparian zone the assessment must include the adjacent lengths of watercourse in the watercourse module. To be clear, where a riparian zone is within the site boundary, the watercourse assessment must include a review of all features across the whole of the riparian zone, even if segments across the riparian zone are outside of the site boundary. This will necessarily include an assessment of the riparian zone vegetation as part of the river condition assessment and an assessment of riparian zone encroachment (on encroachment, see the paragraphs following "strategic significance" in this chapter). Table 11 of the User Guide sets out riparian zone widths for different habitat types.[56] Figure 4 then sets out how to determine whether a length of watercourse should be included or excluded from an assessment, which depends on the location of the site boundary.[57]

Once the condition is known, it is applied to this matrix to achieve the condition score:[58]

---

as follows: "'culvert' means a covered channel or pipe which prevents the obstruction of a watercourse or drainage path by an artificial construction".

56 User Guide Table 11, page 40 https://assets.publishing.service.gov.uk/media/669e45fba3c2a28abb50d426/The_Statutory_Biodiversity_Metric_-_User_Guide__23.07.24_.pdf. Last accessed 1 September 2024

57 User Guide Figure 4, page 41 https://assets.publishing.service.gov.uk/media/669e45fba3c2a28abb50d426/The_Statutory_Biodiversity_Metric_-_User_Guide__23.07.24_.pdf. Last accessed 1 September 2024

58 User Guide Table 6, page 26 https://assets.publishing.service.gov.uk/media/669e45fba3c2a28abb50d4

Good: 3
Fairly Good: 2.5
Moderate: 2
Fairly Poor: 1.5
Poor: 1
Condition Assessment N/A: 1
N/A – Other: 0

For post-development condition assessments the intermediate ("fairly") categories are not permissible unless there is an evidenced reason given in the metric by a competent professional.[59] It is also worth noting that the metric does not account for ongoing anthropogenic pressure (i.e. proximity to humans), and expert ecological judgment will be needed to determine whether a proposed outcome condition for habitat is realistically possible in light of any likely anthropogenic pressure.

"Strategic significance" refers to the local importance of the habitat based on its type and location. Habitat parcels are split in the metric where they lie on a planning authority boundary or a boundary between two areas of different strategic significance. The strategic significance of offsite habitat is to be measured using local documents relevant to the strategic significance for the offsite location rather than the development site.

The strategic significance inherent in ecological connectivity is not directly included in metric calculations (connectivity was a feature in earlier iterations but led to as yet insurmountable technical challenges, although it is understood work is underway to resolve these issues). Strategic significance is instead assessed by reference to the relevant Local

26/The_Statutory_Biodiversity_Metric_-_User_Guide__23.07.24_.pdf. Last accessed 1 September 2024

59 User Guide page 26 https://assets.publishing.service.gov.uk/media/669e45fba3c2a28abb50d426/The_Statutory_Biodiversity_Metric_-_User_Guide__23.07.24_.pdf. Last accessed 1 September 2024

Nature Recovery Strategy ("LNRS"), of which there will be 48 covering all of England.[60] The relevant LNRS must include a local habitat map that identifies opportunities for habitat uplift and a statement of biodiversity priorities, it may also include connectivity and ecological corridors. LNRS' are to be prepared under ss.104-107 of the Environment Act 2021, the Environment (Local Nature Recovery Strategies) (Procedure) Regulations 2023, and information / guidance provided by government.[61] Identified authorities are responsible for producing and implementing an LNRS. Habitat which is enhanced and/or created in an area mapped within the LNRS' Local Habitat Map for measures to be taken to achieve the priorities of the LNRS will generate 15% more biodiversity units in the metric than if the same habitat were enhanced and/or created elsewhere.

The User Guide provides a table summarising the impacts of various criteria on strategic significance:[62]

---

60 See Government announcement 30 June 2023. https://www.gov.uk/government/publications/local-nature-recovery-strategies/local-nature-recovery-strategies. Last accessed 1 September 2024

61 The announcement of 30 June 2023 indicates government will liaise with responsible authorities directly. https://www.gov.uk/government/publications/local-nature-recovery-strategies/local-nature-recovery-strategies#how-they-will-be-prepared. Last accessed 1 September 2024

62 User Guide Table 7 page 28 https://assets.publishing.service.gov.uk/media/669e45fba3c2a28abb50d426/The_Statutory_Biodiversity_Metric_-_User_Guide__23.07.24_.pdf. Last accessed 1 September 2024

Table 7 Statutory metric strategic significance categories and score applied in the metric where an LNRS has been published

Category	Score	Description
High (Formally identified in local strategy)	1.15	This category can be applied when: a) the location of the habitat parcel has been mapped in the Local Habitat Map as an area where a potential measure has been proposed to help deliver the priorities of that LNRS; and b) the intervention is consistent with the potential measure proposed for that location If your project delivers the mapped potential measure set out in the LNRS you should: record strategic significance as low in the baseline record strategic significance as high in post-intervention sheets record that you have applied the published LNRS in your gain plan
Medium	1.10	This was an interim category prior to any LNRS being developed; it can no longer be applied in this context.
Low (Area / compensation not in local strategy)	1	Where the definition for high strategic significance is not met. Even if your project is an area mapped with a potential measure, if it does not deliver the specific actions outlined for your location you should record strategic significance as low.

Where there is no published LNRS, first, the relevant planning authority should have specified (or will during discussions with developers) which alternative documents are to be used for assigning strategic significance. The User Guide gives the following examples (in a non-exhaustive list):[63]

- Draft Local Nature Recovery Strategies
- Local Plans and Neighbourhood Plans
- Local Planning Authority Local Ecological Networks
- Tree Strategies and Woodland Strategies
- Area of Outstanding Natural Beauty Management Plans
- Biodiversity Action Plans
- Species conservation and protected sites strategies
- Green Infrastructure Strategies
- River Basin Management Plans
- Catchment Plans and Catchment Planning Systems
- Shoreline management plans
- Estuary Strategies

These documents are to be used in the first instance, and applied to the descriptions set out in Table 8. If there is no document for which a "high" strategic significance could be used (i.e. there is no document mapping and identifying ecologically important habitat types), Table 8 instructs assessors to assign medium strategic significance when the other criteria in Table 8 are met. Otherwise, the strategic significance score will be "low":[64]

---

63 User Guide page 27 https://assets.publishing.service.gov.uk/media/669e45fba3c2a28abb50d426/The_Statutory_Biodiversity_Metric_-_User_Guide__23.07.24_.pdf. Last accessed 1 September 2024

64 User Guide Table 8 page 29 https://assets.publishing.service.gov.uk/media/669e45fba3c2a28abb50d426/The_Statutory_Biodiversity_Metric_-_User_Guide__23.07.24_.pdf. Last accessed 1 September 2024

Table 8 Statutory metric strategic significance categories and score applied in the metric where an LNRS has not yet been published

Category	Score	Description
High (Formally identified in local strategy)	1.15	The habitat type is mapped and described as locally ecologically important within a specific location, within documents specified by the relevant planning authority. If your project delivers the mapped habitat creation, enhancement or actions set out within specified alternative documents, or enhances an existing habitat identified within specified alternative documents as locally ecologically important, strategic significance can be recorded as high in the post-intervention sheets. If the specified alternative documents identify existing habitat as locally ecologically important within a specified location, strategic significance may be recorded as high in the baseline. You should record the name of the plan the relevant planning authority has specified in the user comments and record that you have used the specified document in your gain plan.
Medium (Location ecologically desirable but not in local strategy)	1.10	This category can be applied when the PA has not identified a suitable document for assessing strategic significance. Users should: • explain how the habitat type is ecologically important within a specific location • demonstrate the importance of that habitat in providing ecological linkage to other strategically significant locations • use professional judgement When the above criteria are met, strategic significance may be recorded as medium in the baseline and post-intervention sheets. can be applied when the LPA has not identified a suitable document for assessing strategic significance.

Low (Area / compensation not in local strategy)	1	Where the definitions for high or medium strategic significance are not met.

In addition, for watercourses there are two more quality components: (1) riparian zone encroachment and (2) watercourse encroachment.

Riparian zone encroachment occurs when any feature or activity of the development proposed within the riparian zone reduces the quantity, quality or ecological function of the riparian habitat.[65] Extant towpaths, footpaths, river crossings, and existing small amenity features and utility units where the total footprint is less than 5% of the riparian zone area are excluded from metric calculations but must still be recorded in the baseline. There is a particular methodology for assessing riparian encroachment (for example, both banks must be assessed separately), applying the thresholds for material encroachment and applicable categorisation in Table 12:[66]

65 User Guide page 41 https://assets.publishing.service.gov.uk/media/669e45fba3c2a28abb50d426/The_Statutory_Biodiversity_Metric_-_User_Guide__23.07.24_.pdf. Last accessed 1 September 2024

66 User Guide Table 12 page 42 https://assets.publishing.service.gov.uk/media/669e45fba3c2a28abb50d426/The_Statutory_Biodiversity_Metric_-_User_Guide__23.07.24_.pdf. Last accessed 1 September 2024

Table 12 Watercourse riparian zone encroachment bands

Riparian zone encroachment band for a bank	Definition for rivers and canals	Definition for Ditches
No encroachment	No encroachment within 10 metres of bank top	No encroachment within 5 metres of bank top
Minor	Any encroachment 8 to 10 metres from the bank top (covering up to 100% of area); or where the footprint of encroachment occupies 0- 10% of the riparian zone area 4 to 10 metres from bank top.	Any encroachment 4 to 5 metres from the bank top (covering up to 100% of area); or where the footprint of encroachment occupies 0-10% of the riparian zone area 2 to 5 metres from bank top.
Moderate	Where the footprint of encroachment occupies between 10% to 25% of the riparian zone area 4 to 10 metres from the bank top.	Where the footprint of encroachment occupies between 10% to 25% of the riparian zone area 2 to 5 metres from the bank top.
Major	Any encroachment 0 to 4 metres from the bank top; or Where encroachment occupies greater than 25% of the total riparian zone area.	Any encroachment 0 to 2 metres from the bank top; or Where encroachment occupies greater than 25% of the total riparian zone area.

Watercourse encroachment is any feature and/or action that adversely affects the natural function of the watercourse, or results in localised changes in habitat, species and migratory pathways.[67] It does not include restorative works that improve the condition of the watercourse or reinstate natural riverine processes. Culverts are not given a category, instead any encroachment into a culvert is automatically attributed 0.68 as a multiplier. A multiplier is applied for any watercourse encroachment, on a sliding scale of severity, from non-material encroachment to major, as follows:[68]

Table 13 Watercourse encroachment bands

Watercourse encroachment band	Multiplier	Description	Examples
No encroachment	1.0	less than 5% of the bank length is an engineered bank revetment and there is no encroachment into the channel	N/A
Minor	0.8	5% to 20% of the bank length is an engineered bank revetment; or there is encroachment across up to 10% of the channel width at any one point	Small headwalls, jetties, pontoons

67 User Guide page 44 https://assets.publishing.service.gov.uk/media/669e45fba3c2a28abb50d426/The_Statutory_Biodiversity_Metric_-_User_Guide__23.07.24_.pdf. Last accessed 1 September 2024

68 User Guide Table 13 page 44 https://assets.publishing.service.gov.uk/media/669e45fba3c2a28abb50d426/The_Statutory_Biodiversity_Metric_-_User_Guide__23.07.24_.pdf. Last accessed 1 September 2024

Major	0.5	greater than 20% of the bank length is an engineered bank revetment; or there is encroachment across greater than 10% of the channel width at any one point	Weirs, large headwalls, bank revetment

There is scope to reduce an impact from major to minor even when it is not possible to fully remove manmade structures along or within a watercourse. Partial restoration, i.e. by removing an in-channel structure or reducing the extent of bank revetment (a revetment is any manmade structure placed along the watercourse bank to protect against erosion caused by wave action, storm surge and currents), are acceptable as enhancement works within the metric. In general, all interventions which return watercourses closer to their natural state, and the development of natural habitats within (and along: riparian vegetation also matters) are considered to be watercourse enhancements within the metric.[69]

Specific Assessments

There are, unsurprisingly, nuances within the overarching tri-partite division of kinds of habitat. There are special notes for urban environments, such as habitat mosaics, accounting for degraded sites, and the inclusion of green roofs and/or green walls in the various metric assessments. Individual trees in particular require special attention.[70]

---

69 See "watercourse enhancement" User Guide page 45 https://assets.publishing.service.gov.uk/media/669e45fba3c2a28abb50d426/The_Statutory_Biodiversity_Metric_-_User_Guide__23.07.24_.pdf. Last accessed 1 September 2024

70 See "Individual trees broad habitat type" User Guide pages 53-57 https://assets.publishing.service.gov.uk/media/669e45fba3c2a28abb50d4

As noted earlier in this chapter, individual trees are recorded using the "tree helper" within the metric and categorised as either urban or rural trees. The tree helper generates data to represent canopy biomass using a calculation derived from BS 5837:2012. The area generated in the metric by the tree helper formulas should not be adjusted. The habitat *underneath* a tree canopy is to be included separately within the metric.

Each individual tree will require its own condition assessment. Individual trees within hedgerows and rural lines are to be recorded as individual trees, each with their own condition assessment, unless there is no loss or change of condition of individual trees, in which case the individual trees within that feature do not need to be recorded separately in the baseline. There is a "lines of trees" option within the hedgerow module, to be used only in rural areas. Lines, blocks or groups of trees within and around the perimeter of urban land should be recorded as habitat type "individual trees". In all circumstances "individual trees" should be used to record ancient and veteran trees, regardless of whether they are within hedgerows, rural lines of trees, and/or and woodlands. Trees within overgrown non-native and ornamental hedges should not be classified using the "individual trees" habitat type, but rather as non-native ornamental hedges within the hedgerow module.[71]

All "small" trees (greater than 7.5cm and less than or equal to 30cm diameter at breast height)[72] which are lost do not need to be recorded as individual trees if they are located within a hedgerow, rural line of trees, wood-pasture, parkland or orchard.

26/The_Statutory_Biodiversity_Metric_-_User_Guide__23.07.24_.pdf. Last accessed 1 September 2024

71 User Guide page 53 https://assets.publishing.service.gov.uk/media/669e45fba3c2a28abb50d426/The_Statutory_Biodiversity_Metric_-_User_Guide__23.07.24_.pdf. Last accessed 1 September 2024.

72 Defined in an earlier footnote: "Diameter at breast height" technically means 1.3 meters above ground level.

Otherwise, trees that have to be removed for any reason, including for disease and/or safety reasons, must still be recorded in the baseline and will be considered "lost" within the metric calculation. This is not an unjustified punitive measure, as all trees have ecological value, even (sometimes especially) dead trees.

Planted trees are recorded in the metric as the size when first planted. Natural growth over time for both planted and retained trees should not be included as a separate gain in its own right within the metric. Instead, that should be incorporated into the overall assessment of the *condition* that can be realistically achieved within the relevant BNG maintenance timeframe, normally 30 years.

Defining the Habitat Intervention Category

The next step within the metric assessment is to input the proposed intervention (habitat retention, enhancement, and/or creation). Habitat intervention works cannot be two intervention categories simultaneously, so a proposed intervention cannot be both retention and enhancement, or creation and enhancement; it must fall within one of the three categories. There is of course scope to carry out a series of interventions which individually fall into any one of the three categories as part of the whole BNG package.

Retention of habitat occurs when there is no loss of habitat and it is retained in its baseline condition, and there is no action to enhance the habitat; this includes the riparian zone in relation to watercourses.[73]

Retention is not always straightforward as an option, as retained habitat may still be degraded by natural or human processes, and so there can be

[73] User Guide page 30. For watercourses see page 45 https://assets.publishing.service.gov.uk/media/669e45fba3c2a28abb50d426/The_Statutory_Biodiversity_Metric_-_User_Guide__23.07.24_.pdf. Last accessed 1 September 2024

cases where retention would not meet the requirement of the metric that retained habitat is kept in baseline condition. In cases where there is a risk of degradation, reliance on "retention" for the purposes of the metric may still mean ongoing interventions for at least 30 years are needed in order to maintain the habitat's baseline condition. Where degradation is a risk but the necessary ongoing interventions are not possible for the requisite 30-year period, the metric assessment will have to record the same area and habitat type as being "created" but in a lower condition than the baseline, the "habitat created in advance" function must be set to 30+ years and the assessor must provide ecological reasoning in the user comments.[74]

Enhancement of habitat occurs when there is an improvement in condition compared to the baseline state, a change to a higher distinctiveness habitat within the same broad habitat group compared to the baseline state, restoration of relict high or very high distinctiveness habitats, or restoration of intertidal habitats. Watercourse enhancement is any intervention which promotes natural functions, processes, and/or the development of natural habitats.[75]

Creation of habitat occurs when there is a loss of baseline habitat (and it is replaced with another), or a change in broad habitat type, such as a change from grassland to woodland. Only area habitat and hedgerows can be "created" in this way; watercourse creation is defined as an intervention which is not enhancement, such as straightening a channel,

[74] User Guide page 30 https://assets.publishing.service.gov.uk/media/669e45fba3c2a28abb50d426/The_Statutory_Biodiversity_Metric_-_User_Guide__23.07.24_.pdf. Last accessed 1 September 2024

[75] User Guide page 31. For watercourses see page 45 https://assets.publishing.service.gov.uk/media/669e45fba3c2a28abb50d426/The_Statutory_Biodiversity_Metric_-_User_Guide__23.07.24_.pdf. Last accessed 1 September 2024

installing a culvert, alteration of the watercourse alignment, etc.[76] While creation of new habitat is the most straightforward type of intervention in terms of use of the metric, it is the most difficult in practice to achieve.

When there is doubt over whether works constitute retention or enhancement, creation should be selected as the intervention category for the purposes of the metric. [77] It is also important to remember BNG is 10% gain over the baseline – i.e. the regime requires 110% post-development biodiversity value in reality. This means when habitat is lost the developer also needs to compensate for the loss of the baseline habitat in addition to achieving 10% net gain. The User Guide gives the example of a developer creating a broadleaved woodland on modified grassland; in this case they would still need to compensate for the loss of the grassland in line with the trading rules.[78]

Risk Multipliers

Three risk multipliers are then applied to the proposed intervention(s): difficulty, temporal risk, and spatial risk.

"Difficulty" (of enhancement and/or creation) is a measure representing uncertainty in the effectiveness of management techniques used to

76 User Guide page 32. For watercourses see page 46 https://assets.publishing.service.gov.uk/media/669e45fba3c2a28abb50d426/The_Statutory_Biodiversity_Metric_-_User_Guide__23.07.24_.pdf. Last accessed 1 September 2024

77 User Guide page 32 https://assets.publishing.service.gov.uk/media/669e45fba3c2a28abb50d426/The_Statutory_Biodiversity_Metric_-_User_Guide__23.07.24_.pdf. Last accessed 1 September 2024

78 User Guide page 32 https://assets.publishing.service.gov.uk/media/669e45fba3c2a28abb50d426/The_Statutory_Biodiversity_Metric_-_User_Guide__23.07.24_.pdf. Last accessed 1 September 2024

enhance or create that specific habitat. There is an automatic score within the metric which is applied based on the habitat intervention category (whether enhancement or creation), and the type of habitat. Professional judgment will need to be applied as well, because the difficulty multiplier will not remediate the risk inherent in proposing habitat intervention that is ecologically unsound.

The "time to target condition" multiplier represents the average number of years it will take for a habitat to reach its intended ecological state (whether target condition or distinctiveness, from the start of works until achievement of the target outcome). Again, this is an automatic adjustment made within the metric. If there is any delay between loss and the start of the habitat intervention works this too needs to be factored into the metric, as does the benefit of certainty for any habitat created in advance (i.e. when offsite units are bought through a habitat bank).[79] A bonus is attributed to habitat created in advance because there is lower risk: it has already been proven to be successful. Where the harm is temporary (less than two years from the start of the impact to restoration to the baseline habitat condition and type) then this harm does not need to be recorded as a loss within the metric. This said, this approach to temporary losses cannot be used where policies or permissions require that a specific baseline is applied.[80]

For offsite BNG only, the "spatial risk" multiplier is also applied. This factors in the distance between the location of biodiversity loss (onsite) and where the offsite habitat is being delivered. The outcome is an

---

79 User Guide page 33 https://assets.publishing.service.gov.uk/media/669e45fba3c2a28abb50d426/The_Statutory_Biodiversity_Metric_-_User_Guide__23.07.24_.pdf. Last accessed 1 September 2024

80 User Guide page 34 https://assets.publishing.service.gov.uk/media/669e45fba3c2a28abb50d426/The_Statutory_Biodiversity_Metric_-_User_Guide__23.07.24_.pdf. Last accessed 1 September 2024

assessment of the impact of habitat creation or enhancement relative to the location of the original habitat loss, applying the multiplier score depending on the situation set out in Table 9 of the User Guide:[81]

Table 9 Spatial risk scores and descriptions

Spatial risk category and score	Area and hedgerow modules	Watercourse modules
Within (1.0)	Compensation is within Local Planning Authority (LPA) boundary or National Character Area (NCA) of impact site Intertidal habitats only: Compensation is within Marine Plan Area of impact site	Compensation is within waterbody catchment
Neighbouring (0.75)	Compensation is outside LPA or NCA of impact site, but within neighbouring LPA or NCA Intertidal habitats only: Compensation is outside Marine Plan Area of impact site, but within neighbouring Marine Plan Area	Compensation is outside waterbody catchment, but within operational catchment
Outside (0.5)	Compensation is outside LPA or NCA of impact site and outside neighbouring LPA or NCA Intertidal habitats only: Compensation is outside Marine Plan Area of impact site and outside neighbouring Marine Plan Area	Compensation is outside operational catchment

81 User Guide Table 9 page 35 https://assets.publishing.service.gov.uk/media/669e45fba3c2a28abb50d426/The_Statutory_Biodiversity_Metric_-_User_Guide__23.07.24_.pdf. Last accessed 1 September 2024

Metric Tool Results

Clearly results should be prepared and submitted following industry standards and practices, ensuring accurate and transparent biodiversity assessments. Uploading completed statutory metric tools to planning portals can sometimes be problematic, the following tips may assist:[82]

- unhide all sheets using the 'view all' button on the start page
- save a copy as a macro disabled excel file (.xlsx)
- check document size is less than 10MB

Appendices and Additional Resources

Appendix A of the metric User Guide provides a detailed guide on how to input data into the statutory metric, navigate through its interface, and troubleshoot common issues.

Versions

The current version of the statutory metric (previously version 4.0) is the official version required for BNG calculations. Earlier versions of the metric are not acceptable in planning applications.[83] The outcomes of calculations for most habitats will not change between metric version 4.0 and the statutory version. DEFRA has published information on what

82 User Guide page 62 https://assets.publishing.service.gov.uk/media/669e45fba3c2a28abb50d426/The_Statutory_Biodiversity_Metric_-_User_Guide__23.07.24_.pdf. Last accessed 1 September 2024

83 DEFRA guidance https://www.gov.uk/guidance/biodiversity-net-gain-what-local-planning-authorities-should-do. Last accessed 1 September 2024.

has changed and how to copy and paste from version 4.0 to the statutory version.[84]

Offsite Units and the Metric

Landowners who sell offsite BNG units must use the metric to prove the units that have been sold have been accurately measured in terms of biodiversity value by filling in the offsite part of the statutory metric for all habitat enhancements they are delivering for that development. A completed metric calculation will have to be submitted to Natural England in any event as the register operator alongside all applications to register offsite units (see Offsite BNG chapter below).

The Small Sites Metric

From 2 April 2024 "small" developments are also required to achieve BNG. A small development is defined by what it is not, being major development as defined in article 2(1) of the Town and Country Planning (Development Management Procedure) (England) Order 2015. The DEFRA guidance is more helpful in defining what is a small site:[85]

- residential development where the number of dwellings is between 1 and 9 on a site of an area 1 hectare or less, or if the number of dwellings is unknown, the site area is less than 0.5 hectares;
- commercial development where floor space created is less than 1,000 square metres or total site area is less than 1 hectare;

---

84 Natural England, "Overview of Metric Changes" February 2024. Available at: https://publications.naturalengland.org.uk/publication/6049804846366720. Last accessed 1 September 2024.

85 DEFRA guidance https://www.gov.uk/guidance/biodiversity-metric-calculate-the-biodiversity-net-gain-of-a-project-or-development Last accessed 1 September 2024.

- development that is not the winning and working of minerals or the use of land for mineral-working deposits; and
- development that is not waste development.

The purpose of the small sites metric is to offer a streamlined and more proportionate version of the statutory metric. As the values are fixed for all habitats assessed in the small sites metric, developers do not have to carry out a condition assessment as part of the pre-development survey of existing habitat.[86] Developers do not need an ecologist to use the small sites metric,[87] although someone with knowledge of the development site and its habitat would be required.

It is not mandatory for small sites to use the small sites metric; developers of small sites are perfectly entitled to use the statutory metric if they prefer. The converse is not true; developers of major development schemes cannot use the small sites metric (as they are not developing a small site).

Further, the small sites metric cannot be used on sites where the onsite habitat includes any of the following:[88]

86 "Developments for on-site gains within small developments do not need to submit habitat surveys." From https://www.gov.uk/guidance/biodiversity-net-gain-what-local-planning-authorities-should-do. Last accessed 1 September 2024.

87 Small Sites Metric User Guide page 6 https://assets.publishing.service.gov.uk/media/669e46e0ab418ab055592a25/The_Small_Sites_Metric__Statutory_Biodiversity_Metric__-__User_Guide__23.07.2024_.pdf. Last accessed 1 September 2024.

88 Small Sites Metric User Guide page 8 https://assets.publishing.service.gov.uk/media/669e46e0ab418ab055592a25/The_Small_Sites_Metric__Statutory_Biodiversity_Metric__-__User_Guide__23.07.2024_.pdf. Last accessed 1 September 2024.

- priority habitats (excluding some hedgerows and arable field margins);
- protected sites; and/or
- European protected species.

If statutory protected sites or priority habitats are located within 500m of the development site boundary, this must be noted within the small sites metric and a warning flag will appear. Depending on the circumstances, the developer may need to hire an ecologist and use the statutory metric instead.

Users can only propose the enhancement and/or creation of very low, low, and medium distinctiveness habitats within the small sites metric.[89] If habitats of higher distinctiveness bands are to be enhanced or created, because of the greater ecological complexity involved, the statutory metric must be used. Further, any enhancement or restoration of rivers or streams must be calculated using the statutory metric.[90] If there is any encroachment on a watercourse or its riparian zone the statutory metric must be used.[91] Finally, advanced or delayed habitat creation is not an

89 See 'distinctiveness' in Table 1 of the Small Sites Metric User Guide page 9 https://assets.publishing.service.gov.uk/media/669e46e0ab418ab055592a25/The_Small_Sites_Metric__Statutory_Biodiversity_Metric__-__User_Guide__23.07.2024_.pdf. Last accessed 1 September 2024.

90 Small Sites Metric User Guide page 12 https://assets.publishing.service.gov.uk/media/669e46e0ab418ab055592a25/The_Small_Sites_Metric__Statutory_Biodiversity_Metric__-__User_Guide__23.07.2024_.pdf. Last accessed 1 September 2024

91 Small Sites Metric User Guide page 24 https://assets.publishing.service.gov.uk/media/669e46e0ab418ab055592a25/The_Small_Sites_Metric__Statutory_Biodiversity_Metric__-__User_Guide__23.07.2024_.pdf. Last accessed 1 September 2024.

option within the small sites metric: in such cases the statutory metric must be used.[92]

If any part of a development site must be completed using the statutory metric, the entire site must be assessed using it.[93]

The small sites metric does not have an offsite section, but developers of small sites can still use offsite units for the purposes of achieving BNG.[94] If offsite units are required, the developer will need to submit the completed small sites metric calculation to the relevant planning authority alongside the biodiversity gain plan which proposes the use of offsite units. The developer should also send the completed output from the small sites metric to the offsite BNG unit provider for the purpose of recording the allocation on the biodiversity gain site register. Offsite habitat can be assessed using the statutory metric, even when the onsite habitat is assessed using the small sites metric.[95]

---

92 Small Sites Metric User Guide page 22 https://assets.publishing.service.gov.uk/media/669e46e0ab418ab055592a25/The_Small_Sites_Metric__Statutory_Biodiversity_Metric__-__User_Guide__23.07.2024_.pdf. Last accessed 1 September 2024.

93 Small Sites Metric User Guide page 8 https://assets.publishing.service.gov.uk/media/669e46e0ab418ab055592a25/The_Small_Sites_Metric__Statutory_Biodiversity_Metric__-__User_Guide__23.07.2024_.pdf. Last accessed 1 September 2024

94 DEFRA guidance https://www.gov.uk/guidance/biodiversity-metric-calculate-the-biodiversity-net-gain-of-a-project-or-development. Last accessed 1 September 2024.

95 Small Sites Metric User Guide page 7 https://assets.publishing.service.gov.uk/media/669e46e0ab418ab055592a25/The_Small_Sites_Metric__Statutory_Biodiversity_Metric__-__User_Guide__23.07.2024_.pdf. Last accessed 1 September 2024

Detailed Overview of the Small Sites Metric

Competency Requirements

Those completing the small sites metric are known as "users". It is the developer's responsibility to select a competent person to complete the small sites metric, who, as noted earlier, doesn't necessarily have to be an ecologist. Users must have the required knowledge, skills, and experience to conduct and review the calculations: the standard for competency for "users" is the British Standard BS 8683:2021 for biodiversity net gain.[96] The planning authority does not need to verify the competency of the user for the small sites metric.[97]

SSM Rules, Principles and Data Inputs

There are three Rules:[98]

Rule 1: The small sites metric trading rules must be followed.

Rule 2: Biodiversity unit outputs cannot be summed, traded, or converted between different unit types. The requirement to deliver at least 10% net gain applies to each type of unit.

---

96 Small Sites Metric User Guide page 6 https://assets.publishing.service.gov.uk/media/669e46e0ab418ab055592a25/The_Small_Sites_Metric__Statutory_Biodiversity_Metric__-__User_Guide__23.07.2024_.pdf. Last accessed 1 September 2024.

97 Small Sites Metric User Guide page 6 https://assets.publishing.service.gov.uk/media/669e46e0ab418ab055592a25/The_Small_Sites_Metric__Statutory_Biodiversity_Metric__-__User_Guide__23.07.2024_.pdf. Last accessed 1 September 2024

98 Small Sites Metric User Guide Table 2 page 11 https://assets.publishing.service.gov.uk/media/669e46e0ab418ab055592a25/The_Small_Sites_Metric__Statutory_Biodiversity_Metric__-__User_Guide__23.07.2024_.pdf. Last accessed 1 September 2024

Rule 3: To accurately apply the statutory metric formula, developers must use the statutory metric or small sites statutory metric for small sites. The tools remove the need for a user to manually calculate the change in biodiversity value. The tool will summarise the results of the calculation and inform a user whether the biodiversity net gain objective has been met.

Table 3 of the Small Sites User Guide sets out the trading rules for the small sites metric:[99]

Table 3 Trading rules (Rule 1) to compensate for losses

Baseline habitat distinctiveness band	Area module (area units)	Hedgerow module (hedgerow units)	Watercourse module (watercourse units)
Medium	Losses must be replaced by area habitat units of medium band habitats within the same broad habitat type	Losses must be replaced with hedgerow units of the same band	Losses must be replaced with watercourse units of the same habitat type
Low	Losses must be replaced with area habitat units of the same or higher band	Losses must be replaced with hedgerow units of the same or of a higher band	Losses must be replaced with watercourse units of a higher band
Very low	Trading rules do not apply	Losses must be replaced with hedgerow units of the same or of a higher band	Not applicable

99 Small Sites Metric User Guide Table 3 page 12 https://assets.publishing.service.gov.uk/media/669e46e0ab418ab055592a25/The_Small_Sites_Metric__Statutory_Biodiversity_Metric__-_User_Guide__23.07.2024_.pdf. Last accessed 1 September 2024

There is also a note on trading in relation to watercourses. Compensation for the loss of any watercourse units should be on a section of watercourse with similar habitat features. The Small Sites Metric User Guide gives as examples:[100]

- impacts on canals cannot be offset on rivers
- impacts on ditches cannot be offset on canals or rivers

Additionally, there are nine principles set out at Table 4:[101]

Table 4 SSM principles

Principle number	Principle detail
Principle 1	The SSM assessment should be completed by a competent person.
Principle 2	The SSM does not change existing biodiversity protections, statutory obligations, or policy requirements. The use of the SSM does not override the ecological mitigation hierarchy and other requirements. This includes consenting or licensing processes, for example those applied over woodlands.
Principle 3	The SSM should be used in accordance with established good practice guidance and professional codes.
Principle 4	The SSM is not a complex or comprehensive ecological model and is not a substitute for expert ecological advice.

100 Small Sites Metric User Guide page 12 https://assets.publishing.service.gov.uk/media/669e46e0ab418ab055592a25/The_Small_Sites_Metric__Statutory_Biodiversity_Metric_-__User_Guide__23.07.2024_.pdf. Last accessed 1 September 2024

101 Small Sites Metric User Guide page 13 https://assets.publishing.service.gov.uk/media/669e46e0ab418ab055592a25/The_Small_Sites_Metric__Statutory_Biodiversity_Metric_-__User_Guide__23.07.2024_.pdf. Last accessed 1 September 2024

Principle 5	Biodiversity units are a proxy for biodiversity and should be treated as relative values.
Principle 6	The SSM is designed to inform decisions in conjunction with locally relevant evidence, expert input, or guidance.
Principle 7	Habitat interventions need to be realistic and deliverable within a relevant project timeframe.
Principle 8	Created and enhanced habitats should be, where practical and reasonable, local to any impact and deliver strategically important outcomes for nature conservation.
Principle 9	The SSM does not enforce a minimum habitat size ratio for compensation of losses. Proposals should aim to: • maintain habitat extent – supporting more, bigger, better and more joined up ecological networks • ensure that proposed or retained habitat parcels are of sufficient size for ecological function

The difference between the statutory metric and the small sites metric is made particularly clear through Table 5 of the Small Sites Metric User Guide, which summarises the data inputs needed (noting habitat type is required for all types of biodiversity units and size is always in metres):[102]

[102] Small Sites Metric User Guide Table 5 page 14 https://assets.publishing.service.gov.uk/media/669e46e0ab418ab055592a25/The_Small_Sites_Metric__Statutory_Biodiversity_Metric_-_User_Guide__23.07.2024_.pdf. Last accessed 1 September 2024

Table 5 Data inputs required for area, hedgerow, and watercourse biodiversity units

Calculation input	Area	Hedgerow	Watercourses
Distinctiveness	Automatically assigned by SSM	Automatically assigned by SSM	Automatically assigned by SSM
Condition and target condition	Required for some created and enhanced habitats only	Required for some created and enhanced habitats only	Required for some created and enhanced habitats only
Strategic significance	Required	Required	Required
Area retained, enhanced, or lost	Required	Not required	Not required
Length retained, enhanced, or lost	Not required	Required	Required

Distinctiveness scores are automatically attributed in the small sites metric as follows (Table 6):[103]

Medium: 4
Low: 2
Very low (hedgerow module): 1
Very low (area module): 0

103 Small Sites Metric User Guide Table 6 page 16 https://assets.publishing.service.gov.uk/media/669e46e0ab418ab055592a25/The_Small_Sites_Metric__Statutory_Biodiversity_Metric_-_User_Guide__23.07.2024_.pdf. Last accessed 1 September 2024

As noted above, no condition assessment is required in the small sites metric. The automatically-attributed condition scores for baseline habitats are as follows (Table 7):[104]

Good: 3
Moderate: 2
Poor: 1
Condition Assessment N/A: 1
N/A – Other: 0

Some habitat types will allow the user to assign a condition post-development. The Small Sites Metric User Guide confirms the default option selected should be the lowest available condition, unless evidence can be provided as to how a higher condition will be achieved.[105]

The same approach for strategic significance as the statutory metric is applied where there is a LNRS.[106] Where there isn't one yet published, the approach under the small sites metric is slightly different, as set out in Table 9:[107]

---

104 Small Sites Metric User Guide Table 7 page 16 https://assets.publishing.service.gov.uk/media/669e46e0ab418ab055592a25/The_Small_Sites_Metric__Statutory_Biodiversity_Metric_-_User_Guide__23.07.2024_.pdf. Last accessed 1 September 2024

105 Small Sites Metric User Guide page 16 https://assets.publishing.service.gov.uk/media/669e46e0ab418ab055592a25/The_Small_Sites_Metric__Statutory_Biodiversity_Metric_-_User_Guide__23.07.2024_.pdf. Last accessed 1 September 2024

106 See Small Sites Metric User Guide pages 17-18 and Table 8 https://assets.publishing.service.gov.uk/media/669e46e0ab418ab055592a25/The_Small_Sites_Metric__Statutory_Biodiversity_Metric_-_User_Guide__23.07.2024_.pdf. Last accessed 1 September 2024

107 Small Sites Metric User Guide Table 9 page 19 https://assets.publishing.service.gov.uk/media/669e46e0ab418ab055592a

Table 9 Statutory metric strategic significance categories where an LNRS has not yet been published

Strategic significance category	**Score applied in the metric**	**Description**
High (Formally identified in local strategy)	1.15	The habitat type is mapped and described as locally ecologically important within a specific location, within documents specified by the relevant planning authority. If your project delivers the mapped habitat creation, enhancement or actions set out within specified alternative documents, or enhances an existing habitat identified within specified alternative documents as locally ecologically important, strategic significance can be recorded as high in the habitat creation and enhancement sections of the SSM. If the specified alternative documents identify existing habitat as locally ecologically important within a specified location, strategic significance may be recorded as high in the baseline. You should record the name of the plan the relevant planning authority has specified in the user comments and record that you have used the specified document in your gain plan.
Low (Area / compensation not in local strategy)	1	Where the definition for high strategic significance is not met.

25/The Small Sites Metric Statutory Biodiversity Metric - User Guide 23.07.2024 .pdf. Last accessed 1 September 2024

Risk Multipliers

Only two risk multipliers are applied to post-development enhancement and/or creation interventions in the small sites metric:[108]

- difficulty of enhancement and/or creation; and
- temporal risk.

The same approach to the risk multipliers as in the statutory metric is taken (including for temporary loss); both the difficulty and temporal risk multipliers are automatically applied in the small sites metric.

Section 10 of the Small Sites Metric User Guide sets out a step-by-step process for completing the metric.[109] Appendix 1 sets out a troubleshooting guide for common issues,[110] and Appendix 2 is a UKHab translation table intended for landscape architects, architects, planning consultants and other planning professionals who might be more familiar with landscape terminologies. It translates landscape terms into terms used in the small sites metric (and the associated distinctiveness category).[111]

---

108 Small Sites Metric User Guide page 22 https://assets.publishing.service.gov.uk/media/669e46e0ab418ab055592a25/The_Small_Sites_Metric__Statutory_Biodiversity_Metric__-__User_Guide__23.07.2024_.pdf. Last accessed 1 September 2024

109 Small Sites Metric User Guide pages 34-43 https://assets.publishing.service.gov.uk/media/669e46e0ab418ab055592a25/The_Small_Sites_Metric__Statutory_Biodiversity_Metric__-__User_Guide__23.07.2024_.pdf. Last accessed 1 September 2024

110 Small Sites Metric User Guide pages 44-47 https://assets.publishing.service.gov.uk/media/669e46e0ab418ab055592a25/The_Small_Sites_Metric__Statutory_Biodiversity_Metric__-__User_Guide__23.07.2024_.pdf. Last accessed 1 September 2024

111 Small Sites Metric User Guide pages 48-53 https://assets.publishing.service.gov.uk/media/669e46e0ab418ab055592a

25/The_Small_Sites_Metric__Statutory_Biodiversity_Metric__-__User_Guide__23.07.2024_.pdf. Last accessed 1 September 2024

CHAPTER FOUR

THE BIODIVERSITY GAIN CONDITION(S) AND BIODIVERSITY GAIN PLAN

The Biodiversity Gain Condition(s)

The statutory metric chapter preceded the biodiversity gain plan chapter because the metric must be used at the application stage to calculate the pre-development biodiversity value of the land within the red line boundary, whereas the biodiversity gain condition only requires the biodiversity gain plan to be submitted after planning permission has been granted.[112] This does not, of course, preclude developers from submitting a draft biodiversity gain plan earlier in the process to ensure any issues are identified early and the subsequent discharge of the biodiversity gain condition process is efficient.

The biodiversity gain condition, (actually potentially a series of conditions in the case of phased development) is imposed on planning permission differently from the normal imposition of conditions under section 70(1)(a) and s.72 of the Town and Country Planning Act 1990. Instead, the planning condition is automatically imposed by Schedule 7A, paragraph 13(1) of the Town and Country Planning Act

---

112 In fact, as a matter of law, the biodiversity gain plan cannot be formally submitted before: by article 37B of the Town and Country Planning (Development Management Procedure) (England) Order 2015 the biodiversity gain plan cannot be submitted earlier than "the day after the day on which formal notification is given of the decision to grant planning permission". In other words, the day after planning permission is granted.

1990. The condition applies to every planning permission granted for the development of land in England (unless the specified exemptions or transitional provisions apply).

The standard biodiversity gain condition imposed under paragraph 13(1) is set out at Schedule 7A, paragraph 13(2):

> "(2) The condition is that the development may not be begun unless-
>
> > (a) a biodiversity gain plan has been submitted to the planning authority (see paragraph 14), and
> >
> > (b) the planning authority has approved the plan (see paragraph 15)."

Planners and legal practitioners must also be aware of the alternative biodiversity conditions for phased development under paragraph 13 which are substituted for the above condition by reg.4 of the Biodiversity Gain (Town and Country Planning) (Modifications and Amendments) (England) Regulations 2024. These alternative conditions do not appear in paragraph 13 of the Town and Country Planning Act 1990 on Westlaw due to their circumstantial application. They apply when (by reg.3; this is the same definition for phased development at Schedule 7A, paragraph 19(1)):

> "(a) the grant of outline planning permission, where the reservation of matters for subsequent approval has the effect of requiring or permitting development to proceed in phases; [or]

(b) the grant of any kind of planning permission[113], where the grant is subject to conditions (whether requiring the subsequent approval of any matters or otherwise) having that effect."

The alternative conditions for phased development in Schedule 7A, paragraph 13 as modified by the Biodiversity Gain (Town and Country Planning) (Modifications and Amendments) (England) Regulations 2024 are as follows:

"13. *General condition of planning permission*

(1) The grant of planning permission of the type mentioned in paragraph 19(1)(a) or (b) for the development of land in England shall be deemed to have been granted subject to the conditions in sub-paragraphs (2) to (6).

(2) The conditions are that-

(a) the development may not be begun unless the requirement in sub-paragraph (3) or (4) (overall plan) has been met,

(b) no phase of development may be begun unless the requirement in sub-paragraph (5) or (6) (phase plan) has been met in respect of that phase, and

(c) where permission has been granted on an application made under section 73 (determination of applications to develop land without compliance with conditions previously attached), no further development of a phase which has been begun may be carried out pursuant to that permission unless the requirement in sub-paragraph (5) or (6) has been met.

113 Defined in s.336(1) of the Town and Country Planning Act 1990 as "permission under Part III or section 293A but does not include permission in principle."

Overall plan

(3) The requirement in this sub-paragraph has been met where-

(a) a biodiversity gain plan for that overall development has been submitted to the planning authority (see modified paragraph 14), and

(b) the planning authority has approved that plan (see modified paragraph 15).

(4) The requirement in this sub-paragraph has been met where-

(a) a biodiversity gain plan for the overall development has been approved for the purpose of complying with the condition in sub-paragraph (2)(a) subject to which planning permission for that overall development was previously granted,

(b) permission has been granted on an application made under section 73, and

(c) the earlier biodiversity gain plan for that overall development is regarded as approved under section 73(2C) and (2D) for the purpose of the permission granted under section 73.

Phase plan

(5) The requirement in this sub-paragraph has been met where-

(a) a biodiversity gain plan for that phase has been submitted to the planning authority (see modified paragraph 14), and

(b) the planning authority has approved that plan (see modified paragraph 15).

(6) The requirement in this sub-paragraph has been met where-

(a) permission has been granted on an application made under section 73, and

(b) an earlier biodiversity gain plan for that phase is regarded as approved under section 73(2C) and (2D) for the purpose of the permission granted under section 73."

The content of a biodiversity gain plan for phased development, the differing approval procedure, and other consequential changes in relation to phased development are set out in the Phased Development section of the Special Cases chapter below. Because this chapter concerns the more straightforward standard biodiversity condition, the biodiversity condition is referred to in the singular.

As can be seen from the above statutory wording (which cannot be changed by planning authorities, because they are not Parliament), the biodiversity condition does not actually impose a requirement to comply with the approved biodiversity gain plan, nor for the gains to be maintained for at least 30 years. Separate arrangements must be made to secure those requirements.

Planning authorities are "strongly encouraged" not to include the biodiversity gain condition, or reasons for applying it, in the list of conditions imposed in the written notice when granting planning permission.[114] Rather, decision makers are told to rely on the separate requirement under the amended article 35 of the Town and Country Planning (Development Management Procedure) (England) Order 2015 to provide information about the biodiversity gain condition within the decision notice on the grant of planning permission.[115] There is suggested text available for this information to be included on the decision

[114] PPG paragraph: 024 Reference ID: 74-024-20240214.

[115] PPG paragraph: 025 Reference ID: 74-025-20240214.

notice,[116] also set out at Appendix B of this book. This is provided with the intention of ensuring consistency in the information included on decision notices.[117]

The biodiversity gain condition is a pre-commencement condition, precluding any development from taking place until a biodiversity gain plan is submitted and approved by the local planning authority. The outcome of a planning judgment on whether this represents a "true condition precedent" is likely to result in the conclusion that it is: it is clearly worded as a pre-commencement condition, the planning permission could only ever be granted with this condition imposed, and the condition concerns matters which determine the effect of the entire development. This means, applying the principle established in the line of cases following *F. G. Whitley & Sons v Secretary of State for Wales* (1992) 64 P.&C.R. 296, if the biodiversity gain condition is not complied with then any material operation relied on as implementing the permission could not properly be described as commencing the development authorised by the permission because it had been implemented in breach of a condition precedent.

This position is supported by the express changes made to s.56 of the Town and Country Planning Act 1990 ("time when development has begun"). This section has been modified to expressly refer to Schedule 7A, paragraph 13 as a relevant provision in subsection 3, meaning for the purposes of paragraph 13 development shall be taken to be begun on the earliest date on which any material operation comprised in the development begins to be carried out (s.56(2)). "Material operation" is defined by statute: ss.56(4) and (5). Section 56 now reads:

---

116 Available to be downloaded at: https://assets.publishing.service.gov.uk/media/663251d969098ded31fca800/BNG_Decision_Notice_Text.odt. Last accessed 1 September 2024.

117 PPG paragraph: 026 Reference ID: 74-026-20240214.

"56.- Time when development begun.

(1) Subject to the following provisions of this section, for the purposes of this Act development of land shall be taken to be initiated-

(a) if the development consists of the carrying out of operations, at the time when those operations are begun;

(b) if the development consists of a change in use, at the time when the new use is instituted;

(c) if the development consists both of the carrying out of operations and of a change in use, at the earlier of the times mentioned in paragraphs (a) and (b).

(2) For the purposes of the provisions of this Part mentioned in subsection (3) development shall be taken to be begun on the earliest date on which any material operation comprised in the development begins to be carried out.

(3) The provisions referred to in subsection (2) are sections 61L(5) and (7), 85(2), 86(6), 87(4), 89, 91, 92, 94 and 108(3E)(c)(i) and paragraph 13 of Schedule 7A.

(4) In subsection (2) *'material operation'* means-

(a) any work of construction in the course of the erection of a building;

(aa) any work of demolition of a building;

(b) the digging of a trench which is to contain the foundations, or part of the foundations, of a building;

(c) the laying of any underground main or pipe to the foundations, or part of the foundations, of a building or to any such trench as is mentioned in paragraph (b);

(d) any operation in the course of laying out or constructing a road or part of a road;

(e) any change in the use of any land which constitutes material development.

(5) In subsection (4)(e) *'material development'* means any development other than-

(a) development for which planning permission is granted by a general development order, a local development order or a Mayoral development order for the time being in force and which is carried out so as to comply with any condition or limitation subject to which planning permission is so granted;

(b) development of a class specified in paragraph 1 or 2 of Schedule 3; and

(c) development of any class prescribed for the purposes of this subsection.

(6) In subsection (5) *'general development order'* means a development order (within the meaning of section 59) made as a general order applicable (subject to such exceptions as may be specified in it) to all land in England and Wales."

The Secretary of State cannot, by development order, make provision for the deemed discharge of the biodiversity gain condition by way of s.74A of the Town and Country Planning Act 1990 ("deemed discharge of planning conditions") (s.74A(2A)). Nor can they do so by way of simplified planning zone under s.84: s.84(5) provides "[a] simplified planning zone scheme may not disapply the condition under paragraph 13 of Schedule 7A (biodiversity gain condition)".

Local planning authorities are also expressly prohibited from removing or altering the biodiversity gain condition even if they consider the change is not material: by the new s.96A(3A) of the Town and Country Planning Act 1990. Local planning authorities are further prohibited from revoking the biodiversity gain condition: s.97(7) of the Town and Country Planning Act 1990 ("power to revoke or modify planning permission or permission in principle"), although the Secretary of State may make regulations providing for the modification of the biodiversity gain condition under s.97 and/or for planning permission modified under s.97 to be subject to other conditions relating to meeting the biodiversity gain objective.

The Secretary of State's power to make regulations under s.100ZA(1) of the Town and Country Planning Act 1990 ("restrictions on power to impose planning conditions in England") has also been curtailed in relation to the biodiversity gain condition. This power enables regulations to be made to provide: (a) conditions of a prescribed description may not be imposed in any circumstances on a relevant grant of planning permission for the development of land in England, or (b) conditions of a prescribed description may be imposed on any such grant only in circumstances of a prescribed description, or (c) no conditions may be imposed on any such grant in circumstances of a prescribed description. Regulations made under this provision cannot include the biodiversity gain condition because the biodiversity gain condition has been expressly excised from the meaning of "condition" for the purposes of s.100ZA (by s.100ZA(13)(c)). This means where s.100ZA(5) says planning permission for the development of the land "may not be granted subject to a pre-commencement condition without the written agreement of the applicant to the terms of the condition", "the condition" referred to in this provision does not include the biodiversity gain condition.

Biodiversity Gain Plan

The biodiversity gain plan sets out how the biodiversity gain objective of at least 10% BNG will be met for the development which was granted planning permission. The BNG regime requires a biodiversity gain plan to be submitted and approved by the planning authority in order to discharge the relevant biodiversity gain condition prior to the commencement of development. A template for this plan has been provided by DEFRA (see Appendix A of this book).[118] Developers should familiarise themselves with this document now, and again at the very outset of considering and designing a development. As will be appreciated, the information requirements of a biodiversity gain plan are onerous and delay, as well as a great number of headaches, can be prevented through early engagement with the requirements of the BNG regime.

Quite how far proactive applicants should go in the provision of BNG information prior to their application to discharge the biodiversity gain condition will depend on the circumstances. Given the desire for swift uncomplicated approval of the biodiversity gain plan to be able to commence development it makes sense to frontload the provision of this information in order to discover and resolve any issues at an early stage in the determination process. This would mean a completed metric calculation of *both* pre-and post-development values (where post-development biodiversity value can be calculated), and a draft biodiversity gain plan submitted alongside the planning application. The provision of draft heads of terms for any necessary s.106 agreement / conservation covenant, as well as a draft Habitat Management and Monitoring Plan (on these see Legal Agreements and Local Governance chapters below) at the application stage are also likely to assist. The more specific the draft biodiversity gain plan is in particular, the more helpful it will be for the planning authority. However, it is worth pointing out while a prudent developer would likely wish to submit a draft biodiversity gain plan ahead of the determination of the planning application, this is not a national information requirement.[119]

---

118 Available as a downloadable pdf: https://defraenvironment.blog.gov.uk/2023/10/26/the-biodiversity-gain-plan-draft-template-and-guidance/. Last accessed 1 September 2024.

119 PPG paragraph: 034 Reference ID: 74-034-20240214.

Information Requirements for Biodiversity Gain Plan

Schedule 7A, paragraph 14(2) provides that a biodiversity gain plan submitted under paragraph 13(2)(a) must include the following matters:

a) information about the steps taken or to be taken to minimise the adverse effect of the development on the biodiversity of the onsite habitat and any other habitat;
b) the pre-development biodiversity value of the onsite habitat;
c) the post-development biodiversity value of the onsite habitat;
d) any registered offsite biodiversity gain allocated to the development and the biodiversity;
e) any biodiversity credits purchased for the development; and
f) such other matters as the Secretary of State may by regulations specify.

Paragraph 14 is amended for phased development (see Phased Development section in the Special Cases chapter below).

New article 37C of the Town and Country Planning (Development Management Procedure) (England) Order 2015 requires yet further information. This article applies to phased development as well, and while this chapter does not consider the amended BNG regime for phased development the relevant provisions are included below, as well as in the Phased Development section of the Special Cases chapter, so that readers have an idea of the overall article:

> *"37C. Additional content of plan*
>
> (1) In addition to the matters referred to in paragraph 14(2) of Schedule 7A to the 1990 Act (biodiversity gain plan), and for the purposes of paragraph 14(3) of Schedule 7A to the 1990 Act (others matters to be included [by the Secretary of State by way of regulations]), a biodiversity gain plan must include the matters referred to in paragraphs (2) to (5) [below].

(2) A biodiversity gain plan must include-

(a) the name and address of-

(i) the person completing, and

(ii) if different, the person submitting,

the plan;

(b) the reference number of the planning permission to which the plan relates;

(c) a description of the development to which the plan relates;

(d) a description of arrangements for maintenance of habitat enhancement to which paragraph 9(3) of Schedule 7A to the 1990 Act applies (habitat enhancement which must be maintained for at least 30 years after the development is completed) and arrangements for monitoring that maintenance;

(e) subject to paragraph (3), a description of the actions to be taken for the purpose of applying the biodiversity gain hierarchy, including any reasons for not following the order of priority.

(3) Paragraph (2)(e) does not apply in relation to any part of the development for which planning permission is granted where the onsite habitat of that part is irreplaceable habitat.

(4) Where development is not to proceed in phases, the biodiversity gain plan must also include-

(a) the relevant date, and if the relevant date is a date which is earlier than that specified in paragraph 5(2)(a) of Schedule 7A to the 1990 Act, the reasons for this;

(b) the completed statutory metric calculation tool or tools (as the case may be), stating the publication date of that tool and showing how the values specified in the biodiversity gain plan have been calculated;

(c) if any activities of the type mentioned in paragraph 6 or 6A of Schedule 7A to the 1990 Act have been carried out on the land-

(i) a statement that such activities have been carried out;
(ii) confirmation of the date immediately before those activities were so carried out;
(iii) a completed statutory metric calculation tool, stating the publication date of that tool and showing the calculation of the biodiversity value of the onsite habitat on that date; and
(iv) any available supporting evidence for the date referred to in paragraph (ii) and for the value referred to in paragraph (iii);

(d) a description of any irreplaceable habitat, corresponding to the descriptions in Table 1 or in column 1 of Table 2 of the Schedule to the Biodiversity Gain Requirements (Irreplaceable Habitat) Regulations 2024, that-

(i) is on the land to which the plan relates, and
(ii) exists on the relevant date;

(e) pre-development plans-

(i) showing thc location of onsite habitat including any irreplaceable habitat on the relevant date;
(ii) drawn to an identified scale and showing the direction of North;

(f) post-development plans-

(i) showing the location of onsite habitat including any irreplaceable habitat;

(ii) drawn to an identified scale and showing the direction of North;

(g) in relation to any part of the development for which planning permission is granted where the onsite habitat of that part is irreplaceable habitat, arrangements for compensation for any impact the development has on the biodiversity of the onsite habitat.

(5) Where development is to proceed in phases-

(a) the biodiversity gain plan required before development may be begun in accordance with paragraph 13(3)(a) of the 1990 Act (as modified by the Biodiversity Gain (Town and Country Planning) (Modifications and Amendments) (England) Regulations 2024) (overall plan) must also include-

(i) the relevant date, and if the relevant date is a date which is earlier than that specified in paragraph 5(2)(a) of Schedule 7A to the 1990 Act, the reasons for this;

(ii) the completed statutory metric calculation tool or tools (as the case may be), stating the publication date of that tool and showing how the values specified in that biodiversity gain plan have been calculated;

(iii) if any activities of the type mentioned in paragraph 6 or 6A of Schedule 7A to the 1990 Act have been carried out on the land-

(aa) statement that such activities have been carried out,

(bb) confirmation of the date immediately before those activities were so carried out,

(cc) a completed statutory metric calculation tool, stating the publication date of that tool and showing the calculation of the biodiversity value of the onsite habitat on that date, and (dd) any available supporting evidence for the date referred to in sub-paragraph (bb) and for the value referred to in sub-paragraph (cc);

(iv) a description of any irreplaceable habitat, corresponding to the descriptions in Table 1 or in column 1 of Table 2 of the Schedule to the Biodiversity Gain Requirements (Irreplaceable Habitat) Regulations 2024, that-

(aa) is on the land to which the plan relates, and

(bb) exists on the relevant date;

(v) pre-development plans-

(aa) showing the location of onsite habitat including any irreplaceable habitat on the relevant date;

(bb) drawn to an identified scale and showing the direction of North;

(vi) in relation to any part of the development for which planning permission is granted where the onsite habitat of that part is irreplaceable habitat, arrangements for compensation for any impact the development has on the biodiversity of the onsite habitat;

(b) the biodiversity gain plan for a phase of development required in accordance with paragraph 13(5)(a) of the 1990 Act (as modified by the Biodiversity Gain (Town and Country Planning) (Modifications and Amendments) (England) Regulations 2024) (phase plan) must also include-

(i) the reference number of any planning permission decision, other than the planning permission to which the biodiversity gain plan relates, which the person submitting the plan considers is relevant to the phase of development;

(ii) the completed statutory metric calculation tool or tools (as the case may be), stating the publication date of that tool and showing how the values specified in that biodiversity gain plan have been calculated;

(iii) a description of any irreplaceable habitat, corresponding to the descriptions in Table 1 or in column 1 of Table 2 of

the Schedule to the Biodiversity Gain Requirements (Irreplaceable Habitat) Regulations 2024, that-

(aa) is on the land to which the plan relates, and

(bb) exists on the relevant date;

(iv) post-development plans for the phase of development-

(aa) showing the location of onsite habitat including any irreplaceable habitat;

(bb) drawn to an identified scale and showing the direction of North;

(v) information about the steps taken or to be taken to minimise the adverse effect of the phase of development on the biodiversity of the onsite habitat;

(vi) in relation to any part of the development to which the biodiversity gain plan relates where the onsite habitat of that part is irreplaceable habitat, arrangements for compensation for any impact the development has on the biodiversity of the onsite habitat.

(6) In this article-

(a) 'post-development biodiversity value of the onsite habitat of the phase of development', and related expressions, have the same meaning as 'post-development biodiversity value of the onsite habitat' in paragraphs 8 and 9 of Schedule 7A to the 1990 Act (post-development biodiversity value) but as if references in those paragraphs to 'the onsite habitat' were references to 'the onsite habitat on the land to which the phase of development relates';

(b) a reference to a development proceeding in phases is a reference to a development where-

(i) outline planning permission has been granted and the reservation of matters for subsequent approval has the effect of requiring or permitting development to proceed in phases, or

(ii) any kind of planning permission has been granted and the grant is subject to conditions (whether requiring the subsequent approval of other matters or otherwise) having that effect."

Submitting the Biodiversity Gain Plan

The plan must be submitted in writing no earlier than the day after planning permission has been granted (article 37B of the Town and Country Planning (Development Management Procedure) (England) Order 2015). This said, as noted above, a prudent developer would want to submit a draft plan alongside the planning application in order to identify any issues and resolve them with the local planning authority prior to determination of the application. Applicants are "encouraged to engage with local planning authorities before submitting their application in order to identify, understand and seek to resolve issues; this will help to improve both the efficiency and effectiveness of the planning application process, reduce issues around validation, and improve the quality of the application."[120] There is no separate application form for the submission of the biodiversity gain plan, though the use of the biodiversity gain plan template is "strongly encouraged".[121] The planning authority has eight weeks to approve or reject the biodiversity gain plan (unless an extension is agreed).[122]

Approving the Biodiversity Gain Plan

Schedule 7A, paragraph 15 provides the planning authority can only lawfully approve the biodiversity gain plan if they are satisfied:

---

120 PPG paragraph: 014 Reference ID: 74-013-20240214.

121 PPG paragraph: 034 Reference ID: 74-034-20240214.

122 Article 37D(1) of the Town and Country Planning (Development Management Procedure) (England) Order 2015.

a) the pre-development biodiversity value of the onsite habitat is as specified in the plan;
b) the post-development biodiversity value of the onsite habitat is at least the value specified in the plan;
c) in the case where the registered offsite biodiversity gain is specified in the plan, as allocated to the development:
    i. the registered offsite biodiversity gain is so allocated (and, if the allocation is conditional, that any conditions attaching to the allocation have been met or will be met by the time the development begins), and
    ii. the registered offsite biodiversity gain has the biodiversity value specified in the plan in relation to the development;
d) that any biodiversity credits specified in the plan as purchased for the development have been so purchased;
e) the biodiversity net gain objective is met; and
f) any other matters specified in the plan under paragraph 14(2)(f).

Article 27 of the Town and Country Planning (Development Management Procedure) (England) Order 2015 has been amended to reflect the BNG regime. The changes made by article 27(4)(a) mean that where there is submission of a biodiversity gain plan for approval under paragraph 13(2)(a) of Schedule 7A then articles 27(1) and (2) do not apply (these set out, respectively, how an application to discharge a condition should be made, what that application must include, and the eight-week time limit for determination of that application). Instead, the new Part 7A of the Town and Country Planning (Development Management Procedure) (England) Order 2015 applies. This provides, in relation to the determination of an application to approve a biodiversity gain plan:

"37D.— Determination

(1) The planning authority must give written notice to the person submitting the biodiversity gain plan of its determination whether to approve that plan within-

(a) the period of eight weeks beginning with the day after the day on which that plan is received by the planning authority, or

(b) such longer period as is agreed, in writing, by the person submitting that plan and the planning authority.

(2) In determining whether to approve a biodiversity gain plan, the planning authority must take into account-

(a) how the biodiversity gain hierarchy is to be applied, and

(b) subject to paragraph (3), where the order of priority specified in that hierarchy is not to be applied—

(i) the reason for that, or

(ii) the absence of a reason.

(3) Paragraph (2) does not apply in relation to any part of the development for which planning permission is granted where the onsite habitat of that part is irreplaceable habitat.

(4) Where the planning authority that has given written notice under paragraph (1) is not the local planning register authority, the planning authority must, within five working days beginning with the day after the day of that written notice, send to the local planning register authority-

(a) a copy of the biodiversity gain plan submitted under paragraph 13 of Schedule 7A to the 1990 Act, including all plans, drawings and other documents submitted with the biodiversity gain plan;

(b) notice of the determination whether to approve the biodiversity gain plan including the date of that notice and the name of the planning authority.

> (5) Where the planning authority makes a determination not to approve the biodiversity gain plan, the notice provided under paragraph (1) must state clearly and precisely their full reasons for the determination, specifying all elements of the biodiversity gain plan which are relevant to the determination.
>
> (6) In this article-
> 'the local planning register authority' has the same meaning as in article 40(1); 'working day' means a day which is not a Saturday, Sunday or public holiday."

The PPG notes decision makers should always consider wider matters when assessing the suitability of proposals for onsite habitat gains, such as: highways safety, designated heritage assets, increasing or restricting access to nearby natural areas (depending on the sensitivity of nearby habitats), and the impact on aviation safety.[123]

It is important to highlight the legal requirement that if a planning authority makes a determination not to approve the biodiversity gain plan, the decision notice must state clearly and precisely their full reasons for the determination (article 37D(5) of the Town and Country Planning (Development Management Procedure) (England) Order 2015),[124]

---

123 PPG paragraph: 021 Reference ID: 74-021-20240214.

124 As per earlier reference to the common law standard for reasons in decision making: reasons for the decision must be intelligible and adequate, enabling one to understand why the matter was decided as it was and what conclusions were reached on the 'principal important controversial issues'. A decision maker's reasoning must not give rise to a substantial doubt as to whether they went wrong in law, for example by misunderstanding a relevant policy or by failing to reach a rational decision on relevant grounds. But the reasons need refer only to the main issues in the dispute, not to every material consideration (per Lord Brown in *South Bucks District Council and another v Porter* (No. 2) [2004] 1 WLR 1953, at page 1964B-G).

specifying all elements of the biodiversity gain plan which are relevant to the determination.

Amending the Biodiversity Gain Plan

It is not possible to amend an approved biodiversity gain plan.[125] Developers can only submit a replacement plan if they need/wish to change the approach to meeting the biodiversity gain objective for the development. This incentivises early engagement of relevant professionals to determine the feasibility of the proposed BNG plan as it is conceivable that onsite gains may not ultimately be achievable due to layout issues, unknown underground infrastructure, or design challenges, or that proposed offsite units are not available and statutory credits need to be purchased instead (which in turn may impact on scheme viability and/or funds available for non-BNG related planning obligations).

Fees

The submission of a biodiversity gain plan to a local planning authority falls under reg.16 of the Town and Country Planning (Fee for Applications, Deemed Applications, Requests and Site Visit) (England) Regulations 2012 (fees for the written confirmation of compliance with a condition or conditions attached to a grant of planning permission). Currently this is £145 per request. The PPG confirms that where a biodiversity gain plan takes longer than 12 weeks to determine, the planning guarantee applies and the fee must be refunded.[126]

125 PPG paragraph: 043 Reference ID: 74-043-20240214.

126 PPG paragraph: 037 Reference ID: 74-037-20240214.

Appeals Against Refusal to Approve / Non-Determination of Biodiversity Gain Plan

Submitting an Appeal

If an application for the approval of the biodiversity gain plan is refused by the local planning authority, the person submitting the plan may appeal to the Secretary of State in the usual way under s.78 of the Town and Country Planning Act 1990. However, it is important to note the normal procedure to appeal under s.78 set out in article 37 of the Town and Country Planning (Development Management Procedure) (England) Order 2015 does not apply to appeals made in relation to a refusal to approve a biodiversity gain plan (see reg.18 of the Biodiversity Gain (Town and Country Planning) (Modifications and Amendments) (England) Regulations 2024). Instead, the new article 37E of Part 7A of the Town and Country Planning (Development Management Procedure) (England) Order 2015 applies.

A person submitting a biodiversity gain plan for approval may also appeal under s.78 if the local planning authority does not make a decision within eight weeks (or the extended period where there is a written agreement to extend the decision making period).

There is no third party right of appeal to the Secretary of State when a biodiversity gain plan is approved, rejected, or not determined.

A notice of appeal must be submitted to the Secretary of State, at the latest, six months from the decision to refuse to approve the biodiversity gain plan or, if no decision has been made, six months from when a decision should have been given article (37E(3) of the Town and Country Planning (Development Management Procedure) (England) Order 2015). There is scope for the Secretary of State to extend this time period, at their discretion (article 37E(2)(a)(ii)). There is no requirement for permission to appeal; it is a statutory right.

Article 37E(4) of the Town and Country Planning (Development Management Procedure) (England) Order 2015 specifies a series of documents which must accompany the appeal form, where the document is relevant to the appeal:

a) a copy of the planning application sent to the local planning authority to which the biodiversity gain plan relates;
b) all plans, drawing and documents sent to the local planning authority relating to that application;
c) all correspondence with the local planning authority relating to the determination whether to approve the biodiversity gain plan;
d) the notice of the determination whether to approve the biodiversity gain plan, if any;
e) the biodiversity gain plan to which the appeal relates;
f) [except where a direction by the Secretary of State under s.321(3) of the Town and Country Planning Act 1990 (matters relating to national security) has been given]...:
    i. the full statement of case of the person who submitted the biodiversity gain plan (if they wish to make additional representations);
    ii. a statement of which procedure (written representations, a hearing or inquiry) the person who submitted the biodiversity gain plan considers should be used to determine the appeal;
    iii. a draft statement of common ground if the person submitting the biodiversity gain plan considers that the appeal should be determined through a hearing or an inquiry.

The terms "full statement of case" and "draft statement of common ground" in article 37E have the same meaning as in article 37(8):

> *"full statement of case"* means, and is comprised of, a written statement which contains full particulars of the case which a person

proposes to put forward and copies of any documents which that person intends to refer to or put in evidence.

"draft statement of common ground" means a written statement containing factual information about the proposal which is the subject of the appeal that the applicant reasonably considers will not be disputed by the local planning authority.

The appellant must also serve the local planning authority with the following documents as soon as reasonably practicable (by article 37E(2)(b)):

- the completed appeal form;
- except where a direction by the Secretary of State under s.321(3) of the Town and Country Planning Act 1990 (matters relating to national security) has been given:
    - the full statement of case of the person who submitted the biodiversity gain plan (if they wish to make additional representations);
    - a statement of which procedure (written representations, a hearing or inquiry) the person who submitted the biodiversity gain plan considers should be used to determine the appeal;
    - a draft statement of common ground if the person submitting the biodiversity gain plan considers that the appeal should be determined through a hearing or an inquiry.

Both steps – serving the mandatory information on the Secretary of State within six months of the relevant start date, and serving the mandatory information on the relevant local planning authority as soon as reasonably practicable – together comprise giving "notice of appeal" to the Secretary of State.

While the person submitting the biodiversity gain plan appeal is asked to indicate their view of the most appropriate procedure for their case (whether written representation, hearing or inquiry), the Secretary of State or their appointed planning inspector will have the final say on which procedure is to be used when determining the appeal.

Determination of the Appeal

As is the usual way, s.78 appeals on a biodiversity gain plan will most often be determined by a planning inspector appointed on behalf of the Secretary of State. Appeals on biodiversity gain plans may be determined as if the application for permission had been made to the Secretary of State in the first instance.[127]

The Secretary of State also has the power to recover the appeal for their own determination (upon being advised by a report from an appointed inspector). Here the standard (albeit dated) criteria for recovering an appeal will apply, summarised as follows in the PPG:[128]

> "[As] set out in a Parliamentary Statement on 30 June 2008. There may be other cases which merit recovery because of the particular circumstances:
>
> - Proposals for development of major importance having more than local significance.
> - Proposals giving rise to substantial regional or national controversy.
> - Proposals which raise important or novel issues of development control, and/or legal difficulties.
> - Proposals against which another government department has raised major objections or has a major interest.

---

127 Section 79(1) of the Town and Country Planning Act 1990, and PPG paragraph: 050 Reference ID: 74-050-20240214.

128 PPG Appeals, paragraph: 005 Reference ID: 16-005-20160713.

- Proposals of major significance for the delivery of the government's climate change programme and energy policies.
- Proposals for residential development of over 150 units or on sites of over 5 hectares, which would significantly impact on the government's objective to secure a better balance between housing demand and supply and create high quality, sustainable, mixed and inclusive communities.
- Proposals which involve any main town centre use or uses where that use or uses comprise(s) over 9,000 square metres gross floorspace (either as a single proposal or as part of or in combination with other current proposals) and which are proposed on a site in an edge of centre or out of centre location that is not in accordance with an up-to-date development plan document.
- Proposals for significant development in the Green Belt. Major proposals involving the winning and working of minerals.
- Proposals which would have an adverse impact on the outstanding universal value, integrity, authenticity and significance of a World Heritage Site.
- Proposals involving traveller sites in the Green Belt, as set out in a statement to Parliament on 17 January 2014.
- Proposals for residential development of over 25 units in areas where a qualifying body has submitted a neighbourhood plan proposal to the local planning authority, but where the relevant plan has not been made, as set out in a statement to Parliament on 7 July 2016.
- Proposals for exploring and developing shale gas, as set out in a statement to Parliament on 16 September 2015."

A recovered appeal is determined via written representations, a hearing or an inquiry in the same way as other planning appeals. It should also be noted recovery of an appeal for the Secretary of State's determination can occur at any stage, even after the site visit, hearing or inquiry has taken place.

Challenging an Appeal Decision

The inspector's/Secretary of State's decision on a s.78 appeal may only be challenged by way of statutory review under s.288 of the Town and Country Planning Act 1990. Potential claimants will need to be aware of the tight timescale for such challenges, which must be brought (including service of the claim) within six weeks of the decision which is the subject of the appeal (s.288(4B)). Because this is a deadline set by statute the courts have no jurisdiction to extend this time period (unlike in judicial review claims).

CHAPTER FIVE

IRREPLACEABLE HABITATS

Irreplaceable habitats are ecologically valuable habitats which are technically very difficult or take a very significant time to restore, recreate or replace once destroyed. The BNG regime sets out special considerations for the content and approval of the biodiversity gain plan when these irreplaceable habitats form part of the development site. Irreplaceable habitats are defined for the purposes of Part 2 of Schedule 7A (being paragraphs 13 to 21) in reg. 2 of the Biodiversity Gain Requirements (Irreplaceable Habitat) Regulations 2024. Regulation 2 refers to two tables in the Schedule, although it should be noted a further consultation on irreplaceable habitats is due to be carried out in late 2024.[129] For now, irreplaceable habitat means habitat in the first column of either table (reg. 2(1)).

In Table 1, which refers to "the List", each specified habitat has the same meaning as in the list published by the Secretary of State under s.41 of the Natural Environment and Rural Communities Act 2006 (by reg.2(2) of the Biodiversity Gain Requirements (Irreplaceable Habitat) Regulations 2024):

[129] As indicated on the DEFRA blog: https://defraenvironment.blog.gov.uk/2023/10/05/irreplaceable-habitats-and-bng-what-you-need-to-know/#:~:text=The%20consultation%20will%20seek%20views,list%20on%20wider%20planning%20policy. Last accessed 1 September 2024.

Table 1 Habitats contained in the List

Habitat
Blanket bog
Lowland fens
Limestone pavements
Coastal sand dunes

In Table 2, each specified irreplaceable habitat in the first column must be construed in accordance with the corresponding row in the second column (by reg.2(3) of the Biodiversity Gain Requirements (Irreplaceable Habitat) Regulations 2024):

Table 2 Other habitats

Habitat	*Description*
Ancient woodland	Ancient woodland is areas of woodland that have been continuously wooded since at least 1600. Ancient woodland includes— (i) Ancient Semi-Natural Woodlands; (ii) Plantations on Ancient Woodland Sites; (iii) Ancient Wood Pasture and Parkland; and (iii) Infilled Ancient Wood Pasture and Parkland.
Ancient trees and veteran trees	Ancient and veteran trees can be found as individual trees or collections of trees in any setting. Ancient trees have passed beyond maturity into an ancient life stage or are old in comparison with other trees of the same species which exhibit one or more of the following— (i) demonstrably great age relative to others of the same species; (ii) changes to their crown and trunk development indicative of the ancient life stage. Veteran trees are mature trees that share physical and other characteristics in common with ancient trees, due to their

	life or environment, but are neither developmentally nor chronologically ancient. All ancient trees are veteran trees, but not all veteran trees are ancient. Veteran and ancient trees which have died are still recognised as such because they retain significant biodiversity value for many decades. Veteran trees exhibit one or more of the following— (i) significant decay features such as deadwood, hollowing or signs of advanced decay in the trunk or major limbs; (ii) a large girth, depending on and relative to species, site and management history; (iii) a high value for nature, especially in hosting rare or specialist fungi, lichens and deadwood invertebrates.
Spartina saltmarsh swards	Spartina (cord-grass) saltmarsh swards colonise a wide range of substrates, from very soft muds to shingle, in areas sheltered from strong wave action. It occurs on the seaward fringes of saltmarshes and creek-sides and may colonise old pans in the upper saltmarsh.
Mediterranean saltmarsh scrub	Mediterranean and thermo-Atlantic halophilous (salt-tolerant) scrub develops in the uppermost levels of saltmarshes, often where there is a transition from saltmarsh to dunes, or in some cases where dunes overlie shingle. The form that most closely resembles the scrub vegetation of the Mediterranean is restricted to south and south-east England and is formed predominantly of bushes of shrubby sea-blite Suaeda vera and sea purslane Atriplex portulacoides.

Following new ecological evidence, Natural England has included spartina saltmarsh swards and Mediterranean saltmarsh scrub within the definition of irreplaceable habitats. This is both because of their rarity and because they are irreplaceable outside their natural range in the south and southeast of England. Other types of saltmarsh habitat were considered replaceable across England.

Regulation 2(4) of the Biodiversity Gain Requirements (Irreplaceable Habitat) Regulations 2024 also empowers Natural England to issue guidance for the purpose of identifying whether a habitat falls within the descriptions in the tables in Schedule 1 of those Regulations. At the time of writing there is no guidance.

Paragraph 186(c)[130] of the NPPF is also relevant to irreplaceable habitats, as this provides strong policy protection when determining planning applications that affect irreplaceable habitats: development resulting in the loss or deterioration of irreplaceable habitats should be refused unless there are wholly exceptional reasons and a suitable compensation strategy exists. Importantly, the definition of irreplaceable habitat for the purposes of the Framework is not that set out above, but rather that which is set out within the Framework's Glossary as follows:

> "Habitats which would be technically very difficult (or take a very significant time) to restore, recreate or replace once destroyed, taking into account their age, uniqueness, species diversity or rarity. They include ancient woodland, ancient and veteran trees, blanket bog, limestone pavement, sand dunes, salt marsh and lowland fen."

This is not a closed list, it is also more expansive a definition on its own terms than the list contained within Tables 1 and 2 of the Schedule to the Biodiversity Gain Requirements (Irreplaceable Habitat) Regulations 2024. There is no further guidance from either DEFRA or MHCLG on the discrepancy between these definitions. An ecologically precautionary

130 "When determining planning applications, local planning authorities should apply the following principles:…(c) development resulting in the loss or deterioration of irreplaceable habitats (such as ancient woodland and ancient or veteran trees) should be refused, unless there are wholly exceptional reasons[67] and a suitable compensation strategy exists". Footnote 67 then provides: "For example, infrastructure projects (including nationally significant infrastructure projects, orders under the Transport and Works Act and hybrid bills), where the public benefit would clearly outweigh the loss or deterioration of habitat."

approach would be to apply the broader definition and paragraph 186(c) in the Framework first: it is the stricter test, uses a broader definition, and results in refusal if there is loss or deterioration of irreplaceable habitat without a wholly exceptional reason. If there is a wholly exceptional reason, then Tables 1 and 2 of the Biodiversity Gain Requirements (Irreplaceable Habitat) Regulations 2024 would then be applied; if it is irreplaceable habitat under either of those Tables, the BNG irreplaceable habitat regime applies. The bespoke compensation strategy agreed as part of the BNG regime would then serve a dual purpose as the "suitable" compensation strategy under paragraph 186(c) as well. If the habitat in question does not fit within the definition under the Regulations, but it still fits within the wider Framework definition, then paragraph 186(c) governs the situation, the BNG regime's irreplaceable habitat provisions do not apply, and a suitable compensation strategy must still be prepared and agreed.

Information Required at Application Stage

Developers must provide a description and plan of any irreplaceable habitat on site at the date of the planning application (articles 7(1A)(c)(vi) and (vii) of the Town and Country Planning (Development Management Procedure) (England) Order 2015, although article 7(1A) does not apply to applications made under s.73 of the Town and Country Act 1990: see Special Cases chapter below). The local planning authority will refuse to validate the application if this information is not provided.

Impact on Metric Calculations

Irreplaceable habitat must still be recorded within the statutory metric under the irreplaceable habitats tab. However, unless there is an enhancement proposed to the irreplaceable habitat, the input will not be assigned a value in the metric, either pre- or post-development.

Adverse impacts to irreplaceable habitats cannot be measured by the statutory metric and they will be removed from the baseline calculation in the statutory metric because all adverse impacts require a bespoke approach. Developers cannot record any bespoke compensation for harm to irreplaceable habitat within the enhancement or creation sheets of the statutory metric: while the presence of irreplaceable habitat on the site has to be recorded, designing the compensation strategy must take place in direct correspondence with the planning authority. Once the bespoke compensation has been agreed, "bespoke compensation agreed" can be selected within the statutory metric which then automatically removes those losses from the calculation.[131]

As the metric calculation will still be based on the total pre-development area of the development site, bespoke compensation delivered onsite could result in area discrepancies because bespoke compensation onsite will not be recorded within the metric's onsite enhancement or creation sheets. The User Guide provides a workaround when bespoke compensation is to be delivered onsite. First, the assessor should record the baseline habitat as "lost". Then they are to record an equal area of created "developed land; sealed surface" (this has a biodiversity value of zero). The assessor must then label the area as "proxy area for bespoke compensation delivered on-site" within the user comments.[132]

Where no adverse effect will be caused to the onsite irreplaceable habitat, while this must still be recorded in the irreplaceable habitat sheet of the metric in this case the biodiversity value of the irreplaceable habitat is not

---

131 Statutory Metric User Guide page 22 https://assets.publishing.service.gov.uk/media/669e45fba3c2a28abb50d426/The_Statutory_Biodiversity_Metric_-_User_Guide__23.07.24_.pdf. Last accessed 1 September 2024.

132 This is a temporary fix and a future update to the statutory metric is likely to include a more permanent solution to this issue. Statutory Metric User Guide page 22 https://assets.publishing.service.gov.uk/media/669e45fba3c2a28abb50d426/The_Statutory_Biodiversity_Metric_-_User_Guide__23.07.24_.pdf. Last accessed 1 September 2024.

fed through to the calculation[133] (and so cannot contribute to additional post-development BNG). Because there is no harm, no bespoke compensation package is necessary. Of course, the planning authority will most likely require evidence there will be no harm to the irreplaceable habitat.

In the best-case-scenario, where enhancement to irreplaceable habitat is proposed, this is fed through to the statutory metric calculation after it is recorded in the irreplaceable habitat sheet of the metric. No bespoke compensation package is necessary where there will be only enhancement. Because the habitat is fed through into the metric's calculation the value of the enhancement will contribute to 10% BNG requirement.

Importantly, not only must enhancement works be ecologically appropriate, to qualify as enhancement works for the purposes of the BNG regime there cannot be any adverse impacts on irreplaceable habitat.[134] This means an "overall" enhancement package where benefits outweigh harms is not permissible. Instead of grouping harms and benefits into a single calculation, where <u>any</u> harm arises, even if subsequently offset leading to overall betterment, that is not "enhancement" and the metric will still require a bespoke compensation plan to be agreed for the adverse impacts to irreplaceable habitat (which, as above, cannot count towards the BNG requirement).

Any buffer zone(s) are accounted for as pre-development baseline / post-development habitat in the metric and will be subject to the 10% BNG requirement in the usual way.

As will be seen from the above variety of potential outcomes for metric calculations, the design, layout and spatial choices concerning

---

133 PPG paragraph: 042 Reference ID: 74-042-20240214.

134 PPG paragraph: 042 Reference ID: 74-042-20240214.

development on sites where irreplaceable habitat is present must be very carefully considered from the outset of the planning process.

Impact on Biodiversity Gain Plan

The biodiversity gain plan must include information on the mitigation of any adverse effect on irreplaceable habitat, including specific information as to how harm has been minimised.[135] Regulation 3 of the Biodiversity Gain Requirements (Irreplaceable Habitat) Regulations 2024 has the effect of removing certain aspects from the biodiversity gain plan for any part of a development site for which planning permission is granted where the onsite habitat of that part is irreplaceable habitat. So, where there is irreplaceable habitat on a site, according to the language of the Regulations, the biodiversity gain plan is amended only in relation to that part of the site. The normal approach would apply to the rest of the onsite habitat. Legal practitioners should be aware that, while the Biodiversity Gain Requirements (Irreplaceable Habitat) Regulations 2024 are in force (from 12 February 2024), the amendments they make to the Town and Country Planning Act 1990 are not apparent on Westlaw because of their conditional application. The amendments have been depicted as either strikethrough or new text below.

Schedule 7A is also modified for the purposes of irreplaceable habitat in relation to phased development (reg. 4 of the Biodiversity Gain Requirements (Irreplaceable Habitat) Regulations 2024). This applies to: (a) the grant of outline planning permission, where the reservation of matters for subsequent approval has the effect of requiring or permitting development to proceed in phases; or (b) the grant of any kind of planning permission, where the grant is subject to conditions (whether requiring the subsequent approval of any matters or otherwise) has that effect. The modified paragraphs 14 and 15 are set out in full in the Phased Development section of the Special Cases chapter below.

[135] PPG paragraph: 042 Reference ID: 74-042-20240214.

Where the development is not phased development, the approach to take for the part of the development site which contains irreplaceable habitat is described in the biodiversity gain plan under Schedule 7A, paragraph 14 of the Town and Country Planning Act 1990 as follows (applying the modifications made by reg. 3(2) of the Biodiversity Gain Requirements (Irreplaceable Habitat) Regulations 2024):

> *"14. Biodiversity gain plan*
>
> (1) For the purposes of paragraph 13(2)(a), a biodiversity gain plan is a plan which-
> (a) relates to development for which planning permission is granted, and
> (b) specifies the matters referred to in sub-paragraph (2).
>
> (2) The matters are-
> (a) information about the steps taken or to be taken to minimise the adverse effect of the development on the biodiversity of the onsite habitat ~~and any other habitat~~,
> (b) the pre-development biodiversity value of the onsite habitat,
> (c) the post-development biodiversity value of the onsite habitat,
> ~~(d) any registered offsite biodiversity gain allocated to the development and the biodiversity value of that gain in relation to the development,~~
> ~~(e) any biodiversity credits purchased for the development~~, and
> (f) such other matters as the Secretary of State may by regulations specify."

So, when it provides information on the onsite irreplaceable habitat, the biodiversity gain plan does not need to describe the application of the biodiversity hierarchy in relation to any other offsite habitat. This is because it cannot: where there is harm in relation to irreplaceable habitat, offsetting that loss in biodiversity value requires a bespoke compensation plan. It may include offsite gains (not statutory credits, see the amendments to Schedule 7A, paragraph 15 below), but that must first be agreed with the planning authority.

Thus, if any harm to irreplaceable habitat still arises despite mitigation, the developer must also include a bespoke compensation plan. This will be designed by a competent professional and secured by way of condition or legal agreement. Compensation for this purpose is not the same concept as compensation under article 6(4) of the Habitats Directive, the latter has a very different legal definition and purpose. Compensation for the purposes of the BNG regime is designed to be flexible and tailored to the specific circumstances of the irreplaceable habitat, the development proposed, and any other relevant circumstances.

There have been amendments made to the approval criteria relating to a biodiversity gain plan (again, specifically in relation to only the part(s) of the site which contain irreplaceable habitat, and again, phased development is treated differently), by reg.3(3) of the Biodiversity Gain Requirements (Irreplaceable Habitat) Regulations 2024. Schedule 7A, paragraph 15 of the Town and Country Planning Act 1990 is amended in such cases as follows:

> *"15. Approval of biodiversity gain plan*
>
> (1) For the purposes of paragraph 13(2)(b) a planning authority to which a biodiversity gain plan is submitted must approve the plan if, and only if, it is satisfied as to the matters specified in sub-paragraph (2).
>
> (2) The matters are-
>
> (a) that the pre-development biodiversity value of the onsite habitat is as specified in the plan,
>
> (b) that the post-development biodiversity value of the onsite habitat is at least the value specified in the plan,
>
> ~~(c) that, in a case where any registered offsite biodiversity gain is specified in the plan as allocated to the development—~~

> ~~(i) the registered offsite biodiversity gain is so allocated (and, if the allocation is conditional, that any conditions attaching to the allocation have been met or will be met by the time the development begins), and~~
>
> ~~(ii) the registered offsite biodiversity gain has the biodiversity value specified in the plan in relation to the development,~~
>
> ~~(d) that any biodiversity credits specified in the plan as purchased for the development have been so purchased,~~
>
> (e) ~~that the biodiversity gain objective is met,~~ [*new text*] that the adverse effect of the development on the biodiversity of the onsite habitat is minimised and appropriate arrangements have been made for the purpose of compensating for any impact; and
>
> (f) any other matters specified in the plan under paragraph 14(2)(f).
>
> [*new paragraph 15(3)*] (3) For the purposes of sub-paragraph (2)(e), arrangements are appropriate only if they secure that there is a compensation plan in place that secures appropriate compensation relative to the baseline habitat type, and which does not include the use of biodiversity credits."

It can be seen from the above that planning authorities can only approve the biodiversity gain if they are satisfied that adverse effects of the development on the irreplaceable habitat have been minimised, and if not eliminated entirely, that "appropriate arrangements" have been made for the purpose of compensating for any impact. Again, this is a much more discretionary regime than that set out under the Habitats Directive. There is, however, a legal limit on the planning authority's discretion here: compensation proposals are only appropriate if the compensation for irreplaceable habitat is relative to the baseline habitat type and does not involve the purchase of statutory biodiversity credits (new paragraph 15(3)). It is important to note the legislation does not prohibit compensation plans from relating to offsite habitat altogether. Rather, it requires bespoke compensation relative to the baseline habitat type which the planning authority considers appropriate, without recourse to statutory credits.

What about development which results in land take from protected sites (i.e. Sites of Special Scientific Interest, Special Protection Areas, Special Areas of Conservation, and Ramsar sites)? Development on such sites is not expressly exempt from the net gain requirement. Because of its deliberately simplified design, the statutory metric does not directly account for impacts on protected species or interests and it does not supplant the protected sites regime(s). In these cases, the BNG regime sits alongside these other legal and/or policy requirements concerning protected areas and their features.

CHAPTER SIX

PLANNING AUTHORITY GOVERNANCE

Identity of Planning Authority

When the decision maker is not the local planning authority they can, in certain circumstances, direct that the body responsible for the purposes of Schedule 7A of the Town and Country Planning Act 1990 is the local planning authority. The general rule is set out in Schedule 7A, paragraph 12B:

> "The general rule is that the local planning authority is-
> (a) the local planning authority which granted the planning permission, or
> (b) the local planning authority which could have granted the planning permission had it not been granted by the Secretary of State or a person appointed by the Secretary of State."

Where the Secretary of State has granted planning permission under s.62A (direct submission of a planning application where there is a designated local planning authority), s.76A / s.77 (call in of a planning application), or an appeal under s.78 of the Town and Country Planning Act 1990, the Secretary of State or their appointed inspector may direct either they or the local planning authority which would have been responsible for granting the planning permission, had it not been granted by the Secretary of State or their appointed inspector, is the planning authority for the purposes of Schedule 7A (Schedule 7A, paragraph 12(1)).

Where the Mayor of London has given a direction under s.2A of the Town and Country Planning Act 1990 and granted the relevant planning permission, the Mayor may direct that the local planning authority to whom the planning application was initially made will be the planning authority for the purposes of Schedule 7A. Otherwise, it will be the Mayor (Schedule 7A, paragraphs 12C(a) and 12D(1)-(2)).

Where the Mayor of London has given a direction under s.2A of the Town and Country Planning Act 1990 but the Secretary of State or an inspector has granted the planning permission under ss.76A, 77, or 78 of the Town and Country Planning Act 1990, then the Secretary of State or inspector (as the final decision maker) will determine whether the Mayor of London or the local planning authority to whom the planning application was made will act as the planning authority for the purposes of Schedule 7A (Schedule 7A, paragraphs 12C(a), 12E(1)-(2) and 12F(1)-(2)).

Where a combined authority has the function to call-in and determine planning applications and the order which grants those powers so provides, the planning authority for the purposes of Schedule 7A is the combined authority. In other cases where a combined authority grants planning permission, the local planning authority to whom the planning application was made will be planning authority for the purposes of Schedule 7A (Schedule 7A, paragraphs 12C(b) and 12G(1)-(2)).

Where other bodies have planning powers to determine planning applications, such as Mayoral Development Corporations and Urban Development Authorities, then they will be the planning authority for the purposes of Schedule 7A if the order which grants those powers says so (and only if paragraphs 12D, 12E, 12F, or 12G do not already apply) (Schedule 7A, paragraphs 12C(c) and 12H(1)-(3)).

Information Requirements at Application Stage

If the developer considers the BNG regime does not apply they must specify what exemptions(s) or transitional provision(s) apply, and why, in the application form (article 7(1A)(b) of the Town and Country Planning (Development Management Procedure) (England) Order 2015). The PPG says that supporting evidence may need to be supplied where it is not obvious that an exemption applies, especially (but not exclusively) when the *de minimis* exemption is claimed.[136]

Where the BNG regime does apply, the Town and Country Planning (Development Management Procedure) (England) Order 2015 has been significantly amended to reflect new procedural requirements that must now be followed for applications for planning permission subject to the BNG regime. Article 7 now provides (save for the minerals-specific provisions which have been removed from the below extract):

> "*7. General requirements: applications for planning permission including outline planning permission*
>
> (1) Subject to paragraphs (3) to (5), an application for planning permission must-
>
>> (a) be made in writing to the local planning authority on a form published by the Secretary of State (or a form to substantially the same effect);
>>
>> (b) include the particulars specified or referred to in the form;
>>
>> (c) except where the application is made pursuant to section 73 (determination of applications to develop land without conditions previously attached) or section 73A(2)(c) (planning permission for development already carried out) of the 1990 Act

136 Paragraph: 010 Reference ID: 74-010-20240214.

or is an application of a kind referred to in article 20(1)(b) or (c), be accompanied, whether electronically or otherwise, by-

(i) a plan which identifies the land to which the application relates;

(ii) any other plans, drawings and information necessary to describe the development which is the subject of the application;

(iia) the information relating to the condition under paragraph 13 of Schedule 7A to the 1990 Act ('the biodiversity gain condition') specified in paragraph (1A);

(iii) except where the application is made by electronic communications or the local planning authority indicate that a lesser number is required, 3 copies of the form; and

(iv) except where they are submitted by electronic communications or the local planning authority indicate that a lesser number is required, 3 copies of any plans, drawings and information accompanying the application.

(1A) Subject to paragraph (1B), an application for planning permission must be accompanied by the following information relating to the biodiversity gain condition-

(a) a statement as to whether the applicant believes that planning permission, if granted, would be subject to the biodiversity gain condition;

(b) where the applicant believes that planning permission, if granted, would not be subject to the biodiversity gain condition, the reasons for that belief;

(c) in cases where the applicant believes that planning permission, if granted, would be subject to the biodiversity gain condition-

(i) the completed statutory metric calculation tool or tools (as the case may be) showing the calculation of the biodiversity value of the onsite habitat, for the purpose of the biodiversity gain plan required to be submitted under paragraph 13 of Schedule 7A to the 1990 Act if permission is granted, on-

(aa) the date of the application, or

(bb) an earlier date proposed by the applicant, and

(cc) in either case, the date immediately before any activities of the type mentioned in paragraph 6 or 6A of Schedule 7A to the 1990 Act have been carried out on the land;

(ii) the biodiversity value or values (as the case may be) referred to in paragraph (i);

(iii) the publication date of the statutory metric calculation tool or tools (as the case may be) used to calculate the values referred to in paragraph (i);

(iv) if an earlier date is proposed by the applicant under paragraph (i)(bb), the reasons why that earlier date is proposed;

(v) if any activities of the type mentioned in paragraph 6 or 6A of Schedule 7A to the 1990 Act have been carried out on the land-

(aa) a statement that such activities have been carried out, (bb) confirmation of the date immediately before those activities were so carried out, and

(cc) any available supporting evidence for the date referred to in sub-paragraph (bb) and for the value referred to in paragraph (i)(cc).

(vi) a description of any irreplaceable habitat, corresponding to the descriptions in Table 1 or in column 1 of Table 2 of the Schedule to the Biodiversity Gain Requirements (Irreplaceable Habitat) Regulations 2024, that-

(aa) is on the land to which the application relates, and

(bb) exists on the date referred to in paragraph (i)(aa) or (bb) (as applicable);

(vii) a plan showing the location, on the date referred to in paragraph (i)(aa) or (bb) (as applicable), of-

(aa) the onsite habitat included in the calculations referred to in paragraph (i), and

(bb) any irreplaceable habitat.

(1B) Paragraph (1A) does not apply to an application for permission to develop land without compliance with conditions previously attached made under section 73 of the 1990 Act.

(2) Any plans or drawings required to be provided by paragraph (1) or (1A) must be drawn to an identified scale and, in the case of plans, must show the direction of North.

(3) Except where article 5(3) applies, an application for outline planning permission does not need to give details of any reserved matters.

...

(6) Where an application is made using electronic communications to transmit a form to the local planning authority, the applicant is taken to have agreed-

(a) to the use of such communications by the local planning authority for the purposes of the application;

(b) that the applicant's address for those purposes is the address incorporated into, or otherwise logically associated with, the application; and

(c) that the applicant's deemed agreement under this paragraph subsists until the applicant gives notice in writing of the withdrawal of consent to the use of electronic communications under article 46."

The planning application forms prescribed by the Secretary of State provide the appropriate sections for this information to be set out.[137]

Despite appearances, the list above under article 7 is not exhaustive. A planning authority may ask for further information in order to assist the consideration of BNG as part of their determination. The provision of this information at an early stage would also assist developers in the long run, as early discussion and agreement on achieving the biodiversity gain objective is likely to smooth the approval of the biodiversity gain condition.

This said, the PPG advises local planning authorities to "take a proportionate approach to these information requirements (which

137 Available at: https://www.gov.uk/government/publications/planning-application-forms-templates-for-local-planning-authorities. Last accessed 1 September 2024.

should be set out in their local lists) focused on only necessary additional information, and integrated with wider information requirements on biodiversity and other environmental matters."[138] This paragraph of the PPG gives examples:

- "on smaller sites where the existing habitats impacted have a low biodiversity value and the scope for onsite enhancements is limited it may not be appropriate to request a substantive amount of information from applicants, and may want to rely on the minimum information requirements;
- it may be appropriate to require information on the proposed balance between onsite gains, offsite gains and biodiversity credits, for proposals involving significant onsite habitat enhancements, and potential requirements for s.106 agreements;
- in some cases, further details (such as landscaping) may only be approved as a subsequent matter (for example approval of conditions following the grant of planning permission) following the grant of planning permission and if offsite gains and credits are proposed to be used, evidence is going to be required in the biodiversity gain plan therefore it may not be proportionate to request all this information at the planning application stage."

Where significant onsite habitat enhancements are proposed, the PPG advises they are

> "likely to form an integral part of the development, and where these are being proposed an application for planning permission would likely be expected to include detailed proposals of these habitat enhancements as part of the plans, drawings and supporting information accompanying the application. (For

[138] PPG paragraph: 013 Reference ID: 74-013-20240214.

outline planning applications, details of landscaping and layout may be reserved for later approval.)" [139]

The PPG also advises planning authorities to integrate information requirements wherever possible, giving examples of the alignment of information requirements for BNG purposes and wider planning policies which conserve and enhance biodiversity and protect the environment, such as urban greening policies.[140]

It is the planning authority's obligation to check the habitat surveys and metric calculations submitted by the developer to ensure they are accurate.[141]

Consultation

Natural England is not a statutory consultee for BNG matters for every single planning application or biodiversity gain plan. Natural England is a statutory consultee under article 18 and Schedule 4 of the Town and Country Planning (Development Management Procedure) (England) Order 2015 for:

- development in or likely to affect a site of special scientific interest.
- development which is not for agricultural purposes and is not in accordance with the provisions of a development plan and involves-
    - the loss of not less than 20 hectares of grades 1, 2 or 3a agricultural land which is for the time being used (or was last used) for agricultural purposes; or

---

139 PPG paragraph: 021 Reference ID: 74-021-20240214.

140 PPG paragraph: 013 Reference ID: 74-013-20240214.

DEFRA guidance. https://www.gov.uk/guidance/biodiversity-net-gain-what-local-planning-authorities-should-do. Last accessed 1 September 2024.

- the loss of less than 20 hectares of grades 1, 2 or 3a agricultural land which is for the time being used (or was last used) for agricultural purposes, in circumstances in which the development is likely to lead to a further loss of agricultural land amounting cumulatively to 20 hectares or more.

- (only where it appears to the local planning authority that an area of particular natural sensitivity or interest may be affected), then development falling within any of the following descriptions-
  - development involving the siting of new establishments;
  - development consisting of modifications to existing establishments [which would require notification under regulation 6(6) of the Control of Major Accident Hazards Regulations 2015 or
  - new developments including transport routes, locations of public use and residential areas in the vicinity of establishments, where the siting or development may be the source of or increase the risk or consequences of a major accident.

There are no specific statutory requirements to consult any other statutory body in relation to biodiversity gain plans, or to publicise the submission of a biodiversity gain plan.[142] The normal arrangements for applications to discharge conditions apply.

Taking Account of BNG During Determination

Because the biodiversity gain plan can only be formally submitted after planning permission has been granted, it is difficult to see many instances where decision makers could reasonably refuse an application on the basis the biodiversity gain objective will not be met. However, both decision makers and developers should still consider whether, and if so, how the biodiversity gain objective will be met during the entire planning process

[142] PPG paragraph: 038 Reference ID: 74-038-20240214.

from pre-application to determination. The PPG states "[t]o ensure the biodiversity gain objective is met and the condition can be discharged successfully, it is important biodiversity net gain is considered throughout the planning process".[143] The implications of certain onsite habitats for developability and viability means developers really should be considering BNG at the site-selection stage. Moreover, prudent developers will want planning authorities to take account of the benefit of the provision of BNG (see the decision of Holgate J. in *Vistry Homes Limited v Secretary of State for Levelling Up, Housing and Communities, St Albans City and District Council, Colney Heath Parish Council* [2024] EWHC 2088 (Admin), set out in more detail below), as well as the additional positive benefits of delivering onsite BNG such as landscaping, amenity, health, and climate change mitigation and adaptation improvements, when determining the planning application.

For planning authorities, matters related to the BNG regime that could appropriately be considered prior to determination of the planning application may include (this is not an exhaustive list), according to the PPG:[144]

- "The appropriate balance expected between onsite gains, offsite gains and the use of statutory biodiversity credits for the development, taking account of the biodiversity gain hierarchy;
- Whether the type and location of any significant onsite habitat enhancements proposed for onsite gains are appropriate, taking into account other policies to support biodiversity (including local nature recovery strategies) and other wider objectives (for example policies for design, open space and recreation, and retention of trees); and
- Any planning conditions which need to be imposed to secure any significant onsite habitat enhancements, including any conditions

[143] PPG paragraph: 002 Reference ID: 74-002-20240214.

[144] PPG paragraph: 019 Reference ID: 74-019-20240214.

> requiring the maintenance of the enhancement for at least 30 years after the completion of the development."

Prior to the determination of the planning application, decision makers and applicants should also discuss any necessary legal agreement, the terms of any habitat management and monitoring plan, and any additional conditions that may be required. Ensuring these matters are dealt with early in the process avoids costs and delay subsequently if the arrangements are unworkable and need to be amended.

Where landscaping and layout are reserved matters, the implications for existing onsite habitats and the contribution to onsite gains will not be known with the requisite certainty at the time of the determination. Where it does not fall within the definition of phased development, to which a special procedure applies, planning authorities in such cases will need to secure means by which they can conclude that, notwithstanding the lack of detail, the biodiversity gain objective will be met through subsequent approvals.

<u>Consideration of BNG as a Benefit of Planning Permission</u>

The vexed question of whether policy-based requirements (or in this case, legal requirements) are capable of constituting a benefit of the development in the planning balance was finally resolved by Holgate J., considering BNG, in *Vistry Homes*. In a detailed set of paragraphs, he said:

> "152. Where a development is required to provide a measure in order to overcome or mitigate, or compensate for, a harm caused by that project, ordinarily that measure could not rationally be described as a benefit. So, for example, where a development would result in a loss of biodiversity, the provision of additional biodiversity on the same site or on other land nearby in order to completely offset that loss, so that in overall terms there is no net

reduction in biodiversity attributable to the development, is not a benefit. It is simply the development 'consuming its own smoke.'

153. But as the name and definition of BNG indicates, that term refers to an improvement in biodiversity. That goes beyond offsetting the adverse impacts of a development scheme. It increases biodiversity in order to help redress a general national problem, which is not caused by the development proposed. On any view, that would be a benefit of the proposed scheme. It is difficult to see how rationally anyone could say otherwise. However, the scale of that benefit and the weight to be attached to it are separate considerations.

154. I do not see why the identification of what is, and what is not, a benefit should be altered, because what would otherwise be recognised as an improvement or benefit is the subject of a requirement imposed by planning policy or by legislation. Whether a measure should be treated as a benefit, depends upon *inter alia* its nature and purpose, including whether it would help to meet a need which is, or is not, related to the development proposed...

155. It is difficult to see how logically a decision-maker could give no weight at all to, for example, the provision of 10% BNG because that equated to the 10% requirement in Schedule 7A . The fact that such a requirement is imposed by legislation is simply a mechanism for ensuring that a wide range of developments contribute to the collective effort of improving biodiversity in England. It does not alter the nature or purpose of the improvement in biodiversity which is provided, or the underlying justification for the requirement to reverse a national decline in biodiversity over many years.

156. It also follows that where a development would provide BNG of 20%, a decision-maker is not entitled to say that only that part

of the BNG which exceeds 10% can qualify as a benefit in deciding whether to grant planning permission.

157. I turn to consider questions of weight. If a decision-maker were to reduce the weight which he *would otherwise give* to a 40% provision of affordable housing because the development will provide the level of housing required by the development plan, that would also be objectionable, certainly in the absence of any logical explanation. The decision-maker should be assessing how the developer's contribution of affordable housing stands in relation to *inter alia* the justification in the development plan for the level of affordable housing required by the policy. Key considerations could include the level and nature of the need for affordable housing in the district and any shortfall in delivery.

158. Similarly in relation to BNG, a decision-maker should consider the nature and purposes of the requirement and of the contribution being made. Schedule 7A of TCPA 1990 imposes a blanket requirement for the provision of 10% BNG for a broad range of development to alleviate a national problem. This benefit is of a generalised nature. It may be contrasted with the benefit of providing affordable housing which is related to (a) the highly specific needs identified by a LPA for its area and (b) ensuring that the release of housing land meets the need for affordable housing as well as general housing. Such considerations may affect the weight to be given to benefits. This is a matter for the decision-maker.

...

161. Having said all this, I do accept Mr Williams' submission that the statutory requirement for BNG of 10% can properly be used as a simple *benchmark* for comparing the BNG to be provided for a proposed development...

> 163. Where the application for permission was made before 14 February 2024 [sic: this is 12 February] the statutory 10% requirement should not be treated as having been applicable, nor should that be the effect of the decision-maker's reasoning. However, it was common ground between the parties that the 10% BNG provision in Schedule7A to the TCPA 1990 may be used in such cases, but only as a benchmark, in assessing the weight to be given to a BNG contribution. It must not be used to reduce the weight that the decision-maker would otherwise have given to the provision of BNG in a particular case."

Consideration of Planning Obligations During Determination Process

Local planning authorities should update their local lists of information requirements if they are able to justify the inclusion of information in relation to planning obligations for development subject to the BNG regime.[145] This is because planning obligations are one of the three mechanisms under paragraph 9 of Schedule 7A to secure the necessary maintenance of significant onsite habitat enhancements for at least 30 years (in addition to planning condition or conservation covenant), as well as potentially for offsite gains as well.

Thus, if planning obligations are proposed to achieve BNG, given that this information is then crucial to enable the planning authority to take account of biodiversity gains during their determination (and to give confidence that subsequently the biodiversity gain condition will be satisfied, and the permission implemented), it is good practice to submit heads of terms with the application, or at least prior to the determination of the application. The PPG notes the early provision of this information may be appropriate, saying "[t]he purpose of planning obligations is to make development acceptable in planning terms. If planning obligations are going to be used for biodiversity net gain, it is good practice to submit

145 PPG paragraph: 013 Reference ID: 74-013-20240214.

information about any potential planning obligations which may need to be entered into should the proposal be granted planning permission."[146]

If pre-application engagement has indicated the need for significant onsite biodiversity gain, then applicants are also "encouraged" to provide a draft habitat management and monitoring plan which sets out the proposals for long term maintenance of habitats to be secured through planning condition or planning obligation.[147]

Habitat Management and Monitoring Plan

Good practice is to provide a detailed habitat management and monitoring plan as a schedule to the legal agreement, or to secure one by way of condition (in relation to onsite gains). A competent professional should write the habitat management and monitoring plan. Further, if the development site contains a watercourse the applicant's expert should have the appropriate additional training and qualifications.

The PAS draft conditions template sets out a series of suggested conditions relating to a habitat management and monitoring plan (or similar document).[148] The PAS template conditions also very helpfully sets out a detailed list of what should be included in the habitat management and monitoring plan (at draft condition 2.2), to be adapted as the planning authority sees fit:

(a) a non-technical summary of the habitat management and monitoring plan;

---

146 PPG paragraph: 015 Reference ID: 74-015-20240214.

147 PPG paragraph: 015 Reference ID: 74-015-20240214.

148 https://www.local.gov.uk/pas/environment/biodiversity-net-gain-bng-local-planning-authorities/pas-biodiversity-net-gain-bng. Last accessed 1 September 2024.

(b) roles and responsibilities of the people or organisation(s) delivering the habitat management and monitoring plan;

(c) the planned habitat creation and enhancement works to create or improve habitat to achieve BNG in accordance with the approved biodiversity gain plan;

(d) the management measures to maintain habitat in accordance with the approved biodiversity gain plan for a period of 30 years from the completion of development; and

(e) the monitoring methodology and frequency in respect of the created and/or enhanced habitat.

Details of reporting the outcomes of the monitoring carried out to the relevant enforcing body should also be specified.

A series of habitat management and monitoring plan templates, a checklist and companion guides have been published by Natural England.[149] The full suite of documents available from Natural England are:

- Habitat Management and Monitoring Plan Template
- Companion Document
- habitat management and monitoring plan Template Checklist
- Small Sites Metric habitat management and monitoring plan Template
- Small Sites Metric habitat management and monitoring plan Template Habitat Guide
- Monitoring Report Template

149 Available at: https://publications.naturalengland.org.uk/publication/5813530037846016. Last accessed 1 September 2024.

- Monitoring Report Quantitative Summary Template

Given the huge potential costs of remedial works, and the uncertainty over what may qualify as a force majeure event, the habitat management and monitoring plan should be used to clarify, so far as possible, foreseeable risks and remedial actions if those risks materialise (i.e. upstream abstraction changes, the impacts of climate change, the risk of invasive species, etc.).

If land ownership changes, the habitat management and monitoring plan may need to be updated.

A draft habitat management and monitoring plan should be submitted with the planning application where either significant onsite BNG or offsite BNG are proposed.[150] An agreed habitat management and monitoring plan should be submitted with the biodiversity gain plan. Who it must be agreed with depends on the nature of the gains and legal agreement. If significant onsite BNG is proposed the habitat management and monitoring plan will have to be agreed with the local planning authority and should be included as a schedule to the s.106 agreement. If offsite BNG is proposed to be secured by way of s.106 agreement the habitat management and monitoring plan will also need to be agreed with the relevant local planning authority (or authorities) and included as a schedule to the s.106 agreement. For offsite gains secured by way of conservation covenant, then the habitat management and monitoring plan will have to be agreed with the designated responsible body.

---

150 https://www.gov.uk/guidance/biodiversity-net-gain-what-local-planning-authorities-should-do. Last accessed 1 September 2024.

Information to Include on Decision Notice

The general principles courts will apply to the interpretation of planning permissions should always be borne in mind by planning decision makers. First, the court's starting point is not deference to the decision maker's judgment: *UBB Waste Essex Ltd v Essex County Council* [2019] EWHC 1924 (Admin), per Lieven J. at [25]. This is because the proper interpretation of a planning permission is a matter of law for the court: *Barnett v Secretary of State for Communities and Local Government* [2009] EWCA Civ 476, per Keene L.J. at [28].

The court will ask itself, objectively, what a reasonable reader would understand the words of the planning permission to mean having regard to their natural and ordinary meaning, the planning purpose, and common sense, and the planning permission when read as a whole: *Trump International Golf Club Scotland Ltd v The Scottish Ministers* [2015] UKSC 74 per Lord Hodge at [34]; *London Borough of Lambeth v Secretary of State for Housing, Communities and Local Government* [2019] UKSC 33, per Lord Carnwath at [16]-[19]; and *UBB*, per Lieven J at [55].

The interpretive exercise should not normally include material outside the planning permission itself. The approach to take when determining whether regard should be had to any material beyond the planning permission was set out by Keene J. (as he then was) in *R v Ashford Borough Council ex parte Shepway District Council* [1999] PLCR 12 at pages 19C to 20D, and applied ever since. The case law on this point was summarised by Steyn J. in *R (Gallagher Ventures Limited v Secretary of State for Housing, Communities and Local Government, Torbay Council* [2021] EWHC 3007 (Admin) (at [5]):

> "i) The general rule is that in construing a planning permission which is clear, unambiguous and valid on its face, regard may only be had to the planning permission itself (including the conditions, if any, on it and the express reasons for those conditions): *Ashford*,

per Keene J. at p.19C-D; *R (Menston Action Group) v City of Bradford Metropolitan District Council* [2016] EWCA Civ 796, per Lindblom L.J. at [11].

ii) The planning permission may incorporate by reference the application. It will only do so if some words sufficient to inform a reasonable reader that the application forms part of the permission appear in the operative part of the permission, showing that the words govern the description of the development permitted. Any document that is properly to be regarded as incorporated by reference is intrinsic to the planning permission and the court should have regard to it when determining the meaning of the planning permission. See *Ashford*, per Keene J. at p.19D-G.

iii) If there is an ambiguity in the wording of the permission, it is permissible to look at extrinsic material to resolve that ambiguity. Extrinsic evidence may be documentary (e.g. the relevant planning officer's report), but it is not confined to documentary evidence: *Wood v Secretary of State for Communities and Local Government* [2015] EWHC 2368 (Admin), per Lindblom J. at [43]."

A cautious approach should be taken to extraneous material, especially if it is not material in the public domain. This is because the courts are interpreting a public document, subject to public consultation, on which the public may well have had a vocal say, and which might be relied on by third parties who did not participate in the determination process (*Trump International*, per Lord Carnwath at [65]-[66]; *Lambeth v SSHCLG*, per Lord Carnwath at [18]; and *UBB*, per Lieven J. at [56]-[57]).

The courts are to assume this hypothetical reasonable reader will have some knowledge of planning law, and understand the role of the planning permission, conditions and any incorporated documents: *UBB*, per Lieven J. at [52] to [53].

Article 35 of the Town and Country Planning (Development Management Procedure) (England) Order 2015 now provides BNG-specific information to include on decision notices for planning authorities (so far as may apply to the BNG regime):

"35.- Written notice of decision or determination relating to a planning application

(1) When the local planning authority give notice of a decision or determination on an application for planning permission or for approval of reserved matters-

(za) where planning permission is granted, the notice must include-

(i) information relating to the condition in paragraph 13 of Schedule 7A to the 1990 Act (biodiversity gain condition) including that there are exemptions, transitional arrangements and requirements relating to irreplaceable habitat,

(ii) information to note the effect of section 73(2D) of the 1990 Act (earlier biodiversity gain plan in relation to a previous planning permission regarded as approved for purposes of paragraph 13 of Schedule 7A),

(iii) details of the planning authority under paragraph 12(1) of Schedule 7A (biodiversity gain in England), and

(iv) where development is to proceed in phases and the modifications in Part 2 of the Biodiversity Gain (Town and Country Planning) (Modifications and Amendments) (England) Regulations 2024 apply, a statement to that effect and to the effect that biodiversity gain plans are required before development may be begun and required before each phase of development may be begun;

(a) where planning permission is granted subject to conditions, the notice must state clearly and precisely their full reasons-

(i) for each condition imposed; and
(ii) in the case of each pre-commencement condition, for the condition being a pre-commencement condition;

(b) where planning permission is refused, the notice must state clearly and precisely their full reasons for the refusal, specifying all policies and proposals in the development plan which are relevant to the decision;

(c) where-
(i) the Secretary of State has given a direction restricting the grant of planning permission for the development for which application is made; or
(ii) the Secretary of State or a government department has expressed the view that the permission should not be granted (either wholly or in part) or should be granted subject to conditions,
the notice must give details of the direction or of the view expressed.

(1A) References in paragraph (1)(a) to a condition do not include a condition under paragraph 13 of Schedule 7A (the biodiversity gain condition).

(2) Where paragraph (1)(a) or (b) applies, the notice must also include a statement explaining, whether, and if so how, in dealing with the application, the local planning authority have worked with the applicant in a positive and proactive manner based on seeking solutions to problems arising in relation to dealing with a planning application.

(3) Where paragraph (1)(a), (b) or (c) applies, the notice must be accompanied by a notification in the terms (or substantially in the terms) set out in Schedule 5."

Local planning authorities have also been provided with model paragraphs for biodiversity gain information on the written decision notice when granting planning permission, which they are encouraged to use.[151] These model paragraphs are at Appendix B of this book, and online.[152]

Applying Other Planning Conditions in Relation to BNG

Section 70(1)(a) of the Town and Country Planning Act 1990 gives planning authorities a very broad power to impose such planning conditions as they see fit.[153] It follows that they may include additional conditions relating to the delivery of BNG. The PPG gives examples of additional potential conditions, such as a planning condition used to secure significant onsite habitat enhancements which are required to be secured and maintained for at least 30 years under paragraph 9 of Schedule 7A, as well as monitoring and reporting arrangements.[154]

A key consideration when imposing conditions in relation to BNG (other than the need for objective clarity and precision in light of the 30-year-long positive obligation) is that they should not be used to secure funding for delivering or monitoring biodiversity net gain due to difficulty in enforcement of the condition's terms. These positive obligations should be secured through s.106 planning obligations, where justified.[155]

---

151 PPG paragraph: 025 Reference ID: 74-025-20240214.

152 Available at; https://assets.publishing.service.gov.uk/media/663251d969098ded31fca800/BNG_Decision_Notice_Text.odt. Last accessed 1 September 2024.

153 See also s.72, which does not affect the generality of s.70(1)(a).

154 PPG paragraph: 027 Reference ID: 74-027-20240214.

155 Justification is assessed by reference to the limitations on the use of planning obligations set out in regulation 122 of the Community Infrastructure Levy Regulations 2010. See also PPG on Use of Planning Conditions, paragraph: 005 Reference ID: 21a-005-20190723.

Significant Onsite Habitat Enhancements

Schedule 7A, paragraph 9(3) of the Town and Country Planning Act 1990 requires that where an applicant relies upon a "significant" increase in onsite habitat biodiversity value, that habitat enhancement must be subject to either a planning condition, s.106 agreement, or conservation covenant in each case requiring that habitat to be maintained for at least 30 years after the development is completed. If a planning condition is used this is separate to the biodiversity gain condition (i.e. that which requires them to achieve at least 10% BNG) and so will have to be imposed by the planning authority.

Schedule 7A does not define "significant" onsite enhancements. The PPG does not either. The DEFRA guidance does, although it does not assist much in terms of defining what a significant gain means: "[s]ignificant enhancements are areas of habitat enhancement which contribute significantly to the proposed development's BNG, relative to the biodiversity value before development".[156] Examples (in a non-exhaustive list) are provided:

- habitats of medium or higher distinctiveness in the statutory metric
- habitats of low distinctiveness which create a large number of biodiversity units relative to the biodiversity value of the site before development
- habitat creation or enhancement where distinctiveness is increased relative to the distinctiveness of the habitat before development
- areas of habitat creation or enhancement which are significant in area relative to the size of the development
- enhancements to habitat condition, for example from poor or moderate to good

[156] DEFRA BNG guidance: https://www.gov.uk/guidance/make-on-site-biodiversity-gains-as-a-developer#significant-on-site-enhancements. Last accessed 1 September 2024.

- creating a wildflower meadow or a nature park

There is a PAS onsite s.106 agreement template available which helpfully includes clauses to secure the requisite funds for local planning authority monitoring of all onsite habitat.[157]

What is the "Completion" Date?

The maintenance period for significant onsite habitat enhancement is at least 30 years after "the development is completed." (Schedule 7A, paragraph 9(3)). This is a potential issue because there is no legal obligation to complete a development.

Clearly, the completion of any onsite works to enhance and/or create habitat (not just completion of the buildings related to the development) must be included in considerations of completion (you cannot maintain what does not yet exist). The PPG suggests that using traditional indicators of completion for residential or commercial development (such as a building regulations notice) may not be appropriate for the purposes of the BNG regime,[158] but does not provide further guidance.

Suggestions include using occupation as the defined "completion" date for the purposes of maintaining onsite BNG.[159] This is the earliest point where the purpose of the development can be said to be achieved (thus,

157 PAS templates available at: https://www.local.gov.uk/pas/environment/biodiversity-net-gain-bng-local-planning-authorities/pas-biodiversity-net-gain-bng. Last accessed 1 September 2024.

158 PPG paragraph: 022 Reference ID: 74-022-20240214.

159 See PAS template: at: https://www.local.gov.uk/pas/environment/biodiversity-net-gain-bng-local-planning-authorities/pas-biodiversity-net-gain-bng. Last accessed 1 September 2024.

it can be described as being completed for all intents and purposes) and it is also a point the developer has a financial incentive to achieve.

Due to the importance of all parties having certainty on when the 30-year maintenance period starts (and ends), and because of the potential hardships caused by a poorly thought through unilaterally imposed "completion date", planning authorities and developers should discuss the matter and ensure any consequential document is clear on when completion of development occurs and thus when the 30-year maintenance period begins.

Whatever parameter is chosen for "completion of development", planning authorities and developers should check timeframes with their ecologist and the planning authority carefully as environmental constraints when establishing and maintaining habitat (planting season, suitable ground conditions, appropriate soil fertility levels, etc.) may mean habitat works are only able to be completed years after, for example, occupation timescales.

Onsite Enhancements and Aerodrome Safeguarding

The Town and Country Planning (Safeguarded Aerodromes, Technical Sites and Military Explosives Storage Areas) Direction 2002 requires consultation with the Civil Aviation Authority, the Secretary of State for Defence, or the aerodrome operator (as the case may be) when development is proposed on the site of or in the neighbourhood of an aerodrome, technical site or military explosives storage area for which a safeguarding map has been prepared. A safeguarding map is:

> (a) a map issued for the purpose of the Direction and certified by the Civil Aviation Authority to be the safeguarding map for the aerodrome or technical site; or

(b) a map issued for the purpose of the Direction and certified by the Secretary of State for Defence to be the safeguarding map for the aerodrome, technical site or military explosives storage area.

The relevant consultee is then premised on the safeguarding map:

(a) in relation to a safeguarding map certified by the Civil Aviation Authority, the consultee is the owner or operator of the aerodrome or technical site identified on that map; or

(b) in relation to a safeguarding map certified by the Secretary of State for Defence, the consultee is the Secretary of State for Defence.

If a local planning authority propose to grant permission contrary to the advice of the consultee, they are obliged to notify:

(a) both the Civil Aviation Authority and the consultee; or
(b) the Secretary of State for Defence (as relevant).

The danger which arises in the context of the BNG regime is the risk of bird strike. The bird strike consultation area of an Officially Safeguarded Aerodrome is a 13km circle depicted on the safeguarding map. Because of the public safety implications where enhancement and/or creation works are proposed which may include features likely to attract birds within safeguarding areas, developers must confirm the relevant aerodrome and consultee (if not one and the same) have been notified of the proposed habitat enhancement and/or creation, had the opportunity to assess the plan for potential hazards to aircraft operations, and what their response was. The planning authority have to be satisfied with any risk to aviation safety based on the works proposed and final outcome of the biodiversity gain plan.[160]

---

[160] PPG paragraph: 023 Reference ID: 74-023-20240214.

Interactions with Local Plan-Making

The BNG regime is predominately a statutory regime. Where a provision in statute conflicts with a provision in a local plan, statute takes priority. Where the local plan goes further than the BNG regime (i.e. requiring 20% BNG), (1) what is required under statute must be provided, and (2) the requirements of the policy must also be provided, unless material considerations indicate otherwise (by s.38(6) of the Planning and Compulsory Purchase Act 2004). This means a developer could not argue at appeal that 10% BNG need not be provided, but they can argue that material considerations mean that 20% need not be.

The PPG says that a local plan-based policy which required a gain of at least 10% from new developments in anticipation of the statutory regime "should no longer apply when determining applications for planning permission subject to biodiversity net gain, although it may continue to be a material consideration"; and "[d]ecision makers should not give weight to local policy which requires biodiversity gains for types of development which would now be exempt under the statutory framework".[161] Unless extant development plan policy has been revoked it remains development plan policy subject to s.38(6) of the Planning and Compulsory Purchase Act 2004, so decision makers cannot ignore such policies: they remain material considerations due to an express statutory direction on decision making. What weight should be given to relevant policies and guidance is a matter for decision makers, but the PPG is also a material consideration and any decision contrary to the PPG requires justification.

Looking ahead, future development plans, supplementary development plan documents, and local guidance should be consistent with the BNG regime. There is nothing precluding plan makers from including additional policies which complement but do not duplicate the BNG regime. Indeed, paragraph 185 of the NPPF encourages plans to – among

[161] PPG paragraph: 020 Reference ID: 74-020-20240214.

other things – identify and pursue opportunities for securing measurable net gains for biodiversity in order to "protect and enhance biodiversity". The PPG confirms planning authorities and neighbourhood planning bodies will want to take account of the BNG regime when preparing new policies in line with paragraph 185.[162]

As to the adoption of development plan policies which go beyond the BNG regime, the PPG says:

> "[p]lan-makers should not seek a higher percentage than the statutory objective of 10% biodiversity net gain, either on an area-wide basis or for specific allocations for development unless justified. To justify such policies they will need to be evidenced including as to local need for a higher percentage, local opportunities for a higher percentage and any impacts on viability for development. Consideration will also need to be given to how the policy will be implemented."[163]

So, it is permissible to adopt local development plan policy requiring greater than 10% BNG but it must be carefully considered, consulted on, and justified by reference to appropriate evidence in line with the PPG, unless good reasons exist to depart from the PPG.

Local Planning Authorities and the Register of Biodiversity Gain Plan Information

Article 37D(4) of The Town and Country Planning (Development Management Procedure) (England) Order 2015 requires that where written notice is given to the person submitting the biodiversity gain plan, the planning authority must provide the local planning register authority (if they are not already the local planning register authority) within five working days after that written notice:

---

162 PPG paragraph: 006 Reference ID: 74-006-20240214.

163 PPG paragraph: 006 Reference ID: 74-006-20240214.

a) a copy of the biodiversity gain plan submitted to the planning authority under paragraph 13 of Schedule 7A, including all plans, drawings and other documents submitted with the biodiversity gain plan; and
b) notice of the determination whether to approve the biodiversity gain plan, if any, including the date of that notice and the name of the planning authority.

Article 40(4ZA) of the Town and Country Planning (Development Management Procedure) (England) Order 2015 requires each local planning register authority to publish the above information on the planning register.

Local Planning Authority Enforcement

Failure to comply with the biodiversity gain condition is a breach of planning control. Onsite provision of habitat is the first priority of the BNG regime. Local planning authorities, accordingly, have the most crucial enforcement role within the entire BNG regime.

Remediating failed BNG works can be extremely costly. For this reason, it is not uncommon for planning authorities to require security for BNG maintenance obligations. Where there are legitimate concerns over the long-term ability of a party to deliver the biodiversity gain, then performance bonds, or sums held in escrow which would survive the bankruptcy, or insolvency of the party responsible for ensuring the biodiversity gain plan is delivered can be sought. The PAS offsite s.106 template includes optional wording providing for the payment of a bond where it has been agreed between the parties that it is necessary. The template provides for the bond sum to decrease each year as relevant monitoring contributions are paid and actions required by the habitat management and monitoring plan (or similar document) are delivered, but planning authorities should seek specialist ecological advice on the appropriateness of any provisions. If appropriate monitoring is not secured in relation to a proposed habitat that requires significant long-term intervention, for example, then there may be a risk of a catastrophic loss of biodiversity value at the end of the relevant 30-year period requiring remediation which the remaining bond sum would not cover. On the other hand, it is right to recognise and reflect in the security sum the actual realisation of benefits as they occur: a scheme which fails at year 29 will have delivered 28 years of requisite BNG, and that must be taken into account.

Where a planning authority agrees it is appropriate to provide for a defence to a breach of planning obligation similar to the statutory defence for breach of a conservation covenant they may look to the PAS offsite template for guidance on the wording of any such clause.[164] Currently this provides that no person is to be liable for breach of obligation if it is shown (1) the breach occurred as a result of a matter beyond the control of the person in default; or (2) the breach occurred as a result of doing, or not doing, something in an emergency in circumstances where it was necessary for that to be done, or not done, in order to prevent loss of life or injury to any person.

Local planning authorities should have local enforcement plans that include their priorities for enforcement action. These should be updated to reflect the new BNG regime, and include enforcement of the initial delivery of habitats as well as enforcement of ongoing management, maintenance and monitoring requirements.

The enforcement tools granted to local planning authorities relevant to BNG are discretionary, and fears over the lack of capacity of overstretched enforcement teams within local planning authorities have accompanied the development of the BNG regime from its very conception. This lack of capacity means enforcement action is often initiated by complaints from local residents. However, local residents

---

164 https://www.local.gov.uk/pas/environment/biodiversity-net-gain-bng-local-planning-authorities/pas-biodiversity-net-gain-bng. Last accessed 1 September 2024.

may well be more likely to complain about a failure to mow "messy" BNG grassland because they want to use it for football and picnics than they are to complain about that grassland achieving moderate condition instead of good condition by year 25, for example (and this is assuming local residents are even aware of the contents of the biodiversity gain plan).

A breach of condition notice is issued under s.187A of the Town and Country Planning Act 1990 as follows (noting, while it is still discretionary, there is no expediency test for the service of a breach of condition notice and no right of appeal):

> "(2) The local planning authority may, if any of the conditions is not complied with, serve a notice (in this Act referred to as a *'breach of condition notice'*) on-
>
> (a) any person who is carrying out or has carried out the development; or
>
> (b) any person having control of the land,
>
> requiring him to secure compliance with such of the conditions as are specified in the notice."

Because habitats may take decades to establish, by the time a breach is apparent the developer is likely to have passed on any ongoing legal liabilities under the BNG regime. The person "having control of the land" may need to then be identified. Management companies incorporated or hired to carry out landscaping and BNG work must be in control of the land on which the BNG units have been provided in order to be liable for any breach of condition. Then there is the question of whether they have the funds and expertise to secure compliance with the breach of condition notice. It is foreseeable that a failure to provide the requisite BNG is precisely because that person lacks sufficient funds and/or expertise.

Further, a breach of condition notice must *specify* the steps which the local planning authority consider ought to be taken, or the activities which the authority consider ought to cease, to secure compliance with the conditions specified in the notice (s.187A(5)). A period for compliance must also be specified (s.187A(7)). The statutory language requires detail, clarity and precision in the drafting of the notice. This is of particular importance given the risk of criminal liability if the notice is not complied with. In *R. v East Lothian Council Ex p Scottish Coal Company Ltd* [2001] 1 P.L.R. 1 (a Scottish case, but considering the same statutory language), Lord Prosser said at [12] this statutory language "is concerned with actual, factual steps". The formulation adopted in the notice in that case, which required that the respondents complied with the stated condition by "ensuring" that its terms were met, was not lawful, because use of the word "ensuring" focused upon the result to be achieved, rather than the means of achieving it (which, according to the statutory language, had to be specified) (per Lord Prosser at [12]). This means local planning authorities could require highly specialist ecological expertise in order to specify the requisite terms of the notice so as to secure compliance with the enforcement regime for breach of condition notices.

If the breach of condition notice is not complied with, it is a criminal offence punishable by an unlimited fine (s.187A(9) and s.187A(12)). There is a statutory defence that the recipient of the notice took all reasonable measures to secure compliance with the conditions specified in the notice, or was no longer in control of the land (s.187A(11)). Criminal proceedings and a hefty fine will not secure BNG. Section 187A does not grant local planning authorities step in rights to remedy a breach of condition.

One option is for local planning authorities to instead serve an enforcement notice, as they would then have the option under s.178(1) to enter the land, carry out the steps which were not carried out within the period for compliance specified in the enforcement notice, and recover the costs of carrying out those steps from the landowner.

Where there is a s.106 agreement or conservation covenant (see Legal Agreements chapter for more details on their content and relevant procedures), the legal enforcement framework is much simpler and significantly more certain, as any failure to comply with the terms of that agreement is a breach and may be enforced in accordance with the terms of that agreement. As above, the decision whether or not to enforce in relation to a breach of a planning obligation is for the enforcing local planning authority: in *Milebush Properties Ltd v Tameside MBC* [2011] P.T.S.R. 1654 the Court of Appeal accepted that enforcement of a s.106 agreement is a matter for the discretion of the local planning authority.

For enforcement purposes legal agreements should contain clauses clearly stating the outcome to be achieved and providing for appropriate monitoring, maintenance, step-in rights, and remedial obligations. In the case of a s.106 agreement step-in rights are automatically granted to the enforcing local planning authority in respect of a breach of a planning obligation: s.106(6)-(7) provide:

> "...if there is a breach of a requirement in a planning obligation to carry out any operations in, on, under or over the land to which the obligation relates, the authority by whom the obligation is enforceable may-
>
> (a) enter the land and carry out the operations; and
>
> (b) recover from the person or persons against whom the obligation is enforceable any expenses reasonably incurred by them in doing so.
>
> (7) Before an authority exercise their power under subsection (6)(a) they shall give not less than twenty-one days' notice of their intention to do so to any person against whom the planning obligation is enforceable."

It can be seen the planning authority's expenses are recoverable from those against whom the planning obligation is enforceable, which, in the case of a s.106 agreement, means not only the current owner but also the original covenantor and all intervening owners, unless the obligation exempts liability once the owner has disposed of their interest.

CHAPTER SEVEN

SPECIAL CASES: SECTION 73, 62A, PHASED, AND MINERALS PERMISSIONS

Section 73 Permissions

The starting point for consideration of s.73 of the Town and Country Planning Act 1990 is that the decision to grant consent results in a fresh planning permission. This means the biodiversity gain condition is automatically imposed on a s.73 consent just as with any other planning permission granted under Part 3 of the Town and Country Planning Act 1990. There are, however, quite a number of modifications of the BNG regime in respect of s.73 permissions.

First, there are the transitional provisions (this also applies to small sites development subject to the change of date to 2 April 2024). The Environment Act 2021 (Commencement No.8 and Transitional Provisions) Regulations 2024 sets out transitional provisions for all other s.73 applications at reg. 4:

> "*4. Transitional provision: section 73 planning permissions*
>
> (1) The biodiversity gain planning condition does not apply in relation to a section 73 planning permission where-
>
> (a) the original planning permission to which the section 73 planning permission relates was granted before 12th February 2024; or
>
> (b) the application for the original planning permission to which the section 73 planning permission relates was made before 12th February 2024.

(2) For the purposes of this regulation-

(a) 'section 73 planning permission' means a planning permission granted on an application made under section 73 of the 1990 Act (determination of applications to develop land without compliance with conditions previously attached);

(b) 'the original planning permission to which the section 73 planning permission relates' means a planning permission which is the first in a sequence of two or more planning permissions, where the second and any subsequent planning permissions are section 73 planning permissions."

From the above, and as set out in the Exemptions chapter, it is clear an application under s.73 which is made after 12 February 2024 is not in scope if the original permission to which the s.73 application relates (1) was granted or (2) the application for the original permission was made before this date. However, from the statutory language, any s.73 application made after 12 February 2024 which relates to a s.73 permission is not exempt. This is because the Environment Act 2021 (Commencement No. 8 and Transitional Provisions) Regulations 2024 confirm that "original planning permission to which the section 73 planning permission relates" is defined as a planning permission which is the first in a sequence of two or more planning permissions, where the second and any subsequent planning permissions are s.73 planning permissions (reg.4(2)(b)).

For completeness, it should be noted that s.73 itself has been amended to ensure that no planning authority has the power to disapply the BNG condition, and to provide for a more efficient procedure when the s.73 application relates to any permission for which there is already an approved biodiversity gain plan (subject to special conditions in relation to phased development set out later):

"73. Determination of applications to develop land without compliance with conditions previously attached.

(1) This section applies, subject to subsection (4), to applications for planning permission for the development of land without complying with conditions subject to which a previous planning permission was granted.

(2) On such an application the local planning authority shall consider only the question of the conditions subject to which planning permission should be granted, and-

(a) if they decide that planning permission should be granted subject to conditions differing from those subject to which the previous permission was granted, or that it should be granted unconditionally, they shall grant planning permission accordingly, and

(b) if they decide that planning permission should be granted subject to the same conditions as those subject to which the previous permission was granted, they shall refuse the application.

...

(2B) Nothing in this section authorises the disapplication of the condition under paragraph 13 of Schedule 7A (biodiversity gain condition).

(2C) Subsection (2D) applies where-

(a) for the purposes of paragraph 13 of Schedule 7A a biodiversity gain plan was approved in relation to the previous planning permission ('the earlier biodiversity gain plan'),

(b) planning permission is granted under this section, and

(c) the conditions subject to which the planning permission is granted under this section-

(i) do not affect the post-development value of the onsite habitat as specified in the earlier biodiversity gain plan, and

(ii) in the case of planning permission for a development where all or any part of the onsite habitat is irreplaceable habitat within the meaning of regulations made under paragraph 18 of Schedule 7A [these are the Biodiversity Gain Requirements (Irreplaceable Habitat) Regulations 2024], do not change the effect of the development on the biodiversity of that onsite habitat (including any arrangements made to compensate for any such effect) as specified in the earlier biodiversity gain plan.

(2D) Where this subsection applies, the earlier biodiversity gain plan is regarded as approved for the purposes of paragraph 13 of Schedule 7A in relation to the planning permission granted under this section.

(4) This section does not apply if the previous planning permission was granted subject to a condition as to the time within which the development to which it related was to be begun and that time has expired without the development having been begun.

(5) Planning permission must not be granted under this section for the development of land in England to the extent that it has effect to change a condition subject to which a previous planning permission was granted by extending the time within which–

(a) a development must be started;

(b) an application for approval of reserved matters (within the meaning of section 92) must be made."

<u>Information Requirements for Section 73 Applications</u>

Article 7(1B) of the Town and Country Planning (Development Management Procedure) (England) Order 2015 excludes applications made under s.73 from the minimum information requirements set out in article (1A) (such as the pre-development biodiversity value of the onsite habitat for biodiversity net gain). It seems this contemplates that the BNG regime would only ever apply to a s.73 application when it also applied to the original planning permission, in which case, there is only one (potentially) implemented permission in contemplation (the original) and, so it would be a straightforward situation of simply checking whether s.73(2D) applies or not. The alternative envisaged would be the opposite: the BNG regime did not apply to the original permission, in which case it would not apply to the s.73 permission (by reg.4 of the Environment Act 2021 (Commencement No.8 and Transitional Provisions) Regulations 2024).

However, as explained above, planning law allows for another scenario where the s.73 permission is itself amending a s.73 permission, and that second s.73 permission would not be exempt from the BNG regime under the transitional provisions. The result would be a requirement to carry out a fresh pre-development baseline metric assessment for the second s.73 permission which would necessarily include all onsite BNG from the implementation of the original and/or subsequent s.73 permission(s). The 10% post-development BNG requirement would then be calculated from this potentially enhanced onsite baseline.

Impacts Due to Section 73 Permission

If any planning permission granted under s.73 would not affect the post-development biodiversity value of onsite habitat, the earlier biodiversity gain plan is regarded as approved for the purpose of the new permission granted under s.73 (by s.73(2D)). Here it does not matter whether the impact is beneficial or harmful: the statutory language "affect" and "change the effect" in s.73(2C) are outcome-neutral. So, even if there is a beneficial effect, a new biodiversity gain plan is still required. It appears the intention here is to ensure additional gains are quantified and secured.

There is an additional requirement in the case of a site containing irreplaceable habitat. For an automatic approval of the biodiversity gain condition under s.73(2C) and (2D) not only can there be no impact on the post-development onsite habitat, including any irreplaceable habitat, the permission granted by way of the s.73 application also cannot affect any compensation arrangement(s) previously agreed in relation to onsite irreplaceable habitat. If there is such an impact (again, this is whether the impact is beneficial or harmful), then fresh consideration of the bespoke compensation plan for the irreplaceable habitat will be required, following the regime for irreplaceable habitat set out in the chapter on Irreplaceable Habitats.

Finally, it is important to think about any potential consequences of a s.73 permission on any extant s.106 agreement or conservation covenant relating to the use of the land. Where there are repercussions, the existing legal agreement should be varied or supplemented to ensure that it remains enforceable when the new s.73 permission is implemented.

Applications Submitted Directly to the Secretary of State under Section 62A

The BNG regime applies to applications made directly to the Secretary of State under section 62A of the Town and Country Planning Act 1990. Section 62A of the 1990 Act allows applicants to apply directly to the Secretary of State for determination of their planning applications where the local planning authority has been designated for special measures. The procedure for s.62A applications and hearings is set out in the Town and Country Planning (Section 62A Applications) (Hearings) Rules 2013; the Town and Country Planning (Section 62A Applications) (Written Representations and Miscellaneous Provisions) Regulations 2013; the Town and Country Planning (Section 62A Applications) (Procedure and Consequential Amendments) Order 2013, and the Section 62A Procedural Guidance.[165]

[165] Guidance available at: https://www.gov.uk/government/publications/planning-applications-process-section-62a-authorities-in-special-measures/procedural-guidance-for-section-62a-authorities-in-special-measures. Last accessed 1 September 2024.

Phased Development

The BNG regime has been significantly amended to account for planning permission with the effect of permitting development which proceed in phases. This is because such development can occur over a long period of time, and full details are unlikely to be known when the development is first proposed. The modifications to the BNG regime for phased development made by reg.3 of the Biodiversity Gain (Town and Country Planning) (Modifications and Amendments) (England) Regulations 2024 apply to:

> (a) the grant of outline planning permission where the reservation of matters for subsequent approval has the effect of requiring or permitting development to proceed in phases;
> (b) a grant of any kind of planning permission, where the grant is subject to conditions (whether requiring the subsequent approval of any matters or otherwise) having that effect.

This is the same definition of phased development set out at Schedule 7A, paragraph 19(1). Together (a) and (b) form the definition of "phased development" for the purposes of the BNG regime. An outline planning permission on its own is not a phased development. There must be something additional about the reservation of matters which has "the effect of requiring or permitting development to proceed in phases" to engage the BNG regime's phased development procedures.

The PPG seems to contemplate the phased development provisions to be clear to apply, giving as an example of phased development a large scale urban extension where the permission "identifies clear phases for development", and a series of subsequent reserved matter approvals concerning the detailed design of each phase. It contrasts this with a small-scale residential development where appearance and landscaping were the only reserved matters.[166] More guidance on the dividing line

166 PPG paragraph 053 Reference ID: 74-053-20240214.

between these two extremes may have been more helpful as the phased development definition would potentially apply to much more than just the obvious large urban extension type of development. However, because the modifications to the BNG regime for phased development are generally more procedural than substantive, the question of whether a permission falls within the phased development regime or not is more likely to be an issue in terms of practicality of compliance with the BNG regime. It is the practicality of applying the BNG regime to phased development which is the issue. Developers often don't know when, nor in what form, phases within an overall development will come forward, so there is a great deal of uncertainty in relation to phased development.

Some clarity (either way), at least in relation to which condition(s) applies, must be provided early on in the process. When granting planning permission the decision maker must state on the written decision notice that the BNG phased development modifications apply (by article 35(za)(iv) of the Town and Country Planning (Development Management Procedure) (England) Order 2015).

Procedural Changes for Phased Development

For phased development the BNG regime contemplates an overall post-development biodiversity value of habitat for the entire development at completion (not after the completion of each phase).[167] As with the "completion of development" issue for the purposes of determining the commencement date for the 30-year maintenance period for significant onsite BNG, this is a potentially serious issue because the phased development may never be completed. Providing all BNG upfront would be financially prohibitive as it uses capital that will only indirectly lead to profit prior to realising any return. It may also generate a 30-year liability on the developer prior to realising any return.

---

167 PPG paragraph 056 Reference ID: 74-056-20240214.

Further, a developer is very unlikely to know exactly when the various phases will be brought forward and delivered, making overall delivery of BNG across the site difficult to coordinate.

It can be seen the uncertainty inherent in the delivery of BNG is also amplified with respect to phased development because it involves assumptions about both the likely future development and habitat enhancements in order to determine projected post-development value. The Biodiversity Gain (Town and Country Planning) (Modifications and Amendments) (England) Regulations 2024 tries to resolve these challenges through modifying the standard biodiversity condition for phased development. Importantly, as noted, the biodiversity gain objective of providing at least 10% net gain applies to the overall development, not to each phase individually.[168] The pre-development biodiversity value of onsite habitat for phased development is calculated in the same way as for any other application.[169] This means the pre-development value of the whole site is to be calculated at the very outset, alongside the overall biodiversity gain plan, and this will not change. The PPG confirms "[l]ater changes to the condition of onsite habitat on a phase prior to its commencement are not relevant to the calculation of the pre-development biodiversity value for phase development."[170]

The contribution of each phase to achieving net gain may vary, allowing for a more flexible approach to the provision of BNG across the site depending on the circumstances of that area of the site and the development proposed.

It will be seen the substantive goal remains the same, but the procedure to be followed is different. The following procedure must instead be followed:

---

168 PPG paragraph 056 reference ID: 74-056-20240214.

169 PPG paragraph 057 reference ID: 74-057-20240214.

170 PPG paragraph 057 Reference ID: 74-057-20240214.

- an "overall biodiversity gain plan" must be submitted to and approved by the planning authority before any development can begin; and
- a "phase biodiversity gain plan" for each phase must also be submitted to and approved by the planning authority before the development of that phase can begin.

The biodiversity gain conditions for phased development (as introduced by reg.4 of the Biodiversity Gain (Town and Country Planning) (Modifications and Amendments) (England) Regulations 2024) are set out earlier in this book. To save having to cross refer back to the Biodiversity Gain Condition(s) and Biodiversity Gain Plan chapter, the Schedule 7A, paragraph 13 biodiversity gain conditions for phased development are:

> "(1) The grant of planning permission of the type mentioned in paragraph 19(1)(a) or (b) for the development of land in England shall be deemed to have been granted subject to the conditions in sub-paragraphs (2) to (6).
>
> (2) The conditions are that-
>
>> (a) the development may not be begun unless the requirement in sub-paragraph (3) or (4) (overall plan) has been met,
>>
>> (b) no phase of development may be begun unless the requirement in sub-paragraph (5) or (6) (phase plan) has been met in respect of that phase, and
>>
>> (c) where permission has been granted on an application made under section 73 (determination of applications to develop land without compliance with conditions previously attached), no further development of a phase which has been begun may be carried out pursuant to that permission unless the requirement in sub-paragraph (5) or (6) has been met.

Overall plan

(3) The requirement in this sub-paragraph has been met where-

(a) a biodiversity gain plan for that overall development has been submitted to the planning authority (see modified paragraph 14), and

(b) the planning authority has approved that plan (see modified paragraph 15).

(4) The requirement in this sub-paragraph has been met where-

(a) a biodiversity gain plan for the overall development has been approved for the purpose of complying with the condition in sub-paragraph (2)(a) subject to which planning permission for that overall development was previously granted,

(b) permission has been granted on an application made under section 73, and

(c) the earlier biodiversity gain plan for that overall development is regarded as approved under section 73(2C) and (2D) for the purpose of the permission granted under section 73.

Phase plan

(5) The requirement in this sub-paragraph has been met where-

(a) a biodiversity gain plan for that phase has been submitted to the planning authority (see modified paragraph 14), and

(b) the planning authority has approved that plan (see modified paragraph 15).

(6) The requirement in this sub-paragraph has been met where-

(a) permission has been granted on an application made under section 73, and

(b) an earlier biodiversity gain plan for that phase is regarded as approved under section 73(2C) and (2D) for the purpose of the permission granted under section 73.

(7) In this Part-

'a section 73 case' means a case where the biodiversity gain plan is required to be submitted for the purpose of complying with a condition in sub-paragraph (2), subject to which permission has been granted on an application made under section 73 (determination of applications to develop land without complying with conditions previously attached)."

DEFRA has published templates for both the overall biodiversity gain plan and a phase biodiversity gain plan. [171]

The PPG contemplates cases (there will probably be many) where it makes more practical sense for phase biodiversity gain plans to be prepared alongside the application for reserved matter(s) approval for that phase.[172]

Article 27(4)(b) of the Town and Country Planning (Development Management Procedure) (England) Order 2015 has been amended to reflect phased development; where there is submission of a biodiversity gain plan for approval under either:

---

[171] Available at: https://www.gov.uk/government/publications/biodiversity-gain-plan-phased-development-templates. Last accessed 10 October 2024.

[172] PPG paragraph 054 Reference ID: 74-054-20240214.

(a) paragraph 13(3)(a) of Schedule 7A (overall biodiversity gain plan); or

(b) paragraph 13(5)(a) of Schedule 7A (phase biodiversity gain plan)

then articles 27(1) and (2) do not apply (these set out, respectively, how an application to discharge a condition should be made, what that application must include, and the eight-week time limit for determination of that application). Instead, in the above two situations, the new Part 7A of the Town and Country Planning (Development Management Procedure) (England) Order 2015 applies (articles 37A to 37E). Article 37C contains relevant provisions for phased development as extracted and set out below, although the full article is of course relevant to all biodiversity gain plans submitted to planning authorities.

Content of Overall Biodiversity Gain Plan

The overall biodiversity gain plan for a phased development (where related to a s.73 permission it may follow a different procedure, set out below) is not the same as a standard biodiversity gain plan. The requirements for a plan submitted to comply with Schedule 7A, paragraph 13(3)(a), are set out in paragraph 14 as modified by reg.5 of the Biodiversity Gain (Town and Country Planning) (Modifications and Amendments) (England) Regulations 2024. These legal requirements are summarised in the PPG.[173] The modified paragraph 14 for an overall gain plan provides:

"14. Biodiversity gain plan: overall plan

(1) For the purposes of paragraph 13(3)(a) (overall plan), a biodiversity gain plan is a plan which-

[173] PPG paragraph: 058 Reference ID: 74-058-20240214.

(a) relates to the development for which planning permission of the type mentioned in paragraph 19(1)(a) or (b) is granted, and (b) subject to sub-paragraph (2A), specifies the matters referred to in sub-paragraph (2).

(2) The matters are-

(a) information about the steps taken or to be taken to minimise the adverse effect of the development on the biodiversity of the onsite habitat [meaning habitat on the land to which the planning permission relates] and any other habitat,

(b) the pre-development biodiversity value ['pre-development biodiversity value' has the meaning given by paragraph 5 of Schedule 7A to the Town and Country Planning Act 1990] of the onsite habitat,

(c) any registered offsite biodiversity gain ['registered offsite biodiversity gain' has the meaning given by paragraph 10 of Schedule 7A to the Town and Country Planning Act 1990] allocated to the development before the date of submission of the biodiversity gain plan and the biodiversity value of that gain in relation to the development,

(d) any registered offsite biodiversity gain proposed to be allocated to the development and the biodiversity value of that gain in relation to the development,

(e) any biodiversity credits [i.e. statutory credits under section 101 of the Environment Act 2021] purchased before the date of submission of the biodiversity gain plan,

(ea) any biodiversity credits proposed to be purchased for the development, (eb) the post-development biodiversity value ['post-development biodiversity value' has the meaning given by paragraph 8 of Schedule 7A to the Town and Country Planning Act 1990] of the onsite habitat for the overall development,

(ec) except in a section 73 case, the post-development biodiversity value of the onsite habitat for each phase of development,

(ed) in a section 73 case, the post-development biodiversity value of the onsite habitat for each phase of development (whether begun or otherwise), and

(f) such other matters as the Secretary of State may by regulations specify.

(2A) Where the onsite habitat of any part of a development is irreplaceable habitat [as defined in reg.2 of the Biodiversity Gain Requirements (Irreplaceable Habitat) Regulations 2024]-

(a) the words 'and any other habitat' in sub-paragraph (2)(a), and
(b) sub-paragraph (2)(c), (d), (e) and (ea),
do not apply in relation to that part of the development.

(3) The Secretary of State may by regulations make provision about-
(a) any other matters to be included in a biodiversity gain plan;
(b) the form of a biodiversity gain plan;
(c) the procedure to be followed in relation to the submission of a biodiversity
gain plan (including the time by which a plan must be submitted);
(d) persons who may or must submit a biodiversity gain plan."

The PPG then provides:

> "Where firm proposals for development and habitat enhancement on each phase have yet to be finalised, assumptions about the likely development and habitat enhancements should be used to determine this post-development value. This value will set the expectations about the biodiversity value of onsite habitats, and the final value will need to be set out in later Phase Biodiversity Gain Plans."[174]

Article 37C of the Town and Country Planning (Development Management Procedure) (England) Order 2015 also applies, in its entirety unless otherwise specified, to phased development (set out in full above in the Biodiversity Gain Plan section of the Biodiversity Gain Condition(s) and Biodiversity Gain Plan chapter). For the purposes of phased development, this contain specific provisions relevant to an overall gain plan (article 37C(5)(a)):

> "(5) Where development is to proceed in phases-
>
> (a) the biodiversity gain plan required before development may be begun in accordance with paragraph 13(3)(a) of the 1990 Act (as modified by the Biodiversity Gain (Town and Country Planning) (Modifications and Amendments) (England) Regulations 2024) (overall plan) must also include-
>
> (i) the relevant date, and if the relevant date is a date which is earlier than that specified in paragraph 5(2)(a) of Schedule 7A to the 1990 Act, the reasons for this;
>
> (ii) the completed statutory metric calculation tool or tools (as the case may be), stating the publication date of that tool and showing how the values specified in that biodiversity gain plan have been calculated;

174 PPG paragraph: 058 Reference ID: 74-058-20240214.

(iii) if any activities of the type mentioned in paragraph 6 or 6A of Schedule 7A to the 1990 Act have been carried out on the land-

(aa) statement that such activities have been carried out,

(bb) confirmation of the date immediately before those activities were so carried out,

(cc) a completed statutory metric calculation tool, stating the publication date of that tool and showing the calculation of the biodiversity value of the onsite habitat on that date, and

(dd) any available supporting evidence for the date referred to in sub-paragraph (bb) and for the value referred to in sub-paragraph (cc);

(iv) a description of any irreplaceable habitat, corresponding to the descriptions in Table 1 or in column 1 of Table 2 of the Schedule to the Biodiversity Gain Requirements (Irreplaceable Habitat) Regulations 2024, that-

(aa) is on the land to which the plan relates, and

(bb) exists on the relevant date;

(v) pre-development plans-

(aa) showing the location of onsite habitat including any irreplaceable habitat on the relevant date;

(bb) drawn to an identified scale and showing the direction of North;

(vi) in relation to any part of the development for which planning permission is granted where the onsite habitat of that part is irreplaceable habitat, arrangements for compensation for any impact the development has on the biodiversity of the onsite habitat;"

<u>Approving an Overall Biodiversity Gain Plan</u>

The planning authority may only approve the overall biodiversity gain plan for a phased development (if it is not a s.73 permission, to which a different procedure might apply: see below) if they are satisfied the requirements of Schedule 7A, paragraph 15 (as modified by reg.7 of the Biodiversity Gain (Town and Country Planning) (Modifications and Amendments) (England) Regulations 2024) are met. The modified paragraph 15 considerations are also summarised in the PPG.[175] Paragraph 15 as modified for the purposes of approving an overall biodiversity gain plan provides:

> "*15. Approval of overall plan*
>
> (1) For the purposes of paragraph 13(3)(a) (overall plan), a planning authority to which a biodiversity gain plan is submitted must approve the plan if, and only if, it is satisfied as to the matters specified in sub-paragraph (2).
>
> (2) The matters are-
>
> (a) that the pre-development biodiversity value of the onsite habitat is as specified in the plan,
>
> (b) where the onsite habitat of any part of a development is irreplaceable habitat, that the adverse effect of the development on the biodiversity of the onsite habitat is minimised and appropriate arrangements have been made for the purpose of compensating for any impact,
>
> (c) except in a section 73 case, and subject to sub-paragraph (3), that the biodiversity gain objective will be met, taking into account-
> (i) the post-development biodiversity value of the onsite habitat for the overall development,
> (ii) the post-development biodiversity value of the onsite habitat for each phase of the development,

175 PPG paragraph: 059 Reference ID: 74-059-20240214.

(iii) the biodiversity value in relation to the development of any registered offsite biodiversity gain allocated or proposed to be allocated to the development (and, if the allocation is conditional, whether any conditions have been met or will be met by the time development begins), and
(iv) any biodiversity credits purchased or proposed to be purchased for the development,

(d) in a section 73 case, and subject to sub-paragraph (3), that the biodiversity gain objective will be met, taking into account-
(i) the post-development biodiversity value of the onsite habitat for the overall development,
(ii) the post-development biodiversity value of the onsite habitat for each phase of the development (whether begun or otherwise),
(iii) the biodiversity value in relation to the development of any registered offsite biodiversity gain allocated or proposed to be allocated to the development (and, if the allocation is conditional, whether any conditions have been met or will be met by the time development begins), and
(iv) any biodiversity credits purchased or proposed to be purchased for the development,

(e) subject to sub-paragraph (3), that-
(i) any biodiversity credits specified in the biodiversity gain plan as having been purchased for the development before the date of submission of that plan have been so purchased,
(ii) in a case where any registered offsite biodiversity gain is specified in the biodiversity gain plan as having been allocated to the development before the date of submission of that plan, that the registered offsite biodiversity gain-
(aa) is so allocated, and
(bb) has the value specified in the biodiversity gain plan in relation to the development, and

(ea) in a section 73 case, that the post-development biodiversity value of the onsite habitat of any phases that have been begun is at least the value specified in the plan most recently approved for that phase, unless the conditions subject to which planning permission has been granted under section 73 affect the post-development biodiversity value of the onsite habitat as specified in that biodiversity gain plan, and

(f) any other matters specified in the plan under paragraph 14(2)(f).

(3) Where the onsite habitat of any part of a development is irreplaceable habitat, sub-paragraph (2)(c)(iii) and (iv), (d)(iii) and (iv), or (e) as the case may be, does not apply in relation to that part of the development.

(4) For the purposes of sub-paragraph (2)(b), arrangements are appropriate only if they secure that there is a compensation plan in place that secures appropriate compensation relative to the baseline habitat type, and which does not include the use of biodiversity credits."

In deciding whether to approve the plan, planning authorities must still take account of the biodiversity gain hierarchy (save for in relation to irreplaceable habitats, to which the biodiversity gain hierarchy does not apply; by article 37D(2) and (3) of the Town and Country Planning (Development Management Procedure) (England) Order 2015).

It is important to note that the phased development modifications to Schedule 7A made by the Biodiversity Gain (Town and Country Planning) (Modifications and Amendments) (England) Regulations 2024 still sit alongside all the amendments that were made to the Town and Country Planning (Development Management Procedure) (England) Order 2015 and the Town and Country Planning (Section

62A Applications) (Procedure and Consequential Amendments) Order 2013 by the Biodiversity Gain (Town and Country Planning) (Modifications and Amendments) (England) Regulations 2024.

Content of Phase Biodiversity Gain Plan

The content of a phase biodiversity gain plan is necessarily more limited in scope than an overall biodiversity gain plan. Instead of setting the overall strategy for the whole site, the phase plan focusses on a phase's contribution to the overall BNG requirement and confirms progress towards the overall biodiversity gain objective for the entire development. A phase biodiversity gain plan submitted under Schedule 7A, paragraph 13(5)(a) must include the following matters, by Schedule 7A, paragraph 14 (as modified by reg.6 of the Biodiversity Gain (Town and Country Planning) (Modifications and Amendments) (England) Regulations 2024) (also summarised in the PPG):[176]

> "*14. Biodiversity gain plan: phase plan*
>
> (1) For the purposes of paragraph 13(5)(a) (phase plan), a biodiversity gain plan is a plan which-
>
> (a) relates to a phase of the development, where planning permission of the type mentioned in paragraph 19(1)(a) or (b) is granted for the development, and
>
> (b) subject to sub-paragraph (2A), specifies the matters referred to in sub-paragraph (2).
>
> (2) The matters are-
>
> (a) the post-development biodiversity value of the onsite habitat for the phase of the development to which the biodiversity gain plan relates,

[176] PPG paragraph: 060 Reference ID: 74-060-20240214.

(b) the post-development biodiversity value of the onsite habitat for each other phase of development (whether begun or otherwise),
(c) any registered offsite biodiversity gain allocated to the development before the date of submission of the biodiversity gain plan and the biodiversity value of that gain in relation to the development,
(d) any registered offsite biodiversity gain which is proposed to be allocated to the development and the biodiversity value of that gain in relation to the development,
(e) any biodiversity credits purchased for the development before the date of submission of the biodiversity gain plan,
(ea) any biodiversity credits proposed to be purchased for the development, and;
(f) such other matters as the Secretary of State may by regulations specify.

(2A) Where the onsite habitat of any part of a development is irreplaceable habitat, sub-paragraph (2)(c) to (ea) does not apply in relation to that part of the development.

(3) The Secretary of State may by regulations make provision about-
(a) any other matters to be included in a biodiversity gain plan;
(b) the form of a biodiversity gain plan;
(c) the procedure to be followed in relation to the submission of a biodiversity gain plan (including the time by which a plan must be submitted);
(d) persons who may or must submit a biodiversity gain plan."

As above in relation to an overall biodiversity gain plan, article 37C of the Town and Country Planning (Development Management Procedure) (England) Order 2015 includes specific provisions concerning a phase biodiversity gain plan:

"(5) Where development is to proceed in phases-

...

(b) the biodiversity gain plan for a phase of development required in accordance with paragraph 13(5)(a) of the 1990 Act (as modified by the Biodiversity Gain (Town and Country Planning) (Modifications and Amendments) (England) Regulations 2024) (phase plan) must also include-

(i) the reference number of any planning permission decision, other than the planning permission to which the biodiversity gain plan relates, which the person submitting the plan considers is relevant to the phase of development;

(ii) the completed statutory metric calculation tool or tools (as the case may be), stating the publication date of that tool and showing how the values specified in that biodiversity gain plan have been calculated;

(iii) a description of any irreplaceable habitat, corresponding to the descriptions in Table 1 or in column 1 of Table 2 of the Schedule to the Biodiversity Gain Requirements (Irreplaceable Habitat) Regulations 2024, that-

(aa) is on the land to which the plan relates, and

(bb) exists on the relevant date;

(iv) post-development plans for the phase of development-

(aa) showing the location of onsite habitat including any irreplaceable habitat;

(bb) drawn to an identified scale and showing the direction of North;

(v) information about the steps taken or to be taken to minimise the adverse effect of the phase of development on the biodiversity of the onsite habitat;

(vi) in relation to any part of the development to which the biodiversity gain plan relates where the onsite habitat of that part is irreplaceable habitat, arrangements for compensation for any impact the development has on the biodiversity of the onsite habitat."

Approving a Phase Biodiversity Gain Plan

The planning authority may only approve the phase biodiversity gain plan if they are satisfied (by Schedule 7A, paragraph 15 (as modified by reg.8 of the Biodiversity Gain (Town and Country Planning) (Modifications and Amendments) (England) Regulations 2024) (also summarised in the PPG):[177]

> "*15. Approval of phase plan*
>
> (1) For the purposes of paragraph 13(5)(a) (phase plan), a planning authority to which a biodiversity gain plan is submitted must approve the plan if, and only if, it is satisfied as to the matters specified in sub-paragraph (2).
>
> (2) The matters are-
>
>> (a) that the post-development biodiversity value of the onsite habitat for the phase of the development to which the biodiversity gain plan relates is at least the value specified in the plan required under regulation 13(5)(a) (phase plan),
>>
>> (b) that the post-development biodiversity value of the onsite habitat for any phase which has been begun is at least the value specified in the biodiversity gain plan most recently approved for that phase, unless in a section 73 case the conditions subject to which planning permission has been granted under section 73 affect the post-development biodiversity value of the onsite habitat as specified in that biodiversity gain plan,
>>
>> (c) subject to sub-paragraph (3), in a case where any registered offsite biodiversity gain is specified in the biodiversity gain plan

[177] PPG paragraph: 061 Reference ID: 74-061-20240214.

as having been allocated to the development before the date of submission of that plan, that-

(i) the registered offsite biodiversity gain is so allocated, and
(ii) the biodiversity value of that gain in relation to the development is as specified in the biodiversity gain plan,

(d) subject to sub-paragraph (3), that any biodiversity credits specified in the biodiversity gain plan as having been purchased for the development before the date of submission of that plan have been so purchased,

(e) where the onsite habitat of a part of the development to which the biodiversity gain plan for the phase relates is irreplaceable habitat, that, having regard to the biodiversity gain plan for the overall development, the adverse effect of the development on the biodiversity of the onsite habitat is minimised and appropriate arrangements have been made for the purpose of compensating for any impact,

(ea) that the biodiversity gain objective will be met for the development, taking into account—

(i) the post-development biodiversity value of the onsite habitat for the overall development,
(ii) the post-development biodiversity value of the onsite habitat for each phase of the development (whether begun or otherwise),
(iii) the biodiversity value in relation to the development of any registered offsite biodiversity gain allocated and proposed to be allocated to the development, and
(iv) any biodiversity credits purchased and proposed to be purchased for the development, and

(f) any other matters specified in the plan under paragraph 14(2)(f).

(3) Where the onsite habitat of any part of the phase of development is irreplaceable habitat, sub-paragraph (2)(c) and (d) do not apply in relation to that part of the phase of development.

(4) For the purposes of sub-paragraph (2)(e), arrangements are appropriate only if they secure that there is a compensation plan in place that secures appropriate compensation relative to the baseline habitat type, and which does not include the use of biodiversity credits."

As with the overall biodiversity gain plan, when deciding whether to approve the phase plan, again, planning authorities must also take account of the biodiversity gain hierarchy except in relation to irreplaceable habitats: articles 37D(2) and (3) of the Town and Country Planning (Development Management Procedure) (England) Order 2015.

Time for Determination and Appeal Provisions

In either case (approval of an overall or a phase biodiversity gain plan) the planning authority still only has eight weeks (or another agreed timescale) to determine the application (article 37D(1)(a) or (b) of the Town and Country Planning (Development Management Procedure) (England) Order 2015).[178] The same procedures set out above in relation to an appeal against refusal or non-determination of a biodiversity gain plan apply.

Phased Development and Irreplaceable Habitats

The modified paragraphs of Schedule 7A contemplate their application to development sites which contain irreplaceable habitat. Modified

[178] See also DEFRA guidance https://www.gov.uk/guidance/biodiversity-net-gain-what-local-planning-authorities-should-do. Last accessed 1 September 2024.

paragraph 14(2A) in relation to both overall and phase biodiversity gain plans amend the wording of paragraph 14(2) "[w]here the onsite habitat of any part of a development is irreplaceable habitat". For overall biodiversity gain plans, articles 37C(5)(a)(iv), (v) and (vi) require certain information in relation to irreplaceable habitat; for phase biodiversity gain plans that additional content is set out at articles 37C(5)(b)(iii), (iv) and (vi).

That would otherwise duplicate the changes made to Schedule 7A, paragraphs 14 and 15 by reg.3 of the Biodiversity Gain Requirements (Irreplaceable Habitat) Regulations 2024. Making this clear is reg.4 of the Biodiversity Gain Requirements (Irreplaceable Habitat) Regulations 2024, which provides that reg.3 does not apply in relation to phased development. This means where the onsite habitat of any part of a development is irreplaceable habitat and the planning permission comprises phased development then paragraphs 14 and 15 remain as set out above (i.e. the modifications under the Biodiversity Gain (Town and Country Planning) (Modifications and Amendments) (England) Regulations 2024, and <u>not</u> as modified by reg.3 of the Biodiversity Gain Requirements (Irreplaceable Habitat) Regulations 2024).

This exception is not dependent on whether or not development under any phase may impact irreplaceable habitat or not: as soon as the overall permission is confirmed to be phased development (see the language of reg.4 of the Biodiversity Gain Requirements (Irreplaceable Habitat) Regulations 2024) then the conditions imposed are those as modified by the Biodiversity Gain (Town and Country Planning) (Modifications and Amendments) (England) Regulations 2024.

<u>Phased Development and Section 73 Permissions</u>

Readers are advised to seek a quiet room and bring a cold towel for their head when delving into this topic. In the first instance, for an overall biodiversity gain plan, paragraph 13(2)(a) requires that paragraphs 13(3) and 13(4) are met. The latter deals with applications under s.73. This requires, first, that a biodiversity gain plan for the overall development was submitted and approved (paragraph 13(4)(a)). Then, when the s.73 permission is granted, paragraph 13(4)(c) allows for the earlier overall biodiversity gain plan to be automatically approved under s.73(2C) and (2D) for the s.73 permission.

Turning to phase biodiversity gain plans, by Schedule 7A, paragraph 13(2)(c) where permission is granted under s.73, no further development of a phase which has been begun may be carried out pursuant to that permission unless the requirements in Schedule 7A, paragraphs 13(5) or 13(6) have been met.

Starting with Schedule 7A, paragraph 13(5), that refers to the standard position where there is no preexisting phase biodiversity gain plan, or a fresh one is required (because the s.73 permission will not satisfy s.73(2C) – but see the paragraph below). In either case, a phase plan relating to the s.73 permission must be submitted and approved. In the alternative, paragraph 13(6) applies where there is an earlier biodiversity gain plan for that phase and s.73(2C) is satisfied, in which case under s.73(2D) the existing phase biodiversity gain plan is to be regarded as approved for the purpose of the permission granted under s.73.

However, the PPG complicates matters. It says if the s.73 permission would impact the post-development value of the phased development's onsite habitat or irreplaceable habitat, a new overall plan must be submitted and approved to ensure the biodiversity gain objective will be achieved. A replacement phase plan is not contemplated in the PPG. This appears to be because even if only one phase under the original planning permission has such impacts, a new overall plan is considered to still be necessary because the development's BNG impacts and delivery will have been determined on the basis of the whole site. The PPG envisages the content of the new overall plan being similar to that of the overall plan for the original planning permission, except that additional information must be provided about the post-development biodiversity value of the onsite habitat of any phase which has already begun. The planning authority must be satisfied that this value is at least the value specified in the phase plan most recently approved for that phase (unless there has been an intervening s.73 permission which has affected this value).[179]

So the position appears to be this. Where there is an extant phase plan, but it cannot be approved under s.73(2D) because it does not satisfy s.73(2C) because the new condition(s) either (or both) affect the post-development value of the onsite habitat as specified in the earlier biodiversity gain plan; or change the effect of the development on the biodiversity of onsite irreplaceable habitat (including any arrangements made to compensate for any such effect) as specified in the earlier biodiversity gain plan, then the developer has to submit a new overall biodiversity gain plan under paragraph 13(3)(a), not a new phase plan under paragraph 13(5)(a). However, a phase plan corresponding to the new overall plan will still be required for that phase (otherwise there would be a breach of paragraph 13(2)(b)), and so a phase plan would also have to be submitted and approved under paragraph 13(5).

Minerals

Planning applications for new minerals permissions are subject to the BNG regime, which applies to them in exactly the same way as any other planning permission.

Reviews of Old Mineral Permissions are not within the scope of the BNG regime as they are not planning permissions granted under Part 3 of the Town and Country Planning Act 1990.

179 PPG paragraph: 062 Reference ID: 74-062-20240214.

CHAPTER EIGHT

LEGAL AGREEMENTS

A legal agreement is always needed where offsite gains form part of the biodiversity gain plan. There are two kinds of legal agreement for offsite BNG: an agreement made under s.106 of the Town and Country Planning Act 1990 (a "s.106 agreement" between the landowner and planning authority which contains planning obligations related to BNG); or a conservation covenant agreement as defined by s.118 of the Environment Act 2021 (a "conservation covenant" between the landowner and a designated responsible body) (by Schedule 7A, paragraph 10(1) of the Town and Country Planning Act 1990). As detailed below, there is also scope for mortgagees, habitat bank operators, other planning authorities, developers and leaseholders to be parties to the legal agreement, but it is important to note that if the offsite gain is secured with a legal agreement with the landowner, the developer is not a mandatory party to any legal agreement.

The provision and maintenance of "significant" onsite habitat enhancement and/or creation must also be the subject of either a planning condition, s.106 agreement, or conservation covenant (Schedule 7A, paragraph 9(3) of the Town and Country Planning Act 1990).

A legal agreement may also be required if onsite gains are not significant, but achieve wider policy aims, i.e. habitat retention or enhancements that "contribute to locally important species or ecological networks".[180] This is expressed in mandatory terms in one set of DEFRA guidance (Enter a

---

180 DEFRA guidance https://www.gov.uk/guidance/legal-agreements-to-secure-your-biodiversity-net-gain. Last accessed 1 September 2024.

legal agreement for biodiversity net gain) but discretionary in another (Make on-site biodiversity gains as a developer); while consistency in guidance would be helpful, ultimately, it will be up to the planning authority to decide whether a legal agreement is necessary.

Both the s.106 agreement or conservation covenant agreement must be in writing, signed by all parties, and executed as a deed. There is guidance from the Land Registry on executing deeds.[181]

Whatever the precise wording and configuration of signatory parties, the legal agreement must contain at least the following commitments:

- Details on the enhancement and/or creation of habitat(s) amounting to the requisite BNG units, including the biodiversity value of pre-enhancement and post-development habitat (calculated using the statutory metric);
- Details on how the offsite BNG habitat will be monitored (when, by whom, how they will access the land and when, how and to whom the resulting monitoring reports will be made);
- An end date for the relevant maintenance and monitoring commitments at least 30 years from when the enhancement and/or creation works are completed (if offsite habitat; if it is significant onsite habitat then this end date is 30 years from the completion of development);
- Provisions concerning any additional consents and/or licences that will be needed;
- Remedial steps to be taken if the plan for habitat enhancement and/or creation does not go as planned;
- Remedial steps in the event of a breach (by whom, when, how, the procedure to be followed, recovery of funds expended in remedial works);

[181] Available at: https://www.gov.uk/government/publications/execution-of-deeds/practice-guide-8-execution-of-deeds. Last accessed 1 September 2024.

- The process for making any necessary changes to the biodiversity gain plan / habitat maintenance and monitoring plan / other document;
- The process for resolving disputes under the legal agreement;
- Funding arrangements (i.e. for ongoing monitoring, for a bond if considered necessary) and a payment schedule if necessary;
- If the enhancement and/or creation work is within the consultation area of an aerodrome, an agreement that the work does not and will not harm aircraft operations.

The intervention work can be completed by anyone, but the legal agreement sets out who is ultimately responsible: a subcontractor cannot be liable for obligations agreed between the signatory parties.

The planning authority has an obligation to check, before they enter into any legal agreement (whether as the relevant local planning authority under a s.106 agreement or the responsible body for the purposes of a conservation covenant) that the landowner has the right licences, consents and permits; that the metric calculations are accurate, and if the enhancement and/or creation of habitat is/are within the consultation area of an aerodrome that it would not harm aircraft operations.[182]

Who Can Be a Party to Legal Agreements

For all s.106 agreements the local planning authority will have to be a party (for out of area offsite units see the section immediately below). For all conservation covenants there will have to be a party acting as the responsible body.

Landowners and/or a person with a lease on the land that is at least the same length as the legal agreement can enter into a legal agreement

182 DEFRA guidance. https://www.gov.uk/guidance/biodiversity-net-gain-what-local-planning-authorities-should-do Last accessed 1 September 2024.

(whether s.106 agreement or conservation covenant) concerning that land for the purposes of complying with the BNG regime. If the lease is shorter than the relevant maintenance period (30 years at a minimum), the freeholder will also need to be included as a party to the legal agreement. There is no requirement for the freeholder to be included as a party to the agreement if they have granted a sufficiently long lease to a BNG provider (i.e. a habitat bank). Nor is there a legal requirement for developers to be included: what matters is that there is an enforceable legal agreement that will ensure the biodiversity gain objective is met. Mortgagees need not be included, but they are suggested as signatories in the PAS templates for good reason: if they take possession in the event of default the obligations fall to them. If a mortgagee is not included as a signatory party, their consent to enter the mortgaged land into the legal agreement should be obtained.

On the other hand, if the developer is proposing gains on land outside the development site's red line boundary for which they are the relevant landowner, then they must secure these gains with a legal agreement to which they are a party.

Matters Specific to Section 106 Agreements

Where a condition provides for onsite monitoring to be carried out by the local planning authority that authority can secure the necessary financial contribution for the onsite BNG monitoring though a s.106 planning obligation. There is a PAS s.l06 agreement template providing for payment of this monitoring fee.[183]

It must be noted the s.106 must relate to the use of land in some way: in *R (Khodari) v Royal Borough of Kensington and Chelsea* [2017] EWCA Civ. 333 Lewison L.J. said at [31]:

[183] https://www.local.gov.uk/pas/environment/biodiversity-net-gain-bng-local-planning-authorities/pas-biodiversity-net-gain-bng. Last accessed 1 September 2024.

> "The references in section 106 to the land must mean land in which the person making the agreement is interested. Although 'the land' in question may be land other than that covered by the planning permission, provide that there is a direct relationship between the two, the person entering into the section 106 agreement must still have an interest in that land."

The Court of Appeal concluded that s.106 was intended to operate as a true restrictive covenant, and so had to control the use of the land itself and not simply control a party to the agreement, even if that control indirectly restricted the use of land. Making provision to monitor the use of the land satisfies this principle.

There is a PAS s.106 template contemplating some BNG provided onsite through condition, and other BNG provided through the registration and allocation of offsite BNG units. The template includes a requirement for the registration of the specified offsite units on the biodiversity gain site register (see also Offsite chapter). It should be noted that offsite units can also be registered in advance and simply required to be allocated on the register in the legal agreement (with spatial details for the offsite units included to preclude the same units from being sold twice).

There has been concern with regards to s.106 agreements relating to the purchase of BNG units arising from land in another local planning authority's area. There is no legal reason why this cannot be done, indeed allowing for this situation is precisely the purpose of the spatial multiplier. All local planning authorities should therefore permit the use of out-of-area units to account for the necessary BNG in principle. It is only if there is an express local policy which requires the purchase of in-area BNG units (and that has been found to be sound at examination in public) where such a restriction might reasonably be made.

There are, however, procedural legal requirements that must be followed for out of area s.106 agreements. The statutory language here is important: s.106(1) refers to any person interested in "land in the area of a local planning authority". "Interested in land" has been held to mean owning an *actual* interest in that land, and so it cannot merely be a developer hoping to acquire an interest later (*Jones v Secretary of State for Wales* (1974) 28 P.&C.R. 280 and *Southampton City Council v Halyard Ltd* [2009] 1 P.&C.R. 5). The planning authority needs to know the contracting party has sufficient interest in the land to enable them to carry out the works under the s.106 agreement.

The position with respect to the contracting local planning authority/(ies) is more nuanced if the development is in one local planning authority's area, but the offsite land is in another's. Local planning authorities have full legal power to enter into the contract in any event (by s.111 of the Local Government Act 1972, although it is noted this must either facilitate, or be conducive or incidental to, the discharge of any of their functions as a local planning authority). The issue is that any local planning authority entering into a s.106 concerning land outside their area is indistinguishable from a private party, as they are not the local planning authority for that area. It must also be noted the statutory power of a local planning authority when carrying out their functions extends only to land in their area (*R (Carralyn Parkes) v Dorset Council v Portland Port Limited, Secretary of State for the Home Department, Secretary of State for Levelling Up, Housing and Communities* [2024] EWHC 1253 (Admin) at [37], [200] and the case law cited therein).

The solution to this is to have both local planning authorities (the one responsible for the permission, and the one in whose area the offsite BNG units are located) included as signatories to the s.106 agreement. Arrangements for the allocation of obligations and payment of money will require legal advice tailored to each specific case. When complying with the requirement of s.106(9)(d) (the agreement must identify the local planning authority by whom the obligation is enforceable), there is scope to take advantage of the power under s.101(1)(b) or s.101(5) of the Local Government Act 1972 (respectively: a local authority may arrange for the discharge of any of their functions by any other local authority;

two or more local authorities may discharge any of their functions jointly), and expressly state within the s.106 agreement which local planning authority will be responsible for monitoring compliance and discharging the enforcement function under s.106(3). This would also enable the alignment of responsibility for enforcement under Part 7 of the Town and Country Planning Act 1990 with enforcement powers under s.106(3).

While the PPG does not preclude the use of unilateral undertakings submitted by developers under s.106, a unilateral undertaking cannot secure the local planning authority's consent to actually carry out an action. Given that monitoring a positive action for at least three decades is a key requirement of the BNG regime, to be effective any unilateral undertaking would have to be very carefully thought through.

The question is likely to turn on whether the unilateral undertaking resolves the planning objection on its own terms. This is to say it cannot require subsequent positive action by the local planning authority and must relate to the use of land. Of note here is *Wimpey Homes (Holdings) Ltd v Secretary of State for the Environment* [1993] 2 P.L.R. 54 where a unilateral obligation to transfer land to the local authority for use as public open space was not permissible because it did not directly impose any restriction on the use of land.

A local planning authority cannot create a s.106 agreement with themselves because they cannot enforce against themselves. Therefore, if they want to secure their own land for the purposes of a s.106 agreement they need to take certain steps. Several have been suggested in the guidance:[184]

[184] DEFRA guidance https://www.gov.uk/guidance/biodiversity-net-gain-what-local-planning-authorities-should-do. Last accessed 1 September 2024.

1. Special purpose vehicle

The local planning authority can set up a special purpose vehicle and enter a s.106 agreement with them. The special purpose vehicle will carry out the habitat enhancement work and the local planning authority must check that they meet their responsibilities.

2. Enter an agreement with the county or district council

If the local planning authority is not a unitary authority, they can enter a s.106 agreement with the county council. The local planning authority will carry out the habitat enhancement work and the county council must check that they meet their responsibilities.

3. Lease the land to a tenant

The local planning authority can lease their land to a tenant and enter a s.106 agreement with them. The tenant will carry out the habitat enhancement work and the local planning authority must check that they meet their responsibilities.

As to the discharge / amendment of a planning obligation, s.106A of the Town and Country Planning Act 1990 (modification and discharge of planning obligations) has been amended to ensure any amendment cannot have the effect of preventing the biodiversity gain objective from being met or even giving rise to a significant risk that the objective will not be met:

> "(6A) Except in such cases as may be prescribed, the authority may not under subsection (6) discharge or modify the planning obligation if the authority considers that doing so would-
>
> (a) prevent the biodiversity gain objective referred to in paragraph 2 of Schedule 7A from being met in relation to any development, or

(b) give rise to a significant risk of that objective not being met in relation to any development."

What gives rise to a significant risk will be a matter for the planning authority's judgment. This provision applies if <u>any</u> development subject to the BNG regime is at risk of not meeting the biodiversity gain objective, and so relevant development for the purposes of s.106A(6A) may go beyond the development underpinning the specific planning obligation in question.

<u>Matters Specific to Conservation Covenants</u>

Section 117 of the Environment Act 2021 provides the definition of a "conservation covenant agreement":

"(1) For the purposes of this Part, a 'conservation covenant agreement' is an agreement between a landowner and a responsible body where-

(a) the agreement contains provision which-

(i) is of a qualifying kind,

(ii) has a conservation purpose, and

(iii) is intended by the parties to be for the public good,

(b) it appears from the agreement that the parties intend to create a conservation covenant, and

(c) the agreement is executed as a deed by the parties.

(2) The reference in subsection (1)(a) to provision of a qualifying kind is to provision-

(a) requiring the landowner-

(i) to do, or not to do, something on land in England specified in the provision in relation to which the landowner holds a qualifying estate specified in the agreement for the purposes of the provision, or

(ii) to allow the responsible body to do something on such land, or

(b) requiring the responsible body to do something on such land.

(3) For the purposes of subsection (1)(a)(ii), provision has a conservation purpose if its purpose is-

(a) to conserve the natural environment of land or the natural resources of land,
(b) to conserve land as a place of archaeological, architectural, artistic, cultural or historic interest, or
(c) to conserve the setting of land with a natural environment or natural resources or which is a place of archaeological, architectural, artistic, cultural or historic interest.

(4) In this Part- a reference to conserving something includes a reference to protecting, restoring or enhancing it;

'qualifying estate' means-

(a) an estate in fee simple absolute in possession, or
(b) a term of years absolute granted for a term of more than seven years from the date of the grant and in the case of which some part of the period for which the term of years was granted remains unexpired;

a reference to 'the qualifying estate', in relation to an obligation under a conservation covenant, is to the estate in land by virtue of which the condition in subsection (1)(a)(i) was met in relation to-

(a) if the obligation is not an ancillary obligation, the provision giving rise to the obligation, or
(b) if the obligation is an ancillary obligation, the provision giving rise to the obligation to which it was ancillary;
(and for this purpose 'ancillary obligation' means an obligation under provision falling within section 118(2)(b));

'natural environment', in relation to land, includes-
its plants, animals and other living organisms;
their habitats;
its geological features"

Section 118 of the Environment Act 2021 then provides:

"(1) A conservation covenant is so much of a conservation covenant agreement as is given statutory effect by this section.

(2) The following provisions of a conservation covenant agreement have statutory effect as a conservation covenant-
(a) provisions in respect of which the conditions in section 117(1)(a) are met, and
(b) provisions ancillary to any provision falling within paragraph (a).

(3) If the agreement includes provision for public access to land to which other provision of the agreement (being provision which meets the conditions in section 117(1)(a)) relates, the provision for public access is to be treated as ancillary to that other provision.

(4) In this Part-
(a) references to an obligation under a conservation covenant are to an obligation of the landowner or the responsible body given statutory effect by this section as part of the conservation covenant, and
(b) references to the land to which an obligation under a conservation covenant relates are, in the case of an obligation given statutory effect by this section by virtue of being ancillary to another provision, to the land to which the obligation under the other provision relates."

Local planning authorities as landowners are able to secure their land with a conservation covenant. The guidance provides examples of how this can be done:[185]

1. The local planning authority carries out the habitat enhancement works and the responsible body checks that they meet their responsibilities.

2. The responsible body carries out the habitat enhancement works under the terms of the conservation covenant, in which case the local planning authority must check that they meet their responsibilities.

3. The local planning authority can lease their land to a tenant and enter into a conservation covenant with them. The tenant will carry out the habitat enhancement work and the local planning authority must check that they meet their responsibilities.

As to responsible bodies, they can be, by s.119 of the Environment Act 2021, either (1) the Secretary of State, (2) a local authority, or (3) another body which has been designated by the Secretary of State as a responsible body under s.119. DEFRA maintains a website of designated responsible bodies.[186] Natural England is a responsible body. Also potentially relevant is the fact that any Secretary of State qualifies as a potential responsible body, not only the Secretary of State for DEFRA: s.5 of the Interpretation Act 1978 provides that, in any Act, unless the contrary intention appears, words and expressions listed in Schedule 1 to the Interpretation Act 1978 are to be construed according to that Schedule.

---

185 DEFRA guidance https://www.gov.uk/guidance/biodiversity-net-gain-what-local-planning-authorities-should-do. Last accessed 1 September 2024.

186 https://www.gov.uk/government/publications/conservation-covenant-agreements-designated-responsible-bodies/conservation-covenants-list-of-designated-responsible-bodies. Last accessed 1 September 2024.

In Schedule 1 the phrase "Secretary of State" means "one of His Majesty's Principal Secretaries of State". In *Re Quinn's Application* [1996] N.I.J.B. 115, at p.118, Kerr J. (as he then was) said:

> "Since the historical position is that the office of the Secretary of State is one [for a discussion of the history of the office see *Harrison v Bush* (1855) 5 E & B 344 at page 352] it appears to me that, in light of the clear terms of section 5 of the Interpretation Act 1978, any powers exercisable by 'the Secretary of State' will, save in exceptional and unambiguously stated circumstances, be exercisable by any of Her Majesty's Secretaries of State."

Before designating a local authority as a responsible body the Secretary of State must be satisfied that it is "suitable" to be a responsible body (s.119(3)). Suitability is not defined, and so it is up to the reasonable discretion of the Secretary of State to determine (see also s.119(7)). However, the Secretary of State must at least publish what they consider to be the suitability criteria (s.119(8)).[187]

Before designating any body other than a local authority the Secretary of State must be: (1) satisfied that it is suitable (s.119(4)(b)), and (2) if it is a public body or a charity, that "at least some" of its main purposes or functions relate to conservation, or, if the body is not a public body or charity, that "at least some" of its main activities relate to conservation (s.119(4)(a) read with s.119(5)). For this purpose conservation need not be ecological conservation. Section 119(9) defines "conservation" for the purposes of designation of a responsible body as conservation of:

> (a) the natural environment or natural resources of land,

[187] This was published (last update 2 May 2024). https://www.gov.uk/government/publications/conservation-covenants-apply-to-become-a-responsible-body/conservation-covenants-criteria-for-being-a-responsible-body. Last accessed 1 September 2024.

(b) places of archaeological, architectural, artistic, cultural or historic interest, or
(c) the setting of land with a natural environment or natural resources or which is a place of archaeological, architectural, artistic, cultural or historic interest.

By s.136(1)-(4) of the Environment Act 2021 all responsible bodies are obliged to make an annual return to the Secretary of State stating: (1) whether there were any conservation covenants under which an obligation was owed to it as the responsible body during the period to which the return relates; (2) if so, the number of conservation covenants and, for each conservation covenant, (3) the area of the land in relation to which the body was owed any obligation as the responsible body. The annual return must also include any additional information required by way of regulations published by the Secretary of State under s.136(4) of the Environment Act. At the time of writing (1 October 2024) no regulations requiring information beyond what is already required under s.136 have been published.

Any responsible body under a conservation covenant may appoint another responsible body to take over its role (unless the covenant provides otherwise) (s.131(1) of the Environment Act 2021). This must be by agreement and executed as a deed by the appointor and appointee (s.131(2)). The local land charges registry, if the conservation covenant is registered in the local land charges register, must also be amended to reflect the new parties; any failure to provide the information necessary to amend the registry means the appointment fails to take effect (s.131(3)). If the necessary information is supplied, but the Registrar then fails to amend the registration, then the appointment will still take effect (s.131(3) only refers to the need to supply the necessary information), but subsequent enforcement of that covenant will be challenging. So all responsible bodies who have appointed another in their stead to take over obligations under a conservation covenant registered in the local land charges register should not rely on their successor responsible body confirming they have provided the necessary information to the

Registrar. They should also check to make sure the registration is actually amended.

By s.119(6) of the Environment Act 2021 the Secretary of State can also revoke a designation at the request of the responsible body, or unilaterally in two cases: (1) if it no longer meets the requirements to be a "suitable" body (s.119(6)(b)), or (2) (other than in the case of a local authority), if the Secretary of State is satisfied that the body no longer meets the following conditions (set out in s.119(5)): if it is a public body or a charity, that "at least some" of its main purposes or functions relate to conservation, or, if the body is not a public body or charity, that "at least some" of its main activities relate to conservation (by s.119(6)(c)).

Notice of revocation must first be given to the responsible body (s.119(6)). The benefits and burdens of a de-designated responsible body under a conservation covenant then transfer to the Secretary of State (s.132(3)), except for any right or liability in respect of an existing breach of obligation (s.132(4)). Where there are ongoing benefits and/or burdens, the Secretary of State then acts as "custodian" of the covenant, and may enforce any obligation / carry out any power given to the responsible body by Part 7 of the Environment Act 2021 (s.132(5) and s.132(7)). The Secretary of State may elect to become the responsible body themselves, by giving notice to every person who is bound by an obligation of the landowner under the covenant (s.132(6)). If they have not elected to become the responsible body and are instead simply the custodian, then the Secretary of State has no liability with respect to performance of any obligation of the responsible body under the covenant (s.132(8)).

Where there are ongoing benefits and/or burdens, by s.132(5) the Secretary of State's custodian role endures until (a) an appointment under s.131(1) made by the Secretary of State has effect, or (b) the Secretary of State gives notice they elect to be the responsible body in relation to the covenant under s.132(6).

It is worth noting there is a statutory "default period" of forever (unless the covenant specifies a shorter period) for the duration of a conservation covenant if the interest in land is an estate in fee simple absolute in possession (i.e. freehold) (by s.121(2)(a) of the Environment Act 2021); or for the remainder of the unexpired fixed-term lease period (s.121(2)(b)). The Environment Act 2021 is silent on whether the statutory default period applies to the original parties when a qualifying lease is surrendered and then regranted within the lease term; this lacunae means it is good practice for leaseholders negotiating a conservation covenant to specify the term. As the conservation covenant runs with the land, any successor in title is also bound by its terms (s.122(2)(b) and s.122(3)). The covenant is not binding on the successor only if (1) the obligation was no longer binding, (2) (when the obligation is a positive one) the person becomes a successor by virtue of holding a term of years absolute of seven years or less from the date of the grant, or (3) the conservation covenant was not registered in the local land charges register when the successor acquired their title in the land (s.122(4) and s.122(5)).

An obligation within a conservation covenant can only be discharged by agreement between the landowner and responsible body (s.127(1) and s.127(3) (landowner obligation) and s.128(1) (obligation on responsible body) of the Environment Act 2021). Similarly, the parties may agree to modify the conservation covenant (provided that the modification does not have the effect of the covenant no longer complying with s.117(1) of the Environment Act 2021) (ss.129(1)-(2)). It is important to note the Upper Tribunal / court (where relevant) has no power under s.84(1)-(2) of the Law of Property Act 1925 to discharge, modify, or make a declaration about a restrictive covenant (by s.130(3) and s.135(2) of the Environment Act 2021), and so any application under these provisions would be bound to fail.

If an obligation has been discharged or modified by agreement, the agreement must be executed as a deed by the parties, and that deed must specify (by s.127(4) (landowner obligation), s.128(2) (obligation on responsible body), and s.129(3) (modification)):

(a) the obligation to which the discharge relates,
(b) the land to which the discharge relates, and
(c) the estate in land by virtue of which the power is exercisable.

If one party seeks to modify or discharge an obligation under the conservation covenant but the other party does not agree, that dispute can be referred to the Upper Tribunal (Lands Chamber). Schedule 18 of the Environment Act 2021 sets out certain requirements and powers (see below). The procedure will be governed by the Tribunal Procedure (Upper Tribunal) (Lands Chamber) Rules 2010.

An interim application to the Upper Tribunal gives scope to put in place a line of defence to proceedings in relation to a breach of an obligation, as s.130(2) of the Environment Act 2021 provides that the respondent to any proceedings to enforce an obligation under a conservation covenant may apply (as part of the enforcement proceedings) to the High Court or the county court for an order giving leave to apply to the Upper Tribunal under Schedule 18 and staying the enforcement proceedings in the meantime.

A variety of powers are granted to either the courts (being the High Court or a county court in the first instance) or Upper Tribunal with respect to conservation covenants. Some applications can go to the courts *or* the Upper Tribunal in the first instance; some can only go to the Upper Tribunal. Which option(s) are possible are set out in the following paragraphs.

First, by s.135(1) of the Environment Act 2021, on the application of any person interested either the court or Tribunal are able to make a declaration as to:

> "(a) whether anything purporting to be a conservation covenant is a conservation covenant,
> (b) whether any land is land to which an obligation under a conservation covenant relates,
> (c) whether any person is bound by, or entitled to the benefit of, an obligation under a conservation covenant and, if so, in respect of what land,
> (d) what, upon the true construction of any instrument by means of which an obligation under a conservation covenant is created or modified, is the nature of the obligation."

Second, under Schedule 18, paragraphs 1(1) or 2(1) of the Environment Act 2021 the Upper Tribunal may by order discharge an obligation in respect of any of the land to which it relates. Either the landowner or the responsible body can make an application. When receiving that application the Upper Tribunal has a wide discretion: it may discharge the obligation when "it considers it reasonable to do so in all the circumstances of the case" (Schedule 18, paragraph 3(1)). When making this judgment it must also consider / disregard the following factors (by paragraphs 3(2)-(4)):

> "[3(2)]...(a) whether there has been any material change of circumstance since the making of the original agreement, in particular-
> (i) change in the character of the land to which the obligation relates or of the neighbourhood of that land;
> (ii) change affecting the enjoyment of the land to which the obligation relates;
> (iii) change affecting the extent to which performance of the obligation is, or is likely in future to be, affordable;
> (iv) change affecting the extent to which performance of the obligation is, or is likely in future to be, practicable;
>
> (b) whether the obligation serves any conservation purpose it had-

(i) when the original agreement was entered into, or

(ii) if the obligation has since been modified (whether by agreement or by the Upper Tribunal), when the obligation was modified,

as the case may be; and

(c) whether the obligation serves the public good.

(3) In considering whether to exercise its power under paragraph 1(1) [application to discharge made by the landowner], the matters to which the Upper Tribunal is to have regard also include-

(a) whether any conservation purpose which the obligation in question had when the original agreement was entered into could be served equally well by an obligation relating to different land in respect of which the applicant holds a qualifying estate; and

(b) whether, if an order under paragraph 1(1) were made, such an alternative obligation could be created by means of a conservation covenant.

(4) In considering, for the purposes of this paragraph, affordability or practicability in relation to performance of an obligation, change in the personal circumstances of a person bound by the obligation is to be disregarded."

Third, on an application to discharge an obligation by a landowner under paragraph 1(1) only, (thus not in relation to an application made by a responsible body under paragraph 2(1)), the Upper Tribunal may also, if both the applicant and the responsible body consent to it, make the discharge conditional on the landowner and responsible body entering into another conservation covenant agreement containing such provision as the Upper Tribunal may specify in their order (Schedule 18, paragraph 5).

Fourth, on an application by a landowner (Schedule 18, paragraph 6(1)) or by a responsible body (paragraph 7(1)), the Upper Tribunal may order the modification of an obligation under a conservation covenant in respect of any of the land to which it relates. The restrictions on this power are as follows: (1) the Upper Tribunal cannot make a modification which, had it been included in the original agreement, would have meant the conservation covenant would not satisfy s.117(1)(a) (by Schedule 18, paragraph 8); (2) the Upper Tribunal must consider it reasonable to modify the obligation in all the circumstances of the case (paragraph 9(1)); and (3) when considering whether to make the modification the Upper Tribunal must bear in mind / exclude from its mind (by paragraphs 9(2)-(3)):

> "[2](a) whether there has been any material change of circumstance since the making of the original agreement, in particular-
>
> (i) change in the character of the land to which the obligation relates or of the neighbourhood of that land;
> (ii) change affecting the enjoyment of the land to which the obligation relates;
> (iii) change affecting the extent to which performance of the obligation is, or is likely in future to be, affordable;
> (iv) change affecting the extent to which performance of the obligation is, or is likely in future to be, practicable;
>
> (b) whether the obligation serves any conservation purpose it had-
>
> (i) when the original agreement was entered into, or
> (ii) if the obligation has since been modified (whether by agreement or by the Upper Tribunal), when the obligation was modified,
>
> as the case may be; and
>
> (c) whether the obligation serves the public good.
>
> (3) In considering, for the purposes of this paragraph, affordability or practicability in relation to performance of an obligation, change

in the personal circumstances of a person bound by the obligation is to be disregarded."

Fifthly and finally, similarly to an application to discharge, in relation to an application by the landowner to modify an obligation under paragraph 6(1) only, (thus not in relation to a paragraph 7(1) application made by a responsible body), the Upper Tribunal may also, and again only provided both parties consent to it, make the modification conditional on the landowner and responsible body entering into a conservation covenant agreement containing such provision as the Upper Tribunal may specify in their order (Schedule 18, paragraph 11(1)).

When making the order under either paragraphs 1(1) / 6(1) (application by landowner) or paragraphs 2(1) / 7(1) (application by responsible body) the Upper Tribunal may order the applicant to pay compensation in respect of the loss of benefit resulting from the order to any person when and for however much as the Upper Tribunal may decide in the order (Schedule 18, paragraphs 4 and 10).

With respect to enforcement proceedings, obviously, a positive obligation is breached when that obligation is not performed. A breach of a negative obligation is defined in the Environment Act 2021 (s.124(1)) as (a) doing something which is prohibited under the conservation covenant, or (b) permitting or suffering another person to do it. Statutory defences to an allegation there has been a breach of the conservation covenant are set out in s.126:

"(1) In proceedings for breach of an obligation under a conservation covenant it is a defence to show-

(a) that the breach occurred as a result of a matter beyond the defendant's control,

(b) that the breach occurred as a result of doing, or not doing, something in an emergency in circumstances where it was necessary for that to be done, or not done, in order to prevent loss of life or injury to any person, or

(c) that at the time of the breach-
(i) the land to which the obligation relates was, or was within an area, designated for a public purpose, and
(ii) compliance with the obligation would have involved a breach of any statutory control applying as a result of the designation.

(2) If the only reason for the application of subsection (1)(c) was failure to obtain authorisation, the defendant must also show that all reasonable steps to obtain authorisation had been taken.

(3) The defence under subsection (1)(c) does not apply if the designation was in force when the conservation covenant was created.

(4) The defence of statutory authority (which applies in relation to the infringement of rights such as easements by a person acting under statutory authority) applies in relation to breach of an obligation under a conservation covenant.

(5) In this section-
'authorisation' means any approval, confirmation, consent, licence, permission or other authorisation (however described), whether special or general;
'statutory control' means control imposed by provision contained in, or having effect under, an Act."

If no defence applies, or a defence fails, then s.125 of the Environment Act 2021 provides for the following remedies to the enforcing party and principles to apply:

"(1) In proceedings for the enforcement of an obligation under a conservation covenant, the available remedies are-
(a) specific performance,
(b) injunction,

(c) damages, and
(d) order for payment of an amount due under the obligation.

(2) On an application for a remedy under subsection (1)(a) or (b), a court must, in considering what remedy is appropriate, take into account any public interest in the performance of the obligation concerned.

(3) Subject to subsection (4), contract principles apply to damages for breach of an obligation under a conservation covenant.

(4) In the case of breach of an obligation of the landowner under a conservation covenant, a court may award exemplary damages in such circumstances as it thinks fit."

Given the timeframes involved, it is also important to note s.125(5) which provides that for the purposes of the Limitation Act 1980 an action founded on an obligation under a conservation covenant will be treated as founded on simple contract. Section 5 of the Limitation Act 1980 provides that an action founded on simple contract shall not be brought after the expiration of six years from the date on which the cause of action accrued.

It should also be noted the provisions set out in Part 7 of the Environment Act 2021 concerning conservation covenants also apply to Crown land (Schedule 19, paragraph 1), subject to the detailed set of provisions within Schedule 19 of the Environment Act 2021.

Relevant Start Dates

The s.106 agreement / conservation covenant starts from the date it is signed. Different dates may be specified within the legal agreement in relation to specific obligations.

For significant and non-significant onsite BNG, the 30-year maintenance period starts when the development, not the habitat enhancement and/or creation work, is completed. No definition of completion of development is provided in statute or guidance, but given the importance of certainty when complying with legal obligations, and the fact that those legal obligations will remain in place well after the original negotiating personalities may have moved on, it is good practice for the parties to discuss the matter and define "completion of development" clearly in either the condition or the legal agreement securing the mandatory 30-year maintenance period.

For offsite BNG, the 30-year maintenance period starts when the habitat enhancement and/or creation work is completed. This refers to completion of the capital works to enhance or create that offsite habitat, i.e. the trees have been planted, the fence has been constructed, the pond has been dug, the arable field has been stripped of excess nutrients in the soil and seeds have been planted, etc.

Enforcement of Legal Agreement

As noted in the Planning Authority Governance chapter, enforcement under a s.106 agreement or conservation covenant is simpler than enforcement action under the Town and Country Planning Act 1990. A failure to comply with the terms of a legal agreement is a breach and may be enforced in accordance with the terms of that agreement and the relevant legal framework. The need for clarity of expression has been emphasised above: whether a matter is enforceable or not, and if so, how and with what consequences, will depend on the wording used on the legal agreement.

Readers are also reminded of the statutory defence to breach of a conservation covenant under s.126 of the Environment Act 2021 set out above, and the automatic grant of step-in rights in the case of a s.106 agreement under s.106(6)-(7):

"...if there is a breach of a requirement in a planning obligation to carry out any operations in, on, under or over the land to which the obligation relates, the authority by whom the obligation is enforceable may—

(a) enter the land and carry out the operations; and

(b) recover from the person or persons against whom the obligation is enforceable any expenses reasonably incurred by them in doing so.

(7) Before an authority exercise their power under subsection (6)(a) they shall give not less than twenty-one days' notice of their intention to do so to any person against whom the planning obligation is enforceable."

CHAPTER NINE

OFFSITE BNG

An offsite biodiversity unit is any BNG provided outside of the red line boundary of the development site (even if the land is directly adjacent to the development site, or within the blue line landownership boundary).[188] There is no central marketplace (as yet) for offsite BNG units, so developers need to search for and purchase units as best they can, although a private marketplace is developing through third party intermediaries. To be clear, the biodiversity gain site register operated by Natural England does not contain contact details of any available gain sites and is not a matchmaking service to connect buyers and sellers. Developers who cannot meet their full BNG requirement onsite must source offsite units in preference to statutory credits from any (or a combination) of the following sources of units:

- directly from a landowner;
- from a habitat bank operator;
- through a broker;
- from a trading platform; and/or
- from a local planning authority who operates their own habitat bank.

The final cost of offsite units will vary. Each unit will have fixed costs, such as (from the non-exhaustive list provided by DEFRA):[189]

188 DEFRA guidance https://www.gov.uk/guidance/make-off-site-biodiversity-gains-as-a-developer. Last accessed 1 September 2024.

189 DEFRA guidance https://www.gov.uk/guidance/sell-biodiversity-units-as-a-land-manager#obligations-and-options-when-you-sell-biodiversity-units-for-off-site-gain. Last accessed 1 September 2024.

- initial creation and enhancement of habitats
- management of the land covering at least 30 years
- monitoring and reporting
- ecologist or other expert's costs
- insurance
- remedial work to correct any habitat management failures
- machinery, tools and other staff to carry out the tasks
- inflation
- lawyer's (and any other expert) fees for drafting the relevant legal agreement

Unit price will be based on the costs incurred when carrying out habitat enhancement and/or creation work, not the number of units those habitats will generate. The variation in price (may) arise from the effect of the distance multiplier in the statutory metric: different developers will value those same units more or less depending on the distance to the development site.

The landowner will need to register their units on the national biodiversity gain sites register, and when they are sold they must be allocated to that specific development on the register (to prevent the same biodiversity units from being sold twice). Units can be registered at any time, whether before, at the same time as, or after units are sold. In all events they must be allocated to the development on the register before the development's biodiversity gain plan can be lawfully approved (by Schedule 7A, paragraph 15(2)(c)(i)).

It is the planning authority's role – not Natural England operating as the register operator – to check that the offsite units being relied on by the developer are registered, allocated to the specific development, and the total value of the offsite BNG units relied on in the biodiversity gain plan matches the total value of the offsite BNG units allocated in the register.[190]

Only offsite units are to be registered on the official biodiversity gain site register, not onsite units, nor statutory credits. The point of the register is to avoid double counting: an offsite provider could sell their units to multiple developers, so a centralised register is necessary to ensure offsite units are only sold once, and attributed to a specific development. Onsite units are not sold, and statutory credits are only generated when they are sold, so there is no risk of double counting with onsite units and statutory credits.

The Biodiversity Gain Sites Register

The register[191] is operated and maintained by Natural England. It lists all registered offsite habitats providing biodiversity units, whether they are allocated to a specific development or not. The purpose of the register is to achieve transparency on offsite biodiversity gains and prevent double counting. Units can only be allocated to one development. The "hands off" approach taken by Natural England as the register operator is made perfectly clear by reg.36(2) of the Biodiversity Gain Site Register Regulations 2024: "[n]o decision of the register operator under these Regulations may be taken as indicating consent or assent to, or any other kind of approval of or acquiescence to, the carrying out of any particular works on the land to which the decision relates." And so, there are only very limited checks carried out before offsite units are registered: (1) whether the applicant for registration holds the requisite interest in the land for 30 years; and (2) the entity proposed to maintain the units is a

---

190 DEFRA guidance. https://www.gov.uk/guidance/biodiversity-net-gain-what-local-planning-authorities-should-do. Last accessed 1 September 2024.

191 Search entry portal available at: https://environment.data.gov.uk/biodiversity-net-gain. Last accessed 1 September 2024.

financially fit entity to carry out that work. As is clear from reg.36(2), the act of Natural England registering units and/or then allocating them is purely administrative. No guarantee whatsoever of the quality of the units and the biodiversity gain plan to achieve them can be assumed from this administrative action being performed. Assessing the submitted biodiversity gain plan and judging whether it will achieve the biodiversity gain objective is entirely the responsibility of the planning authority.

As noted above, units can be registered before they are sold to a specific development, but there must be an underlying legal agreement to maintain those units for at least 30 years at the time the units are registered (and that legal agreement must be provided alongside the application to register the units: regs.5, 6, 7 and 8(4)(a)(i) and 8(4)(b)(i) of the Biodiversity Gain Site Register Regulations 2024). Landowners registering offsite units should ensure the relevant legal agreement contains exit clauses if the units are not subsequently sold to developers, as otherwise they would be obliged to comply with the agreement absent any income.

When pre-registered units are sold, those offsite units must then be "allocated" to that development through an application under reg.12 of the Biodiversity Gain Site Register Regulations 2024. As noted, the biodiversity gain plan cannot be legally approved if the allocation step has not been completed (Schedule 7A, paragraph 15(2)(c)(i) of the Town and Country Act 1990).

In response to any application made (whether for registration, allocation, amendment, or removal from the register) Natural England is entitled to make a request for further information from applicants. If that information is not provided within three months they are entitled to reject the application (reg.s 9(10), 14(10), 18(8), and 25(6) of the Biodiversity Gain Site Register Regulations 2024 respectively).

Finally, if the habitat enhancement and/or creation and management of the offsite units has not commenced by the time the units are allocated, then this work should start within 12 months of allocation.[192]

Applications to Register Units

To have units included on the register, certain requirements must be met (by reg.6 of the Biodiversity Gain Site Register Regulations 2024):

> "*6.- Land eligible to be registered*
>
> (1) Land is eligible to be registered in the biodiversity gain site register in relation to a particular conservation covenant or section 106 agreement if the conditions in paragraphs (2) to (7) are met.
>
> (2) The first condition is that one or more persons are required under the conservation covenant or section 106 agreement to carry out works on the land for the purpose of habitat enhancement.
>
> (3) The second condition is that one or more persons are required under the conservation covenant or section 106 agreement to maintain the habitat enhancement to be achieved by the required enhancement works on the land under the conservation covenant or section 106 agreement for at least 30 years after the completion of those works.
>
> (4) The third condition is that one or more persons are required under the conservation covenant or section 106 agreement to monitor habitats on the land to ensure that the habitat enhancement to be achieved by the required enhancement works on the land under the conservation covenant or section 106

192 DEFRA guidance https://www.gov.uk/guidance/sell-biodiversity-units-as-a-land-manager#obligations-and-options-when-you-sell-biodiversity-units-for-off-site-gain. Last accessed 1 September 2024.

agreement is maintained for the period for which the conservation covenant or section 106 agreement requires it to be maintained.

(5) The fourth condition is that, for the purposes of Schedule 7A to the Town and Country Planning Act 1990, the habitat enhancement to be achieved by the required enhancement works on the land under the conservation covenant or section 106 agreement is made available to be allocated (conditionally or unconditionally, and whether for consideration or otherwise) in accordance with the terms of the covenant, or (as the case may be) in accordance with the terms of one or more planning obligations in the section 106 agreement, to one or more developments for which planning permission is granted.

(6) The fifth condition is that the land is in England.

(7) The sixth condition is that the conservation covenant or (as the case may be) the planning obligations in the section 106 agreement are registered in the local land charges register or the appropriate local land charges register.

(8) For the purposes of paragraphs (2), (3) and (4), a person is only to be regarded as being required under a section 106 agreement to carry out works on land, to maintain the habitat enhancement to be achieved by such works or to monitor habitats on land if that person is required to carry out those works, maintain that habitat enhancement or monitor those habitats (as the case may be) under one or more planning obligations in that section 106 agreement.

(9) In this regulation 'the required enhancement works' on land under a conservation covenant or section 106 agreement are all of the works required to be carried out on that land for the purpose of habitat enhancement under that conservation covenant or (as the case may be) under the planning obligations in that section 106 agreement."

For the purposes of reg.6(7) the "local land charges register" is that which is kept by the Chief Land Registrar under s.3 of the Local Land Charges Act 1975 (as substituted by Schedule 5, paragraph 3 of the Infrastructure Act 2015). The "appropriate local land charges register' is the register of local land charges kept by a local authority where the Chief Land Registrar has not yet assumed functions relating to the registration of local land charges for the area of that local authority.

By reg.7(2) of the Biodiversity Gain Site Register Regulations 2024 an application to register land on the biodiversity gain site register in relation to a conservation covenant can only be made by the following:

> "(a) a person who is required under the covenant to carry out works on the land for the purpose of habitat enhancement;
> (b) a person who is required under the covenant to maintain any habitat enhancement to be achieved by works required to be carried out on the land for that purpose under the covenant; or
> (c) a person by whom a requirement referred to in sub-paragraph (a) or (b) is enforceable."

The responsible body under a conservation covenant may not apply to register offsite units in relation to that covenant (reg.7(3)).

By reg.7(4) an application to register land in the biodiversity gain site register in relation to a s.106 agreement may only be made by a person who is required under a planning obligation in the s.106 agreement:

> "(a) to carry out works on the land for the purpose of habitat enhancement; or
> (b) to maintain any habitat enhancement to be achieved by works required to be carried out on the land for that purpose under a planning obligation in the section 106 agreement."

So, a local planning authority cannot register units unless they are bound by a planning obligation as set out immediately above. Merely having step-in rights under / in connection with a s.106 agreement is not sufficient where that is worded as a power to do something, not an obligation to do it.

There are two potential procedures to register units, depending on whether the offsite units are already registered.

First, if the units are not yet registered, either the developer can (1) require the landowner to register their units, and then the landowner or the developer (with the landowner's permission) applies to allocate those units to the development; or (2) the application to record the allocation of the units to the development is made at the same time as the application to register the units.

Any application to simply register units in relation to an extant conservation covenant or s.106 agreement must contain the following information, declaration, and documents (by reg.8 of the Biodiversity Gain Site Register Regulations 2024):

- evidence that the applicant is entitled under reg.7 to make the application;
- the applicant's name;
- an address to which notices under the Biodiversity Gain Site Register Regulations 2024 may be sent by post to the applicant in connection with the application;
- an email address to which such notices may be sent to the applicant;
- information identifying the location and boundaries of the land to be registered (whether contained in a map or otherwise);

- where the required enhancement works on the land have already commenced, the date on which they commenced;

- the last date (if any) on which, under the terms of the conservation covenant or the planning obligations in the s.106 agreement, there will be any requirement in force to-
  (i) carry out works on the land for the purpose of habitat enhancement, or
  (ii) maintain any habitat enhancement to be achieved by works required to be carried out on the land for that purpose under the conservation covenant or (as the case may be) under the planning obligations in the s.106 agreement;

- where the required enhancement works on the land have not yet commenced-
  (i) the type, size and condition of each habitat on the land, and
  (ii) the projected type, size and condition of each habitat on the land as a result of those works;

- where the required enhancement works on the land have already commenced-
  (i) the type, size and condition of each habitat on the land immediately before the commencement of those works, and
  (ii) the projected type, size and condition of each habitat on the land as a result of those works;

- the name of each person by whom the requirement to carry out any of the required enhancement works on the land is enforceable;

- the name of each person by whom the requirement to maintain any of the habitat enhancement to be achieved by those works is enforceable;

- where any of the habitat enhancement to be achieved by the required enhancement works on the land has been allocated, in accordance with the terms of the conservation covenant or (as the case may be) the terms of a planning obligation in the s.106 agreement, to a development for which planning permission has been granted, the following information in relation to each such allocation-
  (i) information identifying the development;
  (ii) in relation to each habitat to which the allocated habitat enhancement relates, its projected type, size and condition as a result of the works required to be carried out on the land to achieve the allocated habitat enhancement under the conservation covenant or (as the case may be) under the planning obligations in the section 106 agreement;
  (iii) the biodiversity value (for the purposes of Schedule 7A to the Town and Country Planning Act 1990) of the allocated habitat enhancement in relation to the development;

- a declaration by the applicant that-
  (a) where the required enhancement works on the land have already commenced, any consent, licence or other permission necessary for the purpose of carrying out those works was obtained, or
  (b) where the required enhancement works on the land have not yet commenced, any consent, licence or other permission necessary for the purpose of carrying out those works will be obtained before the works are commenced;

- where the application is to register land in relation to a conservation covenant, a copy of-
  (i) the conservation covenant agreement containing that covenant, in the form the agreement was in when executed under s.117 of the Environment Act 2021;

(ii) every agreement discharging an obligation under the covenant or discharging any of the land, or any estate in any of the land, from an obligation under the covenant;
(iii) every agreement modifying an obligation under the covenant;
(iv) every agreement appointing a person to replace a responsible body under the covenant;
(v) every order of the Upper Tribunal modifying or discharging an obligation under the covenant;
(vi) every other decision of a court or tribunal about the effect of the covenant; (vii) every other document which describes any of the required enhancement works on the land and has been produced in accordance with the terms of the conservation covenant;

- where the application is to register land in relation to a s.106 agreement, a copy of-
  (i) the s.106 agreement in the form it was in when entered into under s.106 of the Town and Country Planning Act 1990;
  (ii) every agreement modifying or discharging a planning obligation in the s.106 agreement;
  (iii) every determination, notice or other instrument having the effect of modifying or discharging a planning obligation in the s.106 agreement;
  (iv) every instrument by which the s.106 agreement has otherwise been amended;
  (v) every decision of a court or tribunal about the effect of a planning obligation in the s.106 agreement;
  (vi) every other document which describes any of the required enhancement works on the land and has been produced in accordance with the terms of a planning obligation in the s.106 agreement;
- a copy of every agreement or other document which has been entered into or produced pursuant to the terms of the conservation covenant or a planning obligation in the s.106 agreement and

which describes things to be done in relation to the land for the purpose of-

(i) maintaining any habitat enhancement to be achieved by the required enhancement works on the land, or

(ii) monitoring habitats on the land to ensure that any habitat enhancement to be achieved by the required enhancement works on the land is maintained for the period for which it is required to be maintained under the conservation covenant or a planning obligation in the s.106 agreement;

- a copy of an official search certificate issued under s.9(4) of the Local Land Charges Act 1975 showing the particulars of the registration of the conservation covenant, or (as the case may be) the planning obligations in the s.106 agreement, in the local land charges register or the appropriate local land charges register.

In order for units to be both registered and allocated at the same time (for which the £639 registration fee remains all that is payable, according to the guidance), unless already provided, Natural England will also require the following to be submitted with the application (or within 14 days of Natural England requesting them):[193]

a) the title deeds or lease agreement to prove ownership for all landowners or leaseholders;
b) the completed statutory biodiversity metric tool calculation;
c) the planning permission decision notice; and
d) a habitat management and monitoring plan.

Application to Allocate Pre-Registered Units

If the units are already registered and only need to be allocated, the process simply requires that either the "relevant person" or someone else

193 DEFRA guidance https://www.gov.uk/guidance/register-a-biodiversity-site-and-allocate-to-a-development. Last accessed 1 September 2024.

(with the relevant person's permission) (reg.12(3) of the Biodiversity Gain Site Register Regulations 2024) makes an application to record the allocation of the offsite units to the development on the register. "Relevant person" in terms of allocating units on the register is defined in reg.12(4):

> "(a) where land is registered in the entry in relation to a conservation covenant-
>
> (i) a person who is required under the covenant to carry out works on the land to achieve any of the allocated habitat enhancement,
>
> (ii) a person who is required under the covenant to maintain any of the allocated habitat enhancement, or
>
> (iii) a person by whom a requirement referred to in paragraph (i) or (ii) is enforceable, but not the responsible body under the covenant;
>
> (b) where land is registered in the entry in relation to a section 106 agreement, a person who is required under a planning obligation in the section 106 agreement-
>
> (i) to carry out works on the land to achieve any of the allocated habitat enhancement, or
>
> (ii) to maintain any of the allocated habitat enhancement."

An application to allocate units must contain the following information (by reg.13(1) of the Biodiversity Gain Site Register Regulations 2024):

a) "the name of the applicant;

b) evidence that the applicant is entitled under regulation 12 to make the application;

c) an address to which notices under the Biodiversity Gain Site Register Regulations 2024 may be sent by post to the applicant in connection with the application;

d) an email address to which such notices may be sent to the applicant;

e) the registration number assigned to the entry in question under regulation 11(2)(b);

f) information identifying the development;

g) in relation to each habitat to which the allocated habitat enhancement relates, its projected type, size and condition as a result of the works required to be carried out to achieve the allocated habitat enhancement under-

    (i) where the land is registered in the entry in question in relation to a conservation covenant, the conservation covenant, or

    (ii) where the land is registered in the entry in question in relation to a section 106 agreement, the planning obligations in the section 106 agreement.

h) the biodiversity value for the purposes of Schedule 7A to the Town and Country Act 1990 of the allocated habitat enhancement in relation to the development."

<u>Amending Entries on the Register</u>

Entries can also be amended upon application to Natural England as register operator. Only certain amendments are permitted (see reg.s17(2)-(7) of the Biodiversity Gain Site Register Regulations 2024). Essentially, on the basis that information is incomplete or inaccurate, or the habitat enhancement has wholly or partly ceased to be allocated to the development. Only a "relevant person", or a person who has the consent of every relevant person, can make an application to amend a register entry, as defined in reg.17(9):

"...a 'relevant person', in relation to an application to amend an entry in the biodiversity gain site register, means-

(a) where land is registered in the entry in relation to a conservation covenant-

(i) a person who is required under the covenant to carry out works on the land for the purpose of habitat enhancement,

(ii) a person who is required under the covenant to maintain any habitat enhancement to be achieved by works required to be carried out on the land for that purpose under the covenant, or

(iii) a person by whom a requirement referred to in paragraph (i) or (ii) is enforceable,

but not the responsible person under the covenant;

(b) where land is registered in the entry in relation to a section 106 agreement, a person who is required under a planning obligation in the section 106 agreement-

(i) to carry out works on the land for the purpose of habitat enhancement, or

(ii) to maintain any habitat enhancement to be achieved by works required to be carried out on the land for that purpose under a planning obligation in the section 106 agreement."

Regulation 17(10) sets out specific information requirements for the contents of any application to amend an entry in the register:

"An application to amend an entry in the biodiversity gain site register must-

(a) include the name of the applicant;

(b) include evidence that the applicant is entitled under this regulation to make the application;

(c) include-

(i) an address to which notices under these Regulations in connection with the application may be sent by post to the applicant, and
(ii) an email address to which such notices may be sent to the applicant;

(d) include the registration number assigned to the entry under regulation 11(2)(b);

(e) specify the grounds under paragraph (2)(a), (b), (c) or (d) on which the application is made and explain why the applicant considers those grounds are met;

(f) where the application is made on the grounds in paragraph (2)(d), explain why the applicant considers the information to which the application relates to be incomplete or inaccurate;

(g) specify the amendments which the applicant considers need to be made;

(h) where the application is made on the grounds that information in an entry in the biodiversity gain site register is incomplete or inaccurate as a result of a relevant modification made to a conservation covenant or section 106 agreement, include a copy of the agreement, determination, notice, instrument or decision referred to in paragraph (3)(a) or (b) with which the application is concerned."

Natural England also has the power to unilaterally amend a register entry if it considers that the information in the entry is inaccurate or incomplete (reg.20(1)(b) of the Biodiversity Gain Site Register Regulations 2024). The power to amend unilaterally extends only so far as necessary to "so that the information in question is complete and accurate" (reg.20(2)). An example of "inaccurate" information is given at reg.20(3) of an allocation being recorded contrary to the terms of the relevant conservation covenant or s.106 agreement, but Natural England's powers to unilaterally amend an entry are not limited to this example. Before amending the entry Natural England is to give notice to every "required recipient" of that notice, as follows (by reg.21(2)):

> "A 'required recipient' of a notice of intent under paragraph (1) is a person who the register operator believes, on the basis of any information in the register operator's possession, is-
>
> (a) a person on whom a relevant requirement is imposed under the conservation covenant or section 106 agreement, or
>
> (b) a person by whom any such requirement is enforceable."

Where the land is registered in relation to a conservation covenant, a "relevant requirement" under the conservation covenant is a requirement (by reg.21(3)):

> "(a) to carry out works on the land for the purpose of habitat enhancement, or
>
> (b) to maintain any habitat enhancement to be achieved by works required to be carried out on the land for that purpose under the covenant or obligation."

Where the land is registered in relation to a s.106 agreement, a "relevant requirement" under the s.106 agreement is a requirement (by reg.21(4)):

> "(a) to carry out works on the land for the purpose of habitat enhancement, or
>
> (b) to maintain any habitat enhancement to be achieved by works required to be carried out on the land for that purpose under a planning obligation in the section 106 agreement."

The notice of intent to amend the entry must contain, by reg.21(5), the following information:

> "(a) identify the entry which the register operator intends to

amend;
(b) inform the recipient of the notice that the register operator considers that the information in the entry is inaccurate or incomplete;
(c) explain why the register operator considers that the information in the entry is inaccurate or incomplete;
(d) inform the recipient of the notice that the register operator intends to amend the entry;
(e) inform the recipient of the right to make representations under regulation 22."

The "required recipient" who receives a notice of intent under reg.21 may make representations in writing about why the entry should not be amended. They have only 28 days to make those representations, beginning with the day after the day on which the notice was given (reg.22(1)). Natural England is obliged to bear any representation they receive within that time frame into account when they decide whether or not to amend the entry (reg.22(2)). As Natural England's power to amend the entry extends to such changes to ensure "the information in question is complete and accurate" (by reg.20(2)), they are not limited to the terms of the notice of intent when making their final decision. The obligation to have regard to representations made by those to whom a notice was given also means they have the power to amend the entry in line with those representations. If a significant departure from the changes indicated in the notice of intent is contemplated, and this is not in line with the representations received, then Natural England ought to have regard to the need to act fairly as a public body exercising their power in a way so as to directly affect a person's interests. Fairness may demand that a further notice is given to those affected by the unilateral change giving them another opportunity to make representations.

When it does make its final decision on unilateral amendment (whether that decision is to amend or not), Natural England must give notice to every person who was sent a notice of intent (reg.23), and give reasons for its decision (reg.23(3)(a)) as well as information on the right to appeal (reg.23(3)(b)). Any other person such as a member of the public who was not given a notice of intent may also request the reasons for the amendment in writing, giving their postal and email addresses. Natural England is obliged to send that person its reasons "as soon as practicable" (reg.23(7)).

Removing Entries From the Register

Registered units can also be removed from the register (upon application) when they are not allocated (reg.24(1) of the Biodiversity Gain Site Register Regulations 2024). Only a "relevant person" may make the application. This is defined as (by reg.24(4)):

> "(a) where the land is registered in the entry in question in relation to a conservation covenant-
>
> (i) a person who is required under the covenant to carry out works on the land for the purpose of habitat enhancement,
>
> (ii) a person who is required under the covenant to maintain any habitat enhancement to be achieved by works required to be carried out on the land for that purpose under the covenant, or
>
> (iii) a person by whom a requirement referred to in paragraph (i) or (ii) is enforceable,
>
> but not the responsible person under the covenant;
>
> (b) where the land is registered in the entry in relation to a section 106 agreement, a person who is required under a planning obligation in the section 106 agreement-
>
> (i) to carry out works on the land for the purpose of habitat enhancement, or
>
> (ii) to maintain any habitat enhancement to be achieved by works required to be carried out on the land for that purpose under a planning obligation in the section 106 agreement."

The application to remove the entry must include (by reg.24(5)):

"(a) the name of the applicant;
(b) evidence that the applicant is entitled under this regulation to make the application;
(c) an address to which notices under these Regulations in connection with the application may be sent by post to the applicant;
(d) an email address to which such notices may be sent to the applicant;
(e) the registration number assigned under regulation 11(2)(b) to the entry to which the application relates."

Natural England is obliged to remove the entry if the land is not allocated and all the other requirements of reg.24 have been met (and the fee is paid) (by reg.25(5)). When it accepts an application under reg.24, Natural England must as soon as practicable remove the entry from the register, as well as any map or other document included in the register in relation to that entry (by reg.25(12)).

Any decision made under reg.25 must be communicated to the applicant, with reasons provided, as soon as practicable, and include information on the right to appeal if the applicant is dissatisfied with the decision (reg.25(14)).

Entries can also be unilaterally retired / removed by Natural England if it considers (a) every relevant requirement under the conservation covenant or s.106 agreement has been complied with, (b) the legal agreement is no longer in force, (c) one or more of the relevant requirements under reg.6 have ceased to be met, or (d) false or misleading information has been provided (reg.26(2)).

Where the land is registered in relation to a conservation covenant, a "relevant requirement" for the purpose of reg.26(2)(a) is a requirement (by reg.26(3)):

> "(a) to carry out works on the land for the purpose of habitat enhancement, or
> (b) to maintain any habitat enhancement to be achieved by works required to be carried out on the land for that purpose under the covenant."

Where the land is registered in the entry in relation to a s.106 agreement, a "relevant requirement" for the purpose of reg.26(2)(a) is a requirement (by reg.26(4)):

> "(a) to carry out works on the land for the purpose of habitat enhancement, or
> (b) to maintain any habitat enhancement to be achieved by works required to be carried out on the land for that purpose under a planning obligation in the section 106 agreement."

As with a unilateral amendment to the register, a unilateral decision to remove an entry from the register altogether must be notified in advance to the "required recipient" under reg.27(2), and the notice must include relevant information to enable the recipient to understand the basis for Natural England's intended decision. For these purposes, if Natural England believes s.26(2)(a) applies (that every relevant requirement under the conservation covenant or s.106 agreement has been complied with), then, by reg.27(2):

> "a 'required recipient' of a notice of intent...is a person who the register operator believes, on the basis of any information in the register operator's possession, is-
>
> > (a) a person on whom the last relevant requirement to be in force under the conservation covenant or section 106 agreement was imposed under the covenant or section 106 agreement, or
> > (b) a person by whom that requirement was enforceable."

If Natural England believes s.26(2)(b) applies (the legal agreement is no longer in force), then, by reg.27(3):

> "a 'required recipient' of a notice of intent...is a person who the register operator believes, on the basis of any information in the register operator's possession, is-
>
> (a) a person on whom a relevant requirement under the conservation covenant or section 106 agreement was imposed immediately before the time when the register operator considers the covenant or section 106 agreement ceased to be in force, or
>
> (b) a person by whom any such requirement was enforceable."

If Natural England believes s.26(2)(c) applies (one or more of the relevant requirements under reg.6 have ceased to be met) but also considers that the condition in reg.6(2) is still met (the condition in reg.6(2) is that one or more persons are required under the conservation covenant or s.106 agreement to carry out works on the land for the purpose of habitat enhancement); then, by reg.27(4):

> "a 'required recipient' of a notice of intent...is a person who the register operator believes, on the basis of any information in the register operator's possession, is-
>
> (a) a person on whom a relevant requirement is imposed under the conservation covenant or section 106 agreement, or
>
> (b) a person by whom any such requirement is enforceable."

If Natural England believes s.26(2)(c) applies (one or more of the relevant requirements under reg.6 have ceased to be met) but considers that the condition in reg.6(2) has ceased to be met, then, by reg.27(5):

> "a 'required recipient' of a notice of intent...is a person who the register operator believes, on the basis of any information in the register operator's possession, is-
>
> (a) a person on whom a requirement to carry out works on the land is imposed under the conservation covenant or (as the case may be) under a planning obligation in the section 106 agreement, or

(b) a person by whom any such requirement is enforceable."

It should be noted where the required enhancement works on the land registered in the entry have been completed, by reg.26(5) the fact that the condition in reg.6(2) has, as a consequence, ceased to be met is to be disregarded for the purposes reg.26(2)(c). "Required enhancement works" means the works required to be carried out on the land for the purpose of habitat enhancement under the relevant conservation covenant or s.106 agreement (as relevant) (by reg.26(6)).

Finally, if Natural England believes s.26(2)(d) applies (false or misleading information has been provided), then, by reg.27(6):

> "a 'required recipient' of a notice of intent…is a person who the register operator believes, on the basis of any information in the register operator's possession, is-
>
> (a) a person on whom a relevant requirement is imposed under the conservation covenant or section 106 agreement, or
>
> (b) a person by whom any such requirement is enforceable."

All references to a "relevant requirement" in reg.27, whether to a conservation covenant or s.106 agreement, are to be construed in accordance with reg.26(3) or (4) (set out above).

The notice of intent must (by reg.27(7)):

> "(a) identify the entry which the register operator intends to remove;
>
> (b) inform the recipient of the notice that the register operator intends to remove the entry; (c) set out the grounds under regulation 26(2) on which the register operator intends to remove the entry;
>
> (d) where regulation 26(2)(a) applies, state the last date on which, to the register operator's knowledge, there was any relevant

requirement in force under the conservation covenant or section 106 agreement;
(e) where regulation 26(2)(b) applies, explain why the register operator considers that the conservation covenant or section 106 agreement is no longer in force;
(f) where regulation 26(2)(c) applies, identify the condition or conditions in regulation 6 which the register operator considers is or are no longer met and explain why the register operator considers that to be the case;
(g) where regulation 26(2)(d) applies, specify the information which the register operator considers was false or misleading;
(h) inform the recipient of the notice of the right to make representations under regulation 28."

As with a unilateral decision to amend a register entry, reg.28 gives the recipient of a notice under reg.27 the right to make representations within 28 days (beginning the day after notice was given), to which Natural England must have regard when making their decision (reg.28(2)), and that decision must be communicated (with reasons) to those who received the reg.27 notice, and all those who request those reasons in writing (reg.29). The exact same fairness considerations as noted above in relation to unilaterally amending the register entry apply to decisions to unilaterally remove an entry entirely from the register.

Withdrawing an Application

To withdraw an application, an applicant must request it in writing. The withdrawal of an application is effective only if Natural England receives a written notification of the withdrawal from the applicant before deciding whether to accept or reject the application (regs.7(5), 12(5), 17(11), and 24(6) of the Biodiversity Gain Site Register Regulations 2024).

Fees

There is a fee payable to Natural England as the register operator in respect of any application. The fees vary depending on the nature of the application. These are specified in column (2) of the Table within the Schedule to the Biodiversity Gain Site Register (Financial Penalties and Fees) Regulations 2024:

1	Application referred to in regulation 7(1) of the Biodiversity Gain Site Register Regulations 2024 (application to register land in the biodiversity gain site register)	£639
2	Application referred to in regulation 12(2) of the Biodiversity Gain Site Register Regulations 2024 (application to record the allocation of habitat enhancement to a development in the biodiversity gain site register)	£45
3	Application referred to in regulation 17(1) of the Biodiversity Gain Site Register Regulations 2024 made on the grounds in regulation 17(2)(a) of those Regulations (application to amend information in the biodiversity gain site register which is incomplete or inaccurate as a result of modification of a conservation covenant or section 106 agreement)	£639
4	Application referred to in regulation 17(1) of the Biodiversity Gain Site Register Regulations 2024 made on the grounds in regulation 17(2)(b) or (c) of those Regulations (application to amend information in the biodiversity gain site register because habitat enhancement has ceased wholly or partly to be allocated to a development)	£45
5	Application referred to in regulation 17(1) of the Biodiversity Gain Site Register Regulations 2024 made on the grounds in regulation 17(2)(d) (application to amend information in the biodiversity gain site register which is incomplete or inaccurate for any reason not mentioned in regulation 17(2)(a), (b) or (c))	£639
6	Application referred to in regulation 24(2) of the Biodiversity Gain Site Register Regulations 2024 (application to have an entry removed from the biodiversity gain site register)	£89

The fee must be paid by the applicant before the end of the period of 28 days beginning with the day on which the application is received by Natural England (reg.12(3) of the Biodiversity Gain Site Register (Financial Penalties and Fees) Regulations 2024). However, if the applicant withdraws the application before paying the fee, no fee is payable (reg.12(4)). It would be sensible to assume, for this reason, that no steps will be taken by Natural England on the application until the appropriate fee is paid. Obviously, if no fee is ever paid the application will be rejected.

Appeals Against Registration Decisions

Regulation 30 of the Biodiversity Gain Site Register Regulations 2024 provides for a right to appeal to the First-tier Tribunal against Natural England's decision to reject an application. This is available in the following cases:

1) an application to register land under reg.7;
2) an application to record the allocation of any habitat enhancement to a development under reg.12(2);
3) an application to amend an entry under reg.17(1);
4) where Natural England accepts part but not all of an application to amend an entry under reg.17(1);
5) where Natural England unilaterally amends an entry under reg.20;
6) an application to have an entry removed from the register under reg.24(2); and
7) where Natural England unilaterally removes an entry from the register under reg.26.

The right of appeal is in relation to the person who made the application, however, any "interested person" may also appeal when Natural England acts unilaterally under reg.s 20 or 26. An interested person is defined based on the nature of the legal agreement establishing the relationship between unit seller / buyer / enforcing body.

An interested person in relation to an appeal against the amendment or removal of an entry for land registered in relation to a conservation covenant, by reg.30(8), means a person:

> "(a) who is required under the conservation covenant to carry out works on the land for the purpose of habitat enhancement,
> (b) who is required under the conservation covenant to maintain any habitat enhancement to be achieved by works required to be carried out on the land for that purpose under the covenant, or
> (c) by whom a requirement referred to in sub-paragraph (a) or (b) is enforceable."

By reg.30(9), an interested person in relation to an appeal against the amendment or removal of an entry for land registered in relation to a s.106 agreement means a person:

> "(a) who is required under a planning obligation in the s.106 agreement to carry out works on the land for the purpose of habitat enhancement,
> (b) who is required under a planning obligation in the s.106 agreement to maintain any habitat enhancement to be achieved by works required to be carried out on the land for that purpose under a planning obligation in the s.106 agreement, or
> (c) by whom a requirement referred to in sub-paragraph (a) or (b) is enforceable."

Where Natural England has rejected an application entirely, by reg.31(4) of the Biodiversity Gain Site Register Regulations 2024 the First-tier Tribunal must consider the following statutory grounds of appeal:

> "(a) that Natural England's decision to reject the application was based, wholly or partly, on an error of fact;
> (b) that Natural England's decision to reject the application was wrong in law;

(c) where the decision to reject the application was made under regulations 9(10), 14(10), 18(8) or 25(10), that Natural England's decision to reject the application was unfair or unreasonable for any other reason; and/or
(d) that any decision of Natural England not to exercise its power under regulations 9(6), 14(6), 18(6), or 25(6) (as the case may be), and to reject the application as a result, was unfair or unreasonable for any other reason."

If any of the above grounds has been satisfied, the First-tier Tribunal must (it has no discretion here) quash the decision to reject the application (reg,31(2) of the Biodiversity Gain Site Register Regulations 2024). The First-tier Tribunal then has two options: it will direct either that Natural England must accept the application, or must reconsider the application under reg.s 9, 14, 18 or 25 (as the case may be) in accordance with the First-tier Tribunal's decision.

If the First-tier Tribunal finds that none of the grounds set out in reg.31(4) are made out they must confirm Natural England's decision to reject the application (by reg.31(3)).

Where Natural England has partly accepted an application to amend the register, reg.32(4) of the Biodiversity Gain Site Register Regulations 2024 provides the First-tier Tribunal must consider whether the following grounds apply:

"(a) that the register operator's decision was based, wholly or partly, on an error of fact; and/or
(b) that the register operator's decision was wrong in law."

If the First-tier Tribunal is satisfied that either of the grounds above applies in relation to the Natural England's decision not to make an amendment, it must – again, here it has no discretion – quash Natural England's decision not to make the amendment and either direct Natural England to make the amendment, or direct Natural England to reconsider whether to make the amendment (reg.32(2)). Otherwise, if the First-tier Tribunal is not satisfied that either of the grounds applies, it must confirm Natural England's decision not to make the requested amendment (reg.32(3)).

Finally, if Natural England acts unilaterally (whether that is amending or removing an entry), reg.33(4) of the Biodiversity Gain Site Register Regulations 2024 provides the First-tier Tribunal must consider whether any of the following grounds apply:

> "(a) that the decision appealed against was based, wholly or partly, on an error of fact; (b) that the decision was wrong in law; and/or (c) that the decision was unfair or unreasonable for any other reason."

If the First-tier Tribunal is satisfied that any of the grounds above applies, it must – yet again, here it has no discretion – both quash Natural England's decision, and direct Natural England to reverse the amendment in the biodiversity gain site register or reinstate the removed entry (as the case may be) (reg.33(2)). Otherwise, if the First-tier Tribunal is not satisfied that any of the grounds under reg.33(4) applies, it must confirm Natural England's decision (reg.33(3)).

Penalties for Providing False Information

By reg.3 of the Biodiversity Gain Site Register (Financial Penalties and Fees) Regulations 2024 the register operator (Natural England) may impose a financial penalty of £5,000 on any person when they consider, on the balance of probabilities, that false or misleading information was supplied to it by that person in connection with an application referred to in reg.7(1) of the Biodiversity Gain Site Register Regulations 2024 (applications to register land in the biodiversity gain site register). Before imposing this fine on a person Natural England must provide them with a notice of intent, which (by reg.4) must:

"(a) inform the person that Natural England, as register operator, is satisfied as specified in regulation 3;
(b) specify the information on which Natural England is satisfied was false or misleading;
(c) identify the application in connection with which that information has been or was supplied;
(d) inform the person that Natural England intends to impose a financial penalty of £5000 on the person under [Part 2 of the Biodiversity Gain Site Register (Financial Penalties and Fees) Regulations 2024]; and
(e) give details of the person's right under regulation 5 to object to the imposition of the penalty."

By reg.5(1) of the Biodiversity Gain Site Register (Financial Penalties and Fees) Regulations 2024 a person to whom a notice of intent is given under reg.4 may, within 28 days beginning the day after the notice is given, object to the imposition of the penalty to which the notice relates on the grounds that-

(a) the information specified under reg.4(2)(b) in the notice of intent was not false or misleading; or
(b) there are other compelling reasons why the penalty should not be imposed.

An objection must be made in writing to Natural England and include any evidence which supports the objection (reg.5(2)).

By reg.6(1), where Natural England has given a notice of intent under reg.4, they may impose a financial penalty on that person if it decides to do so within:

(a) the period of 56 days beginning with the day on which Natural England receives an objection made in accordance with reg.5; or

(b) if no such objection is received, the period of 56 days beginning with the day after the day on which the period mentioned in reg.5(1) ended.

A financial penalty is imposed when Natural England gives notice informing that person of their decision to impose the penalty and requiring the penalty to be paid (this is known as a "final penalty notice") (reg. 6(2)). The final penalty notice must contain this mandatory information (by reg. 6(4)):

"(a) state that the amount of the penalty is £5,000;
(b) state the reasons for the imposition of the penalty;
(c) state the period within which the penalty must be paid;
(d) explain the consequences of not paying the penalty within that period;
(e) provide information about how to pay the penalty; and
(f) contain information about the right of appeal under regulation 8."

A person receiving a final penalty notice must pay the fine within 28 days (beginning the day after the final penalty notice was given) (reg.6(3)).

The recipient of any final penalty notice may appeal it to the First-tier Tribunal under reg.8(1). The final penalty notice is suspended until the appeal is finally determined or withdrawn (reg.8(2)). An appeal is a re-hearing of Natural England's decision, but may be determined having regard to matters of which Natural England was unaware (reg.8(3)). The First-tier Tribunal has powers to either quash or confirm the final penalty notice (reg.8(4)). They have no power to amend the final penalty notice.

Either a notice of intent or final penalty notice may be withdrawn "at any time" by Natural England (reg. 7(1)). Withdrawal is effected by Natural England giving notice to the person that the respective notice has been withdrawn (reg.7(2)).

By reg.11(2) of the Biodiversity Gain Site Register (Financial Penalties and Fees) Regulations 2024 notice may be given to a person by either:

(a) sending it by post to the person at the person's proper address, or
(b) sending it to the person by email to the person's appropriate email address.

Regulation 11(3) then provides that when notice is given to a person by email that is to be treated as having been given to that person 24 hours after it was sent.

In light of the fact that there is a potential (at least) 30-year liability, it is critical that Natural England is kept up to date with the contact details of the person referred to in reg.8(1) of the Biodiversity Gain Site Register Regulations 2024. Otherwise, that person could be oblivious to proceedings taking place under the Biodiversity Gain Site Register (Financial Penalties and Fees) Regulations 2024 and be subject to a civil debt recovery order. The default under reg.11(4) of the Biodiversity Gain Site Register (Financial Penalties and Fees) Regulations 2024 is for a person's proper address for a notice sent by post to be the address included under reg.8(2)(b) of the Biodiversity Gain Site Register Regulations 2024 in the application to which the notice relates; and a person's appropriate email address for a notice sent by email is the email address included under reg.8(2)(c) of the Biodiversity Gain Site Register Regulations 2024 in the application to which the notice relates.

CHAPTER TEN

STATUTORY CREDITS

As a last resort, developers can buy statutory credits from Natural England to fulfil their mandatory 10% BNG. This is most often seen where a developer's onsite provision falls short by a small fraction of a unit and it is not possible / economically reasonable to achieve that amount through enhancement and/or creation of offsite habitat.

The option to purchase credits was made available by s.101 of the Environment Act 2021. Section 101 also provides:

> "(6) The Secretary of State may use payments received under arrangements under this section for the following purposes (only)-
>
> (a) carrying out works, or securing the carrying out of works, for the purpose of habitat enhancement (within the meaning of Part 7A of the Town and Country Planning Act 1990) on land in England;
>
> (b) purchasing interests in land in England with a view to carrying out works, or securing the carrying out of works, for that purpose;
>
> (c) operating or administering the arrangements.
>
> (7) The references to works in subsection (6) do not include works which the Secretary of State is required to carry out apart from this section by virtue of any enactment.
>
> (8) The Secretary of State must publish reports relating to the discharge of the Secretary of State's functions under subsections (1) and (6)."

It can be seen there is no legal requirement to spend the income from credits in a specific way (it is discretionary under s.101(6)), or within a specific period, although the Secretary of State for Environment, Food and Rural Affairs must publish a report annually on the use of funds received for statutory credits. DEFRA's BNG guidance does, however, confirm "[t]he government will use the revenue to invest in habitat creation in England."[194]

Where statutory credits are relied on, developers must provide evidence in their biodiversity gain plan that either they approached (at least) three habitat providers who could not assist, or they carried out an online search but could not reasonably source offsite units (see section 8.3 of the biodiversity gain plan template). Planning authorities must be "satisfied" by the evidence provided by the developer that not enough onsite or offsite gains can be made to meet the 10% BNG requirement "before they allow developers to buy statutory credits".[195]

It should be noted where there is a small credit need (less than 0.25 units), less stringent evidence to prove the need to buy credits is required. In this case developers do not need to provide evidence that they approached three local or national suppliers, habitat banks or trading websites and that insufficient offsite options are available.[196]

194 https://www.gov.uk/guidance/understanding-biodiversity-net-gain. Last accessed 1 September 2024.

195 DEFRA guidance https://www.gov.uk/guidance/biodiversity-net-gain-what-local-planning-authorities-should-do. Last accessed 1 September 2024.

196 DEFRA guidance https://www.gov.uk/guidance/statutory-biodiversity-credits. Last accessed 1 September 2024.

Developers are to pay for the credits and submit this proof of purchase alongside the biodiversity gain plan.[197] But if the biodiversity gain plan is not approved, or is approved only after being amended in a way that means statutory credits are no longer required, then the developer is left out of pocket. Credits cannot be refunded or transferred once they are purchased.[198] This means credits should only be purchased as the last stage of compliance with all pre-commencement conditions. If the development cannot be implemented because another pre-commencement condition cannot be discharged then the developer will own statutory credits they cannot benefit from.

To Buy Credits

Natural England operates an online portal service[199] which allows developers to estimate the cost of statutory credits they may need in advance. This enables developers to judge the cost / benefit of different layout and design choices where the purchase of statutory credits might be required. Developers input the relevant information from their completed statutory metric, being credit:

- type (whether area habitat, hedgerow, or watercourse); and
- tier (area A1 to A5, H or W) (the "habitat summary" tab in the statutory metric automatically attributes the habitat shortfall into the right pricing tiers).

197 DEFRA guidance https://www.gov.uk/guidance/statutory-biodiversity-credits. Last accessed 1 September 2024.

198 DEFRA guidance https://www.gov.uk/guidance/statutory-biodiversity-credits. Last accessed 1 September 2024.

199 https://manage-biodiversity-gains.Defra.gov.uk/credits-estimation/credits-tier. Last accessed 1 September 2024.

Developers cannot use an agent or representative to act on their behalf to buy statutory biodiversity credits.[200] They must also familiarise themselves with the relevant timescales to avoid unnecessary delay. The first step is download and complete the relevant form to buy statutory biodiversity credits. This will need to be sent to Natural England to be processed. Natural England will send the form to a third-party supplier for customer due diligence checks (that the developer is who they say they are to carry out anti-money laundering checks). Natural England aims to confirm whether the initial checks have been passed within four weeks of receiving the order. Natural England has given itself up to eight weeks in total to finalise this process. Once the initial checks have been passed, the developer will receive an invoice with instructions on how to pay for the credits.

After the developer has paid, they receive a proof of purchase which is the critical document to send to the planning authority in order to satisfy them the biodiversity gain objective has been met.

If developers require assistance Natural England operates a hotline at 0300 060 3900 with the following operating hours:

- March to September – Monday to Friday, 10am to 4pm
- October to February – Monday to Friday, 10am to 3pm

Alternatively, developers can email the relevant team in Natural England at: biodiversitynetgainenquiries@naturalengland.org.uk

200 DEFRA guidance https://www.gov.uk/guidance/buy-statutory-biodiversity-credits#:~:text=Buying%20statutory%20biodiversity%20credits%20is,to%20buy%20statutory%20biodiversity%20credits. Last accessed 1 September 2024.

Price

The prices for statutory credits (set out below)[201] are deliberately high, incorporating standard creation, maintenance, and monitoring costs plus a markup to avoid undercutting the offsite market and to incentivise the provision of onsite and offsite units. The spatial risk multiplier is applied at 0.5 units per credit (the statutory metric will automatically apply the spatial risk multiplier for any statutory credits on the "unit shortfall summary" tab), making credits the costliest option. For these reasons statutory credit prices cannot be used as a guideline price for offsite units.

Prices for statutory credits are published and reviewed every six months. Changes are announced with at least 10 weeks' notice through publication on DEFRA's website.[202]

The published prices do not include VAT. VAT will be charged in the invoice for any statutory credit purchase. Nor do the prices in the table below include the spatial risk multiplier,[203] so developers will actually end up paying double the cost per unit set out below (because the 0.5 multiplier means the developer must buy two statutory credits for every one biodiversity unit they need). Fractions of a credit, rounded to two decimal places, can be purchased.

Each habitat type in the price table is given a 'tier'. Statutory biodiversity credits are priced in tiers according to habitat type for area-based biodiversity units, which reflects the cost and value of those different area habitats.

---

[201] Also available at https://www.gov.uk/guidance/statutory-biodiversity-credit-prices. Last accessed 1 September 2024.

[202] https://www.gov.uk/guidance/statutory-biodiversity-credit-prices. Last accessed 1 September 2024.

[203] Confirmed in DEFRA guidance https://www.gov.uk/guidance/statutory-biodiversity-credit-prices. Last accessed 1 September 2024.

Area habitats

Low distinctiveness habitats

Habitat distinctiveness	Broad habitat type	Specific habitat type	Price per credit	Tier
Low	All	All	£42,000	A1

Medium distinctiveness habitats

Habitat distinctiveness	Broad habitat type	Specific habitat type	Price per credit	Tier
Medium	Heathland and shrub	All	£42,000	A1
Medium	Grassland	All	£42,000	A1
Medium	Individual trees	All	£42,000	A1
Medium	Urban	All	£42,000	A1
Medium	Cropland	All	£42,000	A1
Medium	Woodland and forest	All	£48,000	A2
Medium	Intertidal sediment	All	£48,000	A2
Medium	Lakes	Reservoirs	£125,000	A4
Medium	Lakes – ponds (non-priority habitat)	Ponds	£125,000	A4

Habitat distinctiveness	Broad habitat type	Specific habitat type	Price per credit	Tier
Medium	Sparsely vegetated land	Other inland rock and scree	£125,000	A4

High distinctiveness habitats

Habitat distinctiveness	Broad habitat type	Specific habitat type	Price per credit	Tier
High	Wetland	Reedbeds	£42,000	A1
High	Grassland	Traditional orchards	£42,000	A1
High	Grassland	Lowland calcareous grassland	£48,000	A2
High	Grassland	Tall herb communities (H6430)	£48,000	A2
High	Grassland	Upland calcareous grassland	£48,000	A2
High	Heathland and shrub	Dunes with sea buckthorn	£48,000	A2
High	Heathland and shrub	Lowland heathland	£48,000	A2
High	Heathland and shrub	Upland heathland	£48,000	A2

Habitat distinctiveness	Broad habitat type	Specific habitat type	Price per credit	Tier
High	Urban	Open mosaic habitats on previously developed land	£48,000	A2
High	Woodland and forest	Wet woodland	£66,000	A3
High	Woodland and forest	Felled	£66,000	A3
High	Woodland and forest	Upland birchwoods	£66,000	A3
High	Intertidal sediment	Littoral mud	£66,000	A3
High	Intertidal sediment	Littoral mixed sediments	£66,000	A3
High	Intertidal sediment	Littoral – biogenic reefs – mussels	£66,000	A3
High	Intertidal sediment	Littoral biogenic reefs – Sabellaria	£66,000	A3
High	Intertidal sediment	Features of littoral sediment	£66,000	A3

Habitat distinctiveness	Broad habitat type	Specific habitat type	Price per credit	Tier
High	Intertidal sediment	Littoral muddy sand	£66,000	A3
High	Wetland mosaic	Floodplain wetland mosaic (CFGM)	£125,000	A4
High	Ponds	Ponds (priority habitat)	£125,000	A4
High	Ponds	Temporary lakes, ponds and pools	£125,000	A4
High	Coastal lagoons	Coastal lagoons	£125,000	A4
High	Rocky shore	High energy littoral rock	£125,000	A4
High	Rocky shore	Moderate energy littoral rock	£125,000	A4
High	Rocky shore	Low energy littoral rock	£125,000	A4
High	Rocky shore	Features of littoral rock	£125,000	A4
High	Coastal saltmarsh	Saltmarshes and saline reedbeds	£125,000	A4

Habitat distinctiveness	Broad habitat type	Specific habitat type	Price per credit	Tier
High	Intertidal sediment	Littoral seagrass	£125,000	A4
High	Sparsely vegetated land	Coastal vegetated shingle	£125,000	A4
High	Sparsely vegetated land	Maritime cliff and slopes	£125,000	A4
High	Sparsely vegetated land	Inland rock outcrop and scree habitats	£125,000	A4
High	Woodland and forest	Upland mixed ashwoods	£125,000	A4
High	Woodland and forest	Native pine woodlands	£125,000	A4
High	Woodland and forest	Lowland mixed deciduous woodland	£125,000	A4
High	Woodland and forest	Lowland beech and yew woodland	£125,000	A4
High	Woodland and forest	Upland oakwood	£125,000	A4

Habitat distinctiveness	Broad habitat type	Specific habitat type	Price per credit	Tier
High	Lakes	High alkalinity lakes	£650,000	A5
High	Lakes	Low alkalinity lakes	£650,000	A5
High	Lakes	Marl lakes	£650,000	A5
High	Lakes	Moderate alkalinity lakes	£650,000	A5
High	Lakes	Peat lakes	£650,000	A5

Linear habitats

Hedgerow

Habitat distinctiveness	Broad habitat type	Specific habitat type	Price per credit	Tier
Various	Hedgerow	All	£44,000	H

Watercourses

Habitat distinctiveness	Broad habitat type	Specific habitat type	Price per credit	Tier
Various	All watercourses	All	£230,000	W

CHAPTER ELEVEN

STACKING AND SELLING

Inclusion of Existing Habitat Creation or Enhancement Works

Habitat creation or enhancement which is required to comply with statutory obligations or policies such as green infrastructure, sustainable drainage, nutrient mitigation, mitigation and/or compensation measures for protected sites and species including suitable alternative natural green space, habitat creation for district-level licensing, and mitigation and enhancement measures outlined in river basin management plans, may all count as part of a development's mandatory 10% BNG.[204]

Whether and how much they can contribute depends on the non-BNG scheme. The biodiversity value uplift from enhancement-only works (i.e. where there is no loss in biodiversity value) count in full towards BNG, meaning the developer can simply cite these works in their biodiversity gain plan if they account for at least their mandatory 10% BNG. There is a small deduction for the environmental harm caused which gives rise to the need for a mitigation and/or compensation scheme (what this means is set out in the summary table on the following page).

The rule of thumb for developers seeking to take advantage of stacking policy is that at least 10% of the development's total BNG must come from activities other than environmental mitigation and compensation. This 10% figure is confusing: it does not mean the whole statutory 10% BNG, it refers to 10% of that 10%. The result is that a developer need

---

204 DEFRA guidance https://www.gov.uk/guidance/what-you-can-count-towards-a-developments-biodiversity-net-gain-bng. Last accessed 1 September 2024.

to prove that 10% of their total BNG units come from gains achieved other than units arising from mitigation and/or compensation action; they can rely on the mitigation or compensation scheme for the remaining 90% of the units they need. The biodiversity gain plan must clearly specify how 10% of these non-stacked BNG units come from habitat creation or enhancement beyond the mitigation / compensation scheme being relied on.

The guidance confirms the same rules apply whether the stacked habitat creation or enhancement occurs onsite or offsite. If something can only count in part offsite, it also counts in part onsite, and vice versa.[205]

Rules for each scheme

Name of scheme	How it can count towards BNG
Sustainable urban drainage (SUDs)	In full (in part when part of nutrient neutrality)
Green infrastructure	In full
River basin management plan (RBMP) enhancement	In full
River basin management plan (RBMP) mitigation	In part
Nutrient neutrality or mitigation	In part
Suitable alternative natural green space (SANG)	In part

205 DEFRA guidance https://www.gov.uk/guidance/what-you-can-count-towards-a-developments-biodiversity-net-gain-bng. Last accessed 1 September 2024.

Name of scheme	How it can count towards BNG
Environmental impact assessment compensation	In part
Mitigation or compensation to a special area of conservation, special protection area, or protected species	In part
Mitigation or compensation to functionally linked land (FLL)	In part
District licensing	In part
Restocking conditions relating to a tree felling licence or a restocking notice	Not allowed
Remediation under the environmental damage regulations	Not allowed

Stacking Biodiversity Units and Nutrient Credits

Both biodiversity units and nutrient credits can be sold from the same land by stacking them, sales are allowed to the same or different developers if eligibility criteria are met. Legal agreements will have to be carefully checked for consistency given the varying obligations and time frames involved (at least 30 years for BNG compared to up to 125 years for nutrient credits).

Landowners should be aware that the current guidance has a "hazard" warning, noting that this represents only "the first phase of the biodiversity net gain (BNG) and nutrient credit markets, up to March 2025".[206]

How BNG and Nutrient Mitigation Work with Other Schemes

BNG and nutrient mitigation may be combined with other environmental schemes, such as public grants and agri-environment schemes, but careful consideration is needed to avoid double-counting. The landowner must calculate the baseline for BNG and/or nutrient mitigation after the original planned habitat works other than BNG / nutrient mitigation have been achieved: to be clear, landowners cannot sell habitat enhancement and/or creation funded by an agri-environment scheme,[207] and should not sell habitat enhancement and/or creation funded by voluntary carbon credit schemes[208] as biodiversity units or nutrient credits.

The guidance confirms that while landowners cannot sell an enhancement funded by an agri-environment scheme as a BNG unit or nutrient credit they can, however, use the same land to create further habitat enhancements on top of an existing agri-environment agreement. To do this, the guidance confirms landowners must:[209]

---

206 DEFRA guidance https://www.gov.uk/guidance/combining-environmental-payments-biodiversity-net-gain-bng-and-nutrient-mitigation Last accessed 1 September 2024.

207 Sustainable Farming Incentive, Countryside Stewardship, Environmental Stewardship, Landscape Recovery

208 Such as the Woodland Carbon Code and Peatland Code. Reputable private sector carbon credits will require evidence of additionality, and so cannot be stacked post-BNG as part of the benefits arising from BNG.

209 DEFRA guidance https://www.gov.uk/guidance/combining-environmental-payments-biodiversity-net-gain-bng-and-nutrient-mitigation Last accessed 1 September 2024.

- take into account what the agri-environment agreement will achieve when calculating the habitat baseline; and
- only sell biodiversity units or nutrient credits that are a result of new works and not those which have already been agreed to sell through delivering sustainable farming standards or as part of a landscape recovery agreement.

Further, landowners can still receive Sustainable Farming Incentive, Countryside Stewardship, Environmental Stewardship, and Landscape Recovery payments on the same land as BNG units and nutrient mitigation if:

- they are on different *parcels* of land; or
- they are on the same parcel of land but the agri-environment payments are not for creating, enhancing or maintaining habitat that would be used for BNG or nutrient mitigation purposes (for example, the payment is for new public access, maintaining heritage features and building walls).

Landowners who receive payments under the Basic Payment Scheme may still use their land to sell biodiversity units and nutrient credits.[210]

Landowners may be able to enhance a protected site on land under their ownership, and sell the resulting BNG units. To do so, first the landowner would need to obtain the consent of Natural England to carry out the work to the protected site and procure and/or renew any requisite consents from Natural England.[211]

---

210 DEFRA guidance https://www.gov.uk/guidance/combining-environmental-payments-biodiversity-net-gain-bng-and-nutrient-mitigation. Last accessed 1 September 2024.

211 DEFRA guidance https://www.gov.uk/guidance/sell-biodiversity-units-as-a-land-manager#obligations-and-options-when-you-sell-biodiversity-units-for-off-site-gain. Last accessed 1 September 2024.

Public grants are also available for landowners to create habitat giving rise to biodiversity gains (in the form of biodiversity units) which can then be sold for private profit. Defra's BNG guidance provides an example: if the landowner has an arable field and received a grant to create a grassland, they could manage that grassland for conservation and sell the resulting biodiversity units, as well as nutrient credits.[212] Further, this guidance confirms landowners can receive public grants to:

- help to get projects ready for investment, including investigation works and/or receiving ecological advice;
- access (additional non-grant) funding which must be repaid in full on sale of the biodiversity units or nutrient credits;
- pay for a specific aspect of the project, which is not part of the habitat creation or enhancement.

Finally, landowners cannot sell habitat created by them when they have received payment for the purposes of restocking trees, marine licensing, or are obliged to carry out that habitat enhancement and/or creation work as remediation under the Environmental Damage (Prevention and Remediation) (England) Regulations 2015.[213]

When a scheme ends landowners should very promptly employ an ecologist to calculate the habitat baseline of the land. This will ensure they gain maximum credit for any future habitat enhancement and/or creation work.

---

212 DEFRA guidance https://www.gov.uk/guidance/combining-environmental-payments-biodiversity-net-gain-bng-and-nutrient-mitigation. Last accessed 1 September 2024.

213 DEFRA guidance https://www.gov.uk/guidance/sell-biodiversity-units-as-a-land-manager#obligations-and-options-when-you-sell-biodiversity-units-for-off-site-gain. Last accessed 1 September 2024.

Selling More Units and Credits

If all goes very well, landowners can sell any additional units achieved beyond the planned biodiversity units set out in the biodiversity gain plan. There is no requirement to wait until the 30 years have expired to enter into a new agreement if the habitat enhancement and/or creations are achieved before the end of the existing legal agreement. First it must be confirmed that the requisite units have been achieved and the habitat is capable of even further biodiversity gains. A new baseline against which to measure the further biodiversity gains must then be calculated using the statutory metric. Then this must all be agreed with the relevant local planning authority or responsible body (as the case may be) responsible for enforcing the original s.106 agreement or conservation covenant. Finally, a new or amended s.106 agreement or conservation covenant is required so that there is a legal agreement in place which covers both the unexpired term for the units already created (because the minimum 30 year period is legally required by way of statute: the parties cannot amend this period themselves, and so the achieved gains must still be maintained for the remaining period within the original 30-year period), and the new term of at least 30 years for the additional "uplift" units.

The agreement concerning these overlapping time periods may be further complicated if there is also an agreement for the land to sell nutrient credits, which can last up to 125 years. If there is also a nutrient credit scheme, any works proposed in a new legal agreement for that land must align with the need to maintain the works (or restriction) underlying the nutrient credit agreement.

It is worth noting that if the local development plan policy requires more than 10%, then the developer cannot comply with development plan policy and sell off all units achieved above 10%. So if the development plan requires 20% BNG, the developer can only sell units that are achieved beyond that 20%.[214]

A developer is able to cross-rely on delivered over-achievement on one site to supplement a calculated under-achievement on another site, but the "bonus" above 10% BNG units achieved on the other site will still be treated as offsite units and the full procedure for offsite units must be followed.

214 DEFRA guidance https://www.gov.uk/guidance/make-on-site-biodiversity-gains-as-a-developer. Last accessed 1 September 2024.

CHAPTER TWELVE

NATIONALLY SIGNIFICANT INFRASTRUCTURE PROJECTS

At present, the BNG regime in relation to NSIPs is very broad brush. When it is in force, the Secretary of State must be satisfied that the biodiversity gain objective is met when determining whether to grant development consent for all NSIP applications decided under the Planning Act 2008.

When in force, s.99 and Schedule 15 of the Environment Act 2021 will amend ss.37, 103-105, 120, 232 and insert a new Schedule 2A into the Planning Act 2008. Schedule 2A, paragraph 1 confirms the amendment would apply to non-excluded NSIPs in England. Excluded NSIPs are to be defined by subsequent regulations (Schedule 2A, paragraph 1(2)).

Schedule 2A, paragraph 2 then confirms the biodiversity gain objective is to be set for NSIPs through a "biodiversity gain statement" which will be a statement of government policy. This must define the biodiversity gain objective which must be met, and during what period for specified descriptions of NSIP development (paragraph 2(2)). It may also specify how development of any description may or must meet the biodiversity gain objective (paragraph 2(3)).

Paragraph 3(1) then defines a biodiversity gain objective for the purposes of Schedule 2A as "an objective that the biodiversity value attributable to development to which a biodiversity gain statement relates exceeds the pre-development biodiversity value of the onsite habitat by a percentage specified in the statement". This increase must be at least 10% (paragraph

3(2)), although the Secretary of State may amend the statement's specified percentage through regulations (paragraph 3(3)).

Paragraph 4 creates a possibility for a very different procedure than the BNG regime under the Town and Country Planning Act 1990, as this provides that a biodiversity gain statement may stipulate the method of calculating biodiversity value. It may be the statutory metric (paragraph 4(2)(b)), but it may also be a bespoke metric "set out in a document produced by the Secretary of State for the purposes of the statement" (paragraph 4(2)(a)) or another metric altogether (paragraph 4(2)(c)). Only the first two must be published in an "appropriate manner" and, if not already, be laid before Parliament (paragraph 4(3), which refers to any metric used under paragraph 4(2)(a); the statutory metric is already subject to the same requirement).

Schedule 2A, paragraph 5(1)(a) then says that the biodiversity gain statement may set out how the onsite habitat is defined and, under paragraph 5(1)(b), the date at which a habitat's value must be assessed. Sub-paragraph 5(2) allows for a different pre-development date to be specified if activities carried out on the land before the application have resulted in a reduction in the biodiversity value of the onsite habitat. By paragraph 5(3) any biodiversity gain statement must include a provision dealing with cases where the application relates to land already registered in the biodiversity gain site register. In such cases the pre-development biodiversity value of the onsite habitat will have to include the biodiversity value of the habitat enhancement which is, on the date specified under paragraph 5(1)(b), recorded in the register as habitat enhancement to be achieved on the land (thus ensuring no overall loss in BNG).

Paragraphs 6-8 then set out what may or must be included in a biodiversity gain statement, including provisions concerning irreplaceable habitats, and what evidence the person making the development consent order application will have to produce so as to demonstrate how the biodiversity gain objective is met. The maintenance of habitat enhancement work is envisaged as being secured, where necessary, through conservation covenants or requirements imposed by the development consent order: the biodiversity gain statement is to provide the relevant details.

For NSIPs subject to an existing national policy statement, Schedule 2A, paragraph 9(2) says that, following commencement of the Schedule, the Secretary of State must amend the statement when it is next reviewed so as to include a biodiversity gain statement. In the time between the Schedule coming into force and the review of the national policy statement, a "separate biodiversity gain statement" may be issued which would have the same effect as a statement integrated within a national policy statement (paragraphs 9(3) and 9(7)). This separate statement must be subject to consultation with whomever the Secretary of State considers appropriate (paragraph 9(4)) and then laid before Parliament and published in a manner deemed appropriate by the Secretary of State (paragraph 9(6)). If the existing national policy statement is inconsistent with the separate statement, the Secretary of State is given the power to amend the existing national policy statement to remove the inconsistency (paragraph 9(8)). This separate biodiversity gain statement would then be revoked when the national policy statement is reviewed and the biodiversity gain content is integrated into the nationally policy statement (paragraph 9(9)), although if an existing national policy statement is withdrawn in relation to any description of development, any separate biodiversity gain statement relating to that description of development would come into effect "as if it were a biodiversity gain statement issued under paragraph 10(2)" (paragraph 9(10)).

For NSIPs not covered by a national policy statement, Schedule 2A, paragraph 10(2) then provides that a biodiversity gain statement may be produced for development which is not covered by a national policy statement. This is also subject to requirements for consultation, laying before Parliament and publication in an appropriate manner (paragraphs 10(3) and 10(5)). Any subsequent national policy statement published for that type of development must include a biodiversity gain statement, and (if there is one) any statement issued under paragraph 10(2) will be revoked (paragraph 10(7)).

Finally, paragraph 11 provides that regulations may be made to apply Schedule 2A to NSIPs within the English marine region (being the English offshore region and the English inshore region, excluding waters in England: paragraph 11(3)). Development carried out at an inter-tidal location may also be the subject of regulations made under paragraph 11 (by paragraph 11(4)).

APPENDIX A

BIODIVRSITY GAIN PLAN TEMPLATE[215]

Department
For Environment Food
& Rural Affairs

Biodiversity gain plan

Submit a biodiversity gain plan to show how your development will achieve biodiversity net gain.

When to use this form

A biodiversity gain plan shows how a development will achieve 10% biodiversity net gain (BNG). Submit this form to your local planning authority after they approve your planning application.

Unless your development is exempt, you cannot start the development until the LPA approves your biodiversity gain plan and statutory metric calculation tool.

1. Submission details

1.1 Date
For example, 3/11/2023

[ ]

[215] From https://www.gov.uk/government/publications/biodiversity-gain-plan.

1.2 Planning application reference number

1.3 Local planning authority (LPA)

1.4 Development site address

If the site does not have an address, enter the OS grid reference.

1.5 Describe the development

Tell us about the proposed development and any changes of use (250 words).

2. Developer details

2.1 Applicant name

2.2 Company name

2.3 Address

2.4 Email address

2.5 Telephone number

2.6 Declaration

By signing this declaration, you confirm that the information you give is complete and correct. Any opinions are your genuine opinions.

2.7 Signature

2.8 Date

3. Responsible person details

Tell us about who is responsible for completing the biodiversity gain plan. For example, a consultancy ecologist or planning agent.

3.1 Name

3.2 Company name

3.3 Address

3.4 Email address

3.5 Telephone number

3.6 Declaration

By signing this declaration, you confirm that the information you give is complete and correct. Any opinions are your genuine opinions.

3.7 Signature

3.8 Date

4. Biodiversity net gain strategy

4.1 Is the relevant date for the pre-development biodiversity value the same date as the planning application?

☐ Yes

☐ No

4.2 If no, what earlier date did you agree with the LPA?

☐

4.3 How have you met the guidance on 'what counts towards your BNG'?

Find out what you can count towards a development's BNG

☐

4.4 How will you avoid or minimise impacts to habitats?

Tell us about the steps you've taken on site, including to avoid or minimise the impact on irreplaceable habitats.

☐

4.5 Did you use your local nature recovery strategy to inform the strategic significance of habitats?

This includes other specified strategies if you do not have a local nature recovery strategy.

☐ Yes

☐ No

4.6 How will you achieve the target net gain percentage?

☐ Onsite

☐ Offsite

☐ Both

4.7 Are any of your onsite enhancements considered 'significant'?

Find out what counts as a significant onsite enhancement.

☐ Yes

☐ No

4.8 If yes, tell us about the significant onsite enhancements

Include the appropriate planning condition or how you've secured the habitat.

4.9 How many offsite biodiversity units do you need to meet 10% net gain?

4.10 Explain why you're using offsite biodiversity units

Only answer this question if you're planning to use offsite biodiversity units (250 words).

4.11 Explain why you're planning to use statutory biodiversity credits

Only answer this question if you're planning to use statutory biodiversity credits (250 words).

4.12 Do you have a habitat management and monitoring plan?

☐ Yes

☐ No

4.13 Have you used the statutory metric tool?

☐ Yes

☐ No

4.14 Statutory metric calculation

Send your statutory metric calculation to the LPA and enter the file name.

4.15 Condition assessments

Send your condition assessments to the LPA and enter the file name.

4.16 Pre-development habitat survey report and map

Send your baseline habitat survey report and map to the LPA. Enter the file name.

4.17 Post-development habitat map or landscape plan

Send your post-development habitat survey report and map to the LPA. Enter the file name.

4.18 Have you included an approved habitat degradation in the baseline?

If yes, include the relevant consenting body and reference number.

☐ Yes

☐ No

Consenting body

Reference number

5. Irreplaceable habitats

5.1 Does the development impact any irreplaceable habitats?

If yes, tell us if you've submitted an approved compensation plan.

☐ Yes

☐ No

5.2 Have you submitted an approved compensation plan?

☐ Yes

☐ No

6. Onsite habitat enhancements

Answer this section if your development includes onsite habitat enhancements.

6.1 Survey date

For example, 3/11/2023

6.2 Survey constraints

For example, access issues, weather, or seasonal constraints.

6.3 Total pre-development biodiversity value

Enter the number from the headline results in your statutory metric calculation.

Number of area habitat biodiversity units

Number of hedgerow biodiversity units

Number of watercourse biodiversity units

6.4 Total post-development biodiversity value

Enter the number from the headline results in your statutory metric calculation.

Number of area habitat biodiversity units

Number of hedgerow biodiversity units

Number of watercourse biodiversity units

☐

6.5 Total net change in biodiversity units

Enter the number from the headline results in your statutory metric calculation.

Area habitat biodiversity units

☐

Area habitat biodiversity units % change

☐

Hedgerow biodiversity units

☐

Hedgerow biodiversity units % change

☐

Watercourse biodiversity units

☐

Watercourse biodiversity units % change

☐

6.6 Will you register and allocate any biodiversity units from your site to other developments?

If yes or provisionally, give details.

☐ Yes

☐ No

6.7 Give details

Tell us about the amount of biodiversity units and the development location (250 words).

☐

7. Offsite habitat enhancements

Answer this section if your development includes offsite habitat enhancements.

7.1 Tell us about the offsite habitat enhancements

Include whether you're delivering the offsite enhancements or buying biodiversity units.

7.2 Biodiversity gain site register reference number

7.3 How have you secured the offsite habitat enhancements?

Tell us about any responsible bodies and whether you've used an S106 or conservation covenant.

7.4 Total baseline biodiversity value

Enter the number from the headline results in your statutory metric calculation.

Number of area habitat biodiversity units

Number of hedgerow biodiversity units

Number of watercourse biodiversity units

7.5 Total biodiversity value post-intervention

Enter the number from the headline results in your statutory metric calculation.

Number of area habitat biodiversity units

Number of hedgerow biodiversity units

Number of watercourse biodiversity units

7.6 Total net change in biodiversity units

Enter the number from the headline results in your statutory metric calculation.

Area habitat biodiversity units

☐

Area habitat biodiversity units % change

☐

Hedgerow biodiversity units

☐

Hedgerow biodiversity units % change

☐

Watercourse biodiversity units

☐

Watercourse biodiversity units % change

☐

8. Statutory biodiversity credits

Answer this section if you need to use statutory biodiversity credits.

8.1 Do you need to use statutory biodiversity credits?

☐ Yes

☐ No

8.2 How many statutory biodiversity credits do you need?

Tell us the unit shortfall by tier, including the spatial risk multiplier. Enter the number from the headline results in your statutory metric calculation.

A1

☐

A2

☐

A3

A4

A5

H

W

8.3 What evidence is there that no units are available through the market?

Send a message from at least 3 habitat providers, or a search result from online registers.

8.4 Proof of purchase

Send proof of purchase and enter the reference number.

9. Trading summary

9.1 Distinctiveness group

Tell us if you met the BNG trading rules on habitat compensation for each distinctiveness group. If you did not meet the trading rules, tell us if you agreed bespoke habitat compensation.

Check the rules on habitat compensation in the statutory metric user guide.

Very high

High

Medium

Low

10. Sharing data (optional)

10.1 Can we share your ecological survey data with the Local Environmental Records Centre or other bodies?

☐ Yes

☐ No

APPENDIX B

SUGGESTED TEXT FOR BIODIVERSITY GAIN INFORMATION ON THE WRITTEN DECISION NOTICE[216]

Purpose of this document

The purpose of this document is to assist local planning authorities to comply with the requirements on Biodiversity Net Gain set out below, by providing suggested text for use on decision notices. The use of this suggested text is discretionary, and local planning authorities should make decisions on the content of their decisions notices and may wish to get their own legal advice. The Department for Levelling Up, Housing and Communities will keep this guidance under review based on practical feedback from local planning authorities and other relevant stakeholders.

Suggested text has been provided for the following scenarios:

1. Where the local planning authority at the time of granting planning permission considers that approval of a Biodiversity Gain Plan will be required before development commences.
2. Where the local planning authority at the time of granting planning permission considers that approval of a Biodiversity Gain Plan will not be required before development commences.
3. Where the local planning authority is unable to indicate at the time of granting planning permission whether the approval of a

216 From https://www.gov.uk/guidance/biodiversity-net-gain#determination-of-the-biodiversity-gain-plan.

Biodiversity Gain Plan will be required before development commences.

The third scenario could occur if, for example key aspects of the development, such as onsite layout and landscaping, are not known at the time of the grant of planning permission. In cases such as this it may not be possible to determine whether permission attracts the de minimis exemption so that the biodiversity gain condition does not apply. For instance, outline planning permission may have been granted for a small development on previously developed land – with landscaping, layout and scale of the development being deferred to reserve matter approval.

It is acknowledged that elements of the suggested text go beyond the statutory requirements. Local planning authorities wishing to use the suggested text should decide which option is appropriate for each written notice and may wish to adapt it depending on the nature of the permission granted, as well as include details of their own advice or other services which they offer to applicants.

Footnotes have been provided in the document to signpost guidance to local planning authorities when setting up the text in their back-office system. Local planning authorities should keep the information they provide on decision notices under review to ensure that it is consistent with any changes to the legislative framework.

Article 35 of the Town and Country Planning (Development Management Procedure) (England) Order 2015 (as amended by The Biodiversity Gain (Town and Country Planning) (Modifications and Amendments) (England) Regulations 2024) requires that where planning permission is granted, the written notice of the decision must include:

(i) information relating to the condition in paragraph 13 of Schedule 7A to the Town and Country Planning Act 1990 (biodiversity gain condition) including that there are exemptions, transitional arrangements and requirements relating to irreplaceable habitat,

(ii) information to note the effect of section 73(2D) of the 1990 Act (earlier Biodiversity Gain Plan in relation to a previous planning permission regarded as approved for purposes of paragraph 13 of Schedule 7A)
(iii) details of the planning authority under paragraph 12(1) of Schedule 7A (biodiversity gain in England), and
(iv) where development is to proceed in phases and the modifications in Part 2 of the Biodiversity Gain (Town and Country Planning) (Modifications and Amendments) (England) Regulations 2024 apply, a statement to that effect and to the effect that Biodiversity Gain Plans are required before development may be begun (the overall plan) and required before each phase of development may be begun (phase plans).

The purpose of these decision notice requirements is to signpost the applicant to the statutory framework for Biodiversity Net Gain.

Suggested Text where the local planning authority considers that approval of a Biodiversity Gain Plan will be required before development commences

Biodiversity Net Gain

The effect of paragraph 13 of Schedule 7A to the Town and Country Planning Act 1990 is that planning permission granted for the development of land in England is deemed to have been granted subject to the condition ("the biodiversity gain condition") that development may not begin unless:

(a) a Biodiversity Gain Plan has been submitted to the planning authority, and
(b) the planning authority has approved the plan.

The planning authority, for the purposes of determining whether to approve a Biodiversity Gain Plan if one is required in respect of this permission would be [*insert name of the planning authority*[217]].

There are statutory exemptions and transitional arrangements which mean that the biodiversity gain condition does not always apply. These are listed below.

Based on the information available this permission is considered to be one which will require the approval of a biodiversity gain plan before development is begun because none of the statutory exemptions or transitional arrangements listed below are considered to apply.

[the following is suggested text for inclusion in the decision notice where the local planning authority considers that the permission falls within paragraph 19 of Schedule 7A to the Town and Country Planning Act 1990].

The permission which has been granted has the effect of requiring or permitting the development to proceed in phases. The modifications in respect of the biodiversity gain condition which are set out in Part 2 of the Biodiversity Gain (Town and Country Planning) (Modifications and Amendments) (England) Regulations 2024 apply.

In summary: Biodiversity gain plans are required to be submitted to, and approved by, the planning authority before development may be begun (the overall plan), and before each phase of development may be begun (phase plans).]

---

217 'name of the planning authority' – this will usually be the local planning authority which granted permission but other provisions may apply where the local planning authority was not the decision-maker for the planning application. See paragraph 12 of Schedule 7A of the Town and Country Planning Act 1990, and Part 1A of The Biodiversity Gain (Town and Country Planning) (Consequential Amendments) Regulations 2024.

Statutory exemptions and transitional arrangements in respect of the biodiversity gain condition.

1. The application for planning permission was made before 12 February 2024.

2. The planning permission relates to development to which section 73A of the Town and Country Planning Act 1990 (planning permission for development already carried out) applies.

3. The planning permission was granted on an application made under section 73 of the Town and Country Planning Act 1990 and

    (i) the original planning permission to which the section 73 planning permission relates* was granted before 12 February 2024; or

    (ii) the application for the original planning permission* to which the section 73 planning permission relates was made before 12 February 2024.

4. The permission which has been granted is for development which is exempt being:

    4.1 Development which is not 'major development' (within the meaning of article 2(1) of the Town and Country Planning (Development Management Procedure) (England) Order 2015) where:

    i) the application for planning permission was made before 2 April 2024;
    ii) planning permission is granted which has effect before 2 April 2024; or
    iii) planning permission is granted on an application made under section 73 of the Town and Country Planning Act 1990 where the original permission to which the section 73 permission relates* was exempt by virtue of (i) or (ii).

4.2 Development below the de minimis threshold, meaning development which:

i) does not impact an onsite priority habitat (a habitat specified in a list published under section 41 of the Natural Environment and Rural Communities Act 2006); and

ii) impacts less than 25 square metres of onsite habitat that has biodiversity value greater than zero and less than 5 metres in length of onsite linear habitat (as defined in the statutory metric).

4.3 Development which is subject of a householder application within the meaning of article 2(1) of the Town and Country Planning (Development Management Procedure) (England) Order 2015. A "householder application" means an application for planning permission for development for an existing dwellinghouse, or development within the curtilage of such a dwellinghouse for any purpose incidental to the enjoyment of the dwellinghouse which is not an application for change of use or an application to change the number of dwellings in a building.

4.4 Development of a biodiversity gain site, meaning development which is undertaken solely or mainly for the purpose of fulfilling, in whole or in part, the Biodiversity Gain Planning condition which applies in relation to another development, (no account is to be taken of any facility for the public to access or to use the site for educational or recreational purposes, if that access or use is permitted without the payment of a fee).

4.5 Self and Custom Build Development, meaning development which:

i) consists of no more than 9 dwellings;

ii) is carried out on a site which has an area no larger than 0.5 hectares; and

iii) consists exclusively of dwellings which are self-build or custom housebuilding (as defined in section 1(A1) of the Self-build and Custom Housebuilding Act 2015).

4.5 Development forming part of, or ancillary to, the high speed railway transport network (High Speed 2) comprising connections between all or any of the places or parts of the transport network specified in section 1(2) of the High Speed Rail (Preparation) Act 2013.

* "original planning permission means the permission to which the section 73 planning permission relates" means a planning permission which is the first in a sequence of two or more planning permissions, where the second and any subsequent planning permissions are section 73 planning permissions.

Irreplaceable habitat

If the onsite habitat includes irreplaceable habitat (within the meaning of the Biodiversity Gain Requirements (Irreplaceable Habitat) Regulations 2024) there are additional requirements for the content and approval of Biodiversity Gain Plans.

The Biodiversity Gain Plan must include, in addition to information about steps taken or to be taken to minimise any adverse effect of the development on the habitat, information on arrangements for compensation for any impact the development has on the biodiversity of the irreplaceable habitat.

The planning authority can only approve a Biodiversity Gain Plan if satisfied that the adverse effect of the development on the biodiversity of the irreplaceable habitat is minimised and appropriate arrangements have been made for the purpose of compensating for any impact which do not include the use of biodiversity credits.

The effect of section 73D of the Town and Country Planning Act 1990

If planning permission is granted on an application made under section 73 of the Town and Country Planning Act 1990 (application to develop land without compliance with conditions previously attached) and a Biodiversity Gain Plan was approved in relation to the previous planning permission ("the earlier Biodiversity Gain Plan") there are circumstances when the earlier Biodiversity Gain Plan is regarded as approved for the purpose of discharging the biodiversity gain condition subject to which the section 73 planning permission is granted.

Those circumstances are that the conditions subject to which the section 73 permission is granted:

i) do not affect the post-development value of the onsite habitat as specified in the earlier Biodiversity Gain Plan, and
ii) in the case of planning permission for a development where all or any part of the onsite habitat is irreplaceable habitat the conditions do not change the effect of the development on the biodiversity of that onsite habitat (including any arrangements made to compensate for any such effect) as specified in the earlier Biodiversity Gain Plan.

Suggested Text where the local planning authority considers that approval of a Biodiversity Gain Plan will not be required before development commences

Biodiversity Net Gain

The effect of paragraph 13 of Schedule 7A to the Town and Country Planning Act 1990 is that planning permission granted for development of land in England is deemed to have been granted subject to the condition (biodiversity gain condition) that development may not begin unless:

(a) a Biodiversity Gain Plan has been submitted to the planning authority, and
(b) the planning authority has approved the plan.

The planning authority, for the purposes of determining whether to approve a Biodiversity Gain Plan, if one is required in respect of this permission would be [*insert name of the planning authority*[218]].

There are statutory exemptions and transitional arrangements which mean that the biodiversity gain condition does not always apply. These are listed below.

Based on the information available this permission is considered to be one which will not require the approval of a biodiversity gain plan before development is begun because one or more of the statutory exemptions or transitional arrangements in the list below is/are considered to apply. [INSERT the list indicating the exemptions which are considered to apply]

Statutory exemptions and transitional arrangements in respect of the biodiversity gain condition.

1. The application for planning permission was made before 12 February 2024.
2. The planning permission relates to development to which section 73A of the Town and Country Planning Act 1990 (planning permission for development already carried out) applies.
3. The planning permission was granted on an application made under section 73 of the Town and Country Planning Act 1990 and
    (i) the original planning permission to which the section 73 planning permission relates* was granted before 12 February 2024; or

[218] 'name of the planning authority' – this will usually be the local planning authority which granted permission but other provisions may apply where the local planning authority was not the decision-maker for the planning application. See paragraph 12 of Schedule 7A of the Town and Country Planning Act 1990, and Part 1A of The Biodiversity Gain (Town and Country Planning) (Consequential Amendments) Regulations 2024.

(ii) the application for the original planning permission* to which the section 73 planning permission relates was made before 12 February 2024.

4. The permission which has been granted is for development which is exempt being:

4.1 Development which is not 'major development' (within the meaning of article 2(1) of the Town and Country Planning (Development Management Procedure) (England) Order 2015) where:

iv) the application for planning permission was made before 2 April 2024;

v) planning permission is granted which has effect before 2 April 2024; or

vi) planning permission is granted on an application made under section 73 of the Town and Country Planning Act 1990 where the original permission to which the section 73 permission relates* was exempt by virtue of (i) or (ii).

4.2 Development below the de minimis threshold, meaning development which:

iii) does not impact an onsite priority habitat (a habitat specified in a list published under section 41 of the Natural Environment and Rural Communities Act 2006); and

iv) impacts less than 25 square metres of onsite habitat that has biodiversity value greater than zero and less than 5 metres in length of onsite linear habitat (as defined in the statutory metric).

4.6 Development which is subject of a householder application within the meaning of article 2(1) of the Town and Country Planning (Development Management Procedure) (England) Order 2015. A "householder application" means an application for planning permission for development for an existing dwellinghouse, or development within the curtilage of such a dwellinghouse for any purpose incidental to the enjoyment of the dwellinghouse which is not an application for change of use or an application to change the number of dwellings in a building.

4.7 Development of a biodiversity gain site, meaning development which is undertaken solely or mainly for the purpose of fulfilling, in whole or in part, the Biodiversity Gain Planning condition which applies in relation to another development, (no account is to be taken of any facility for the public to access or to use the site for educational or recreational purposes, if that access or use is permitted without the payment of a fee).

4.8 Self and Custom Build Development, meaning development which:

iv) consists of no more than 9 dwellings;
v) is carried out on a site which has an area no larger than 0.5 hectares; and
vi) consists exclusively of dwellings which are self-build or custom housebuilding (as defined in section 1(A1) of the Self-build and Custom Housebuilding Act 2015).

4.5 Development forming part of, or ancillary to, the high speed railway transport network (High Speed 2) comprising connections between all or any of the places or parts of the transport network specified in section 1(2) of the High Speed Rail (Preparation) Act 2013.

* "original planning permission means the permission to which the section 73 planning permission relates" means a planning permission which is the first in a sequence of two or more planning permissions, where the second and any subsequent planning permissions are section 73 planning permissions.

Irreplaceable habitat

If the onsite habitat includes irreplaceable habitat (within the meaning of the Biodiversity Gain Requirements (Irreplaceable Habitat) Regulations 2024) there are additional requirements for the content and approval of Biodiversity Gain Plans.

The Biodiversity Gain Plan must include, in addition to information about steps taken or to be taken to minimise any adverse effect of the development on the habitat, information on arrangements for compensation for any impact the development has on the biodiversity of the irreplaceable habitat.

The planning authority can only approve a Biodiversity Gain Plan if satisfied that the adverse effect of the development on the biodiversity of the irreplaceable habitat is minimised and appropriate arrangements have been made for the purpose of compensating for any impact which do not include the use of biodiversity credits.

The effect of section 73D of the Town and Country Planning Act 1990

If planning permission is granted on an application made under section 73 of the Town and Country Planning Act 1990 (application to develop land without compliance with conditions previously attached) and a Biodiversity Gain Plan was approved in relation to the previous planning permission ("the earlier Biodiversity Gain Plan") there are circumstances when the earlier Biodiversity Gain Plan is regarded as approved for the purpose of discharging the biodiversity gain condition subject to which the section 73 planning permission is granted.

Those circumstances are that the conditions subject to which the section 73 permission is granted:

i) do not affect the post-development value of the onsite habitat as specified in the earlier Biodiversity Gain Plan, and

ii) in the case of planning permission for a development where all or any part of the onsite habitat is irreplaceable habitat the conditions do not change the effect of the development on the biodiversity of that onsite habitat (including any arrangements made to compensate for any such effect) as specified in the earlier Biodiversity Gain Plan.

[the following is suggested text for inclusion in the decision notice where the local planning authority considers that the permission falls within paragraph 19 of Schedule 7A to the Town and Country Planning Act 1990.]

The permission which has been granted has the effect of requiring or permitting the development to proceed in phases. The modifications in respect of the biodiversity gain condition which are set out in Part 2 of the Biodiversity Gain (Town and Country Planning) (Modifications and Amendments) (England) Regulations 2024 would apply if the permission were subject to the biodiversity gain condition.

In summary: Biodiversity gain plans would be required to be submitted to, and approved by, the planning authority before development may be begun (the overall plan), and before each phase of development may be begun (phase plans).]

Suggested Text where it is not known whether at the time of granting planning permission whether approval if a Biodiversity Gain Plan will be required before development commences

Biodiversity Net Gain

The effect of paragraph 13 of Schedule 7A to the Town and Country Planning Act 1990 is that planning permission granted for the development of land in England is deemed to have been granted subject to the condition "(the biodiversity gain condition") that development may not begin unless:

(a) a Biodiversity Gain Plan has been submitted to the planning authority, and
(b) the planning authority has approved the plan.

There are statutory exemptions and transitional arrangements which mean that the biodiversity gain condition does not always apply. These are listed below.

The planning authority, for the purposes of determining whether to approve a Biodiversity Gain Plan if one is required in respect of this permission would be [*insert name of the planning authority*[219]].

On the basis of the information provided to determine the application, it is not possible to indicate whether it is considered that this planning permission is one which will require the approval of a biodiversity gain plan before development is begun. This is due to [insert reasons why e.g. landscaping, layout and scale of the development has been reserved for subsequent approval so it cannot be determined whether the permission would be subject to the de minimis exemption].

Before commencing development, you should consider whether a Biodiversity Gain Plan needs to be submitted and approved. Commencing development which is subject to the biodiversity gain condition without an approved Biodiversity Gain Plan could result in enforcement action for breach of planning control.

---

219 'name of the planning authority' – this will usually be the local planning authority which granted permission but other provisions may apply where the local planning authority was not the decision-maker for the planning application. See paragraph 12 of Schedule 7A of the Town and Country Planning Act 1990, and Part 1A of The Biodiversity Gain (Town and Country Planning) (Consequential Amendments) Regulations 2024.

Statutory exemptions and transitional arrangements in respect of the biodiversity gain condition.

1. The application for planning permission was made before 12 February 2024.

2. The planning permission relates to development to which section 73A of the Town and Country Planning Act 1990 (planning permission for development already carried out) applies.

3. The planning permission was granted on an application made under section 73 of the Town and Country Planning Act 1990 and
   (i) the original planning permission to which the section 73 planning permission relates* was granted before 12 February 2024; or
   (ii) the application for the original planning permission* to which the section 73 planning permission relates was made before 12 February 2024.

4. The permission which has been granted is for development which is exempt being:

   4.1 Development which is not 'major development' (within the meaning of article 2(1) of the Town and Country Planning (Development Management Procedure) (England) Order 2015) where:
      vii) the application for planning permission was made before 2 April 2024;
      viii) planning permission is granted which has effect before 2 April 2024; or
      ix) planning permission is granted on an application made under section 73 of the Town and Country Planning Act 1990 where the original permission to which the section 73 permission relates* was exempt by virtue of (i) or (ii).

4.2 Development below the de minimis threshold, meaning development which:

v) does not impact an onsite priority habitat (a habitat specified in a list published under section 41 of the Natural Environment and Rural Communities Act 2006); and

vi) impacts less than 25 square metres of onsite habitat that has biodiversity value greater than zero and less than 5 metres in length of onsite linear habitat (as defined in the statutory metric).

4.3 Development which is subject of a householder application within the meaning of article 2(1) of the Town and Country Planning (Development Management Procedure) (England) Order 2015. A "householder application" means an application for planning permission for development for an existing dwellinghouse, or development within the curtilage of such a dwellinghouse for any purpose incidental to the enjoyment of the dwellinghouse which is not an application for change of use or an application to change the number of dwellings in a building.

4.4 Development of a biodiversity gain site, meaning development which is undertaken solely or mainly for the purpose of fulfilling, in whole or in part, the Biodiversity Gain Planning condition which applies in relation to another development, (no account is to be taken of any facility for the public to access or to use the site for educational or recreational purposes, if that access or use is permitted without the payment of a fee).

4.5 Self and Custom Build Development, meaning development which:

vii) consists of no more than 9 dwellings;

viii) is carried out on a site which has an area no larger than 0.5 hectares; and

ix) consists exclusively of dwellings which are self-build or custom housebuilding (as defined in section 1(A1) of the Self-build and Custom Housebuilding Act 2015).

4.6 Development forming part of, or ancillary to, the high speed railway transport network (High Speed 2) comprising connections between all or any of the places or parts of the transport network specified in section 1(2) of the High Speed Rail (Preparation) Act 2013.

* "original planning permission means the permission to which the section 73 planning permission relates" means a planning permission which is the first in a sequence of two or more planning permissions, where the second and any subsequent planning permissions are section 73 planning permissions.

Irreplaceable habitat

If the onsite habitat includes irreplaceable habitat (within the meaning of the Biodiversity Gain Requirements (Irreplaceable Habitat) Regulations 2024) there are additional requirements for the content and approval of Biodiversity Gain Plans.

The Biodiversity Gain Plan must include, in addition to information about steps taken or to be taken to minimise any adverse effect of the development on the habitat, information on arrangements for compensation for any impact the development has on the biodiversity of the irreplaceable habitat.

The planning authority can only approve a Biodiversity Gain Plan if satisfied that the adverse effect of the development on the biodiversity of the irreplaceable habitat is minimised and appropriate arrangements have been made for the purpose of compensating for any impact which do not include the use of biodiversity credits.

The effect of section 73D of the Town and Country Planning Act 1990

If planning permission is granted on an application made under section 73 of the Town and Country Planning Act 1990 (application to develop land without compliance with conditions previously attached) and a Biodiversity Gain Plan was approved in relation to the previous planning permission ("the earlier Biodiversity Gain Plan") there are circumstances when the earlier Biodiversity Gain Plan is regarded as approved for the purpose of discharging the biodiversity gain condition subject to which the section 73 planning permission is granted.

Those circumstances are that the conditions subject to which the section 73 permission is granted:

i) do not affect the post-development value of the onsite habitat as specified in the earlier Biodiversity Gain Plan, and
ii) in the case of planning permission for a development where all or any part of the onsite habitat is irreplaceable habitat the conditions do not change the effect of the development on the biodiversity of that onsite habitat (including any arrangements made to compensate for any such effect) as specified in the earlier Biodiversity Gain Plan.

[the following is suggested text for inclusion in the decision notice where the local planning authority considers that the permission falls within paragraph 19 of Schedule 7A to the Town and Country Planning Act 1990.]

The permission which has been granted has the effect of requiring or permitting the development to proceed in phases. The modifications in respect of the biodiversity gain condition which are set out in Part 2 of the Biodiversity Gain (Town and Country Planning) (Modifications and Amendments) (England) Regulations 2024 will apply if the permission is subject to the biodiversity gain condition.

In summary: Biodiversity gain plans will be required to be submitted to, and approved by, the planning authority before development may be begun (the overall plan), and before each phase of development may be begun (phase plans).

'The Electronic Communications Code: A Practical Guide – Second Edition' by Kerry Bretherton KC, James Castle, Mark Loveday
'A Practical Guide to the Independent School Standards – September 2023 Edition' by Sarah McKimm
'A Practical Guide to Estate Administration and Crypto Assets' by Richard Marshall
'A Practical Guide to Parental Alienation in Private and Public Law Children Cases' by Sam King QC & Frankie Shama
'Contested Heritage – Removing Art from Land and Historic Buildings' by Richard Harwood QC, Catherine Dobson, David Sawtell
'The Limits of Separate Legal Personality: When Those Running a Company Can Be Held Personally Liable for Losses Caused to Third Parties Outside of the Company' by Dr Mike Wilkinson
'A Practical Guide to Transgender Law' by Robin Moira White & Nicola Newbegin
'A Practical Guide to 'Stranded Spouses' in Family Law' by Mani Singh Basi
'A Practical Guide to Residential Freehold Conveyancing' by Lorraine Richardson
'A Practical Guide to Pensions on Divorce for Lawyers' by Bryan Scant
'A Practical Guide to Challenging Sham Marriage Allegations in Immigration Law' by Priya Solanki
'A Practical Guide to Digital Communications Evidence in Criminal Law' by Sam Willis
'A Practical Guide to Legal Rights in Scotland' by Sarah-Jane Macdonald
'A Practical Guide to New Build Conveyancing' by Paul Sams & Rebecca East
'A Practical Guide to Inherited Wealth on Divorce' by Hayley Trim
'A Practical Guide to Practice Direction 12J and Domestic Abuse in Private Law Children Proceedings' by Rebecca Cross & Malvika Jaganmohan
'A Practical Guide to Confiscation and Restraint' by Narita Bahra QC, John Carl Townsend, David Winch
'A Practical Guide to the Law of Forests in Scotland' by Philip Buchan
'A Practical Guide to Health and Medical Cases in Immigration Law' by Rebecca Chapman & Miranda Butler
'A Practical Guide to Bad Character Evidence for Criminal Practitioners by Aparna Rao
'A Practical Guide to Extradition Law post-Brexit' by Myles Grandison et al
'A Practical Guide to Hoarding and Mental Health for Housing Lawyers' by Rachel Coyle

'Stephens on Contractual Indemnities' by Richard Stephens

'A Practical Guide to the EU Succession Regulation' by Richard Frimston

'A Practical Guide to Solicitor and Client Costs – Second Edition' by Robin Dunne

'Constructive Dismissal – Practice Pointers and Principles' by Benjimin Burgher

'A Practical Guide to Religion and Belief Discrimination Claims in the Workplace' by Kashif Ali

'A Practical Guide to the Law of Medical Treatment Decisions' by Ben Troke

'Fundamental Dishonesty and QOCS in Personal Injury Proceedings: Law and Practice' by Jake Rowley

'A Practical Guide to the Law in Relation to School Exclusions' by Charlotte Hadfield & Alice de Coverley

'A Practical Guide to Divorce for the Silver Separators' by Karin Walker

'The Right to be Forgotten – The Law and Practical Issues' by Melissa Stock

'A Practical Guide to Planning Law and Rights of Way in National Parks, the Broads and AONBs' by James Maurici QC, James Neill et al

'A Practical Guide to Election Law' by Tom Tabori

'A Practical Guide to the Law in Relation to Surrogacy' by Andrew Powell

'A Practical Guide to Claims Arising from Fatal Accidents – Second Edition' by James Patience

'A Practical Guide to Asbestos Claims' by Jonathan Owen & Gareth McAloon

'A Practical Guide to Stamp Duty Land Tax in England and Northern Ireland' by Suzanne O'Hara

'A Practical Guide to the Law of Farming Partnerships' by Philip Whitcomb

'A Practical Guide to the Law of Unlawful Eviction and Harassment – Second Edition' by Stephanie Lovegrove

'A Practical Guide to Costs in Personal Injury Claims – Second Edition' by Matthew Hoe

'A Practical Guide to the General Data Protection Regulation (GDPR) – Second Edition' by Keith Markham

'A Practical Guide to Working with Litigants in Person and McKenzie Friends in Family Cases' by Stuart Barlow

'Protecting Unregistered Brands: A Practical Guide to the Law of Passing Off' by Lorna Brazell

'A Practical Guide to Secondary Liability and Joint Enterprise Post-Jogee' by Joanne Cecil & James Mehigan

'A Practical Guide to the Pre-Action RTA Claims Protocol for Personal Injury Lawyers' by Antonia Ford

'A Practical Guide to Neighbour Disputes and the Law' by Alexander Walsh

'A Practical Guide to Coercive Control for Legal Practitioners and Victims' by Rachel Horman

'A Practical Guide to the Law of Driverless Cars – Second Edition'

by Alex Glassbrook, Emma Northey & Scarlett Milligan

'A Practical Guide to TOLATA Claims' by Greg Williams

'A Practical Guide to Elderly Law – Second Edition' by Justin Patten

'A Practical Guide to Responding to Housing Disrepair and Unfitness Claims' by Iain Wightwick

'A Practical Guide to the Law of Bullying and Harassment in the Workplace' by Philip Hyland

'How to Be a Freelance Solicitor: A Practical Guide to the SRA-Regulated Freelance Solicitor Model' by Paul Bennett

'A Practical Guide to Prison Injury Claims' by Malcolm Johnson

'A Practical Guide to Advising Clients at the Police Station' by Colin Stephen McKeown-Beaumont

'A Practical Guide to Antisocial Behaviour Injunctions – Second Edition' by Iain Wightwick

'Practical Mediation: A Guide for Mediators, Advocates, Advisers, Lawyers, and Students in Civil, Commercial, Business, Property, Workplace, and Employment Cases' by Jonathan Dingle with John Sephton

'The Mini-Pupillage Workbook' by David Boyle

'A Practical Guide to Crofting Law' by Brian Inkster

'A Practical Guide to the Law of Domain Names and Cybersquatting' by Andrew Clemson

'A Practical Guide to the Law of Gender Pay Gap Reporting' by Harini Iyengar

'NHS Whistleblowing and the Law' by Joseph England

'Employment Law and the Gig Economy' by Nigel Mackay & Annie Powell

'A Practical Guide to Noise Induced Hearing Loss (NIHL) Claims' by Andrew Mckie, Ian Skeate, Gareth McAloon

'An Introduction to Beauty Negligence Claims – A Practical Guide for the Personal Injury Practitioner' by Greg Almond

'Intercompany Agreements for Transfer Pricing Compliance' by Paul Sutton

'Zen and the Art of Mediation' by Martin Plowman

'A Practical Guide to Adoption for Family Lawyers' by Graham Pegg

'A Practical Guide to Industrial Disease Claims' by Andrew Mckie & Ian Skeate
'A Practical Guide to Conducting a Sheriff Court Proof' by Andrew Stevenson
'A Practical Guide to Vicarious Liability' by Mariel Irvine
'A Practical Guide to Applications for Landlord's Consent and Variation of Leases' by Mark Shelton
'A Practical Guide to Relief from Sanctions Post-Mitchell and Denton' by Peter Causton
'A Practical Guide to Equity Release for Advisors' by Paul Sams
'A Practical Guide to Financial Services Claims' by Chris Hegarty
'A Practical Guide to Financial Ombudsman Service Claims' by Adam Temple & Robert Scrivenor
'A Practical Guide to Running Housing Disrepair and Cavity Wall Claims – Second Edition' by Andrew Mckie & Ian Skeate
'A Practical Guide to Holiday Sickness Claims – Second Edition' by Andrew Mckie & Ian Skeate
'Arguments and Tactics for Personal Injury and Clinical Negligence Claims' by Dorian Williams
'A Practical Guide to Drone Law' by Rufus Ballaster, Andrew Firman, Eleanor Clot
'On Experts: CPR35 for Lawyers and Experts' by David Boyle
'An Introduction to Personal Injury Law' by David Boyle

These books and more are available to order online direct from the publisher at www.lawbriefpublishing.com, where you can also read free sample chapters. For any queries, call us on 0844 587 2383 or email us at mail@lawbriefpublishing.com.

Our books are all generally in stock at www.amazon.co.uk with free next day delivery for Prime members, and at good legal bookshops such as Wildy & Sons.

We are regularly launching new books in our series of practical day-to-day practitioners' guides. Visit our website and join our free newsletter to be kept informed and to receive special offers, free chapters, etc.

You can also follow us on Twitter at www.twitter.com/lawbriefpub.

www.ingramcontent.com/pod-product-compliance
Lightning Source LLC
LaVergne TN
LVHW052252200926
848481LV00002B/345